Peace
Weavers

Peace
Weavers

Uniting the Salish Coast through Cross-Cultural Marriages

CANDACE WELLMAN

WSU
PRESS

Washington State University Press
Pullman, Washington

WASHINGTON STATE UNIVERSITY

Washington State University Press
PO Box 645910
Pullman, Washington 99164-5910
Phone: 800-354-7360
Fax: 509-335-8568
Email: wsupress@wsu.edu
Website: wsupress.wsu.edu

Library of Congress Cataloging-in-Publication Data

Names: Wellman, Candace, author.
Title: Peace weavers : uniting the Salish coast through cross-cultural
    marriages / by Candace Wellman.
Description: Pullman, Washington : Washington State University Press,
2017. | Includes bibliographical references and index.
Identifiers: LCCN 2016047759 | ISBN 9780874223460 (alk. paper)
Subjects: LCSH: Salish Indians--Marriage customs and rites--Washington
    (State)--Whatcom County. | Interracial marriage--Washington
    (State)--Whatcom County--History--19th century. | Whatcom County
    (Wash.)--Race relations--History--19th century.
Classification: LCC E99.S2 W39 2017 | DDC 305.8009797/73--dc23
LC record available at https://lccn.loc.gov/2016047759

On the cover: *Native View*, painting by Steve Mayo, www.stevemayoart.com

Dedication

To three generations of my family who have lived with,
and supported, my project for eighteen years: Mike, Christine,
Ame and Ron, Jim and Amy, Jake, and Addy

To Judy, Sue, Rita, and Suzann, my dear Gonzaga Girlz
who always, always believed

To my own grandmothers, Katherine Amend Huffman Kiesz
and Elizabeth Berrigan LeBlanc

And to all the indigenous grandmothers
whose stories wait to be told

Contents

Illustrations

Acknowledgments

O VER THE YEARS, I have been helped by perhaps two hundred people and institutions who believed in this project. Without them, the book *Peace Weavers* would not exist. The contributions of dozens do not appear here because some biographies wait for another book, but I do not value their help any less. The following names represent those who have contributed to this book and they deserve my deepest gratitude.

Chief Tsi'li'xw James, Frances Lane James, George Adams, Juanita Jefferson, Tammy Cooper-Woodrich, and Adelina Singson shared their knowledge and wisdom and supported my long cross-cultural research. Donna Sands and other Whatcom Genealogical Society volunteers inspired the project when they would not let go of the injustice they saw until I did something about it. Mike Vouri, Janet Oakley, Tim Wahl and Dr. Wayne Suttles encouraged me to keep digging from the beginning and shared their personal work. Author David D. Busch believed I could write a book and shared his knowledge of the publishing industry, as did Dr. Coll Thrush. Molly Masland edited early drafts. Jeff Jewell of the Whatcom Museum supplied his vast knowledge of historical photographs in the collection.

My thanks go to the present and past staffs of the Washington State Archives, Northwest Region, the Center for Pacific Northwest Studies at Western Washington University, and the Whatcom County Historical Society. All of them supported my project in every way for nearly two decades. Thanks also go to Lummi Nation Archives staff, Lummi Island Library, Whatcom County Law Library, Seattle Archdiocese Archives, Oatlands Plantation, State Library of Virginia, Virginia Historical Society, Chilliwack City Archives, Gloucester City Archives, the public libraries of Bellingham, Seattle, Fredericksburg (VA), and Fayetteville (AR), Orcas Island Historical Museum, Anacortes Museum, Island County Museum, San Juan Historical Society and Museum, Oregon Historical Society, Special Collections Room of the University of Washington Libraries, U.S.

Military Academy archives, and Arkansas United Methodist Church Archives.

Thanks to these other individuals who gave support, read drafts, or shared memories, research materials, and family photographs: Carole Teshima, Carleton Howard, Edward Pyeatt, Robert Keen, Tim Baker, Roger Newman, Carol Besette, Niler Pyeatt, Barbara Landis, Jane Frost, Julie Johannsen, Laurie Cepa, Carol Ericson, Sallie Lee Fitzhugh, Sonny and Cindi Berry, Martha Holcomb, Virginia Brumbaugh, Sherry Guzman, Boyd Pratt, Dave Adams, Col. James Gibson, Forrest Tennant, Steve Tennant, Robert Krick, Ruth Williams, Don and Cathy Munks, Vaughn Ploeger, Patricia Scott, Chad Waukechon, Alan Caldwell, Dr. Elizabeth Upton, Dr. Jack Miller, Vi Hilbert, Charlene Oerding, Pete McLallen, George and Ridgely Copland, Kris Day-Vincent, Juanita Rouleau, George and Patricia Weeks, Denise McClanahan, Bettie Wood, Mary Jane King, Cheri Sexton, Janell Swearingen, Nancy Britton, Rev. Charlotte Osborn, Helen Almojera, Tony Dardeau, Nick Peroff, Mary Helen Cagey, Ernestine Gensaw, Lorraine McConaghy, Llyn De Danaan, Jamie Valadez, Dr. Susan Armitage, Dr. Jean Barman, Dr. Alexandra Harmon, Janis Olsen, Troy Lugenbill, Mary Michaelson, Catalina Renteria, Dr. Melissa Upton Cyders, Edradine Hovde, Marilee Hagee, Dr. Charles Bolton, Rita Rosenkranz, Tim Kavanaugh, Dr. Bill Lang, Linda Lawson, Mae Moss, Julie Owens, Sam Pambrun, Patricia Roppel, Allan Richardson, Belinda Thomas, Darrell Hillaire, Kim Ferbrache, Lynette Miller, Michael Mjelde, Patricia Neal, Catherine Replogle, Cheri Rapp, Ruth Solomon, Maxine Stremler, Irene Jernigan, Molly and Richard Walker, Kathy Duncan, Mina Kyle, and Alice Keller.

Many thanks also go to Robert Clark, Beth DeWeese, and Caryn Lawton of the WSU Press, who have shown immense patience while shepherding me through the publishing process.

My apologies to anyone I have omitted. Feel free to let me know and I will instantly tender my thanks.

Preface

I HAVE SPENT NEARLY TWO DECADES in the company of Nellie, Caroline, Mary, Clara, their husbands, families, and other inter-married couples. Some observations can be made about researching these women whose lives have been hidden behind too common Euro-American assumptions that they were unknowable and irrelevant to Western history. There was so much to find, but apart from their families and friends, no one looked.

Some information was irretrievable. Government records at all levels were sometimes incomplete, contradictory, missing, or clearly inaccurate. Access to Bureau of Indian Affairs individual records that are closed to outsiders depended on the generosity of family. Men talked and wrote about other men's activities and ignored women's lives. Critical oral history either didn't exist, or I never met the person who carried it. Photos that once existed no longer do, or families wished to keep them private. Local published histories ended a reservation family's story when the founding intermarried father died, implying that the family no longer existed. Biographies had to be written within these limitations.

The most powerful discovery was that assumptions can stunt a biography's accuracy and completeness. When assumptions on paper and within the researcher go unquestioned, pathways to undiscovered information are overlooked or the researcher wastes time on erroneous or extraneous trails that could have been avoided. One must dissect what has been written, re-confirm stated facts, and follow all possible points of research. Some assumptions that I encountered were:

- The husband's birth family wanted nothing to do with his wife and children.
- Only Hudson's Bay Company forts spawned intermarriage clusters.
- All white men abandoned their indigenous families.

- Nineteenth century indigenous women generally left no trace behind.
- Communities began when the first white woman arrived.
- The intermarried couple was not "really" married if there was no paper record.
- Everything in an earlier publication is accurate.

Many people I encounter in the general public continue to ask "But were they *really* married?" It took a territorial chief justice who understood that marriage is ultimately a contract between two people to stop persecution of the intermarried Washingtonians as fornicators. Many, if not most, people have never considered the equal right of the woman and her family to define her relationship. They look at these historic unions only from the husband's European cultural perspective until prompted to rethink their bias toward a paper-based society.

It is my hope that the great-great-great granddaughters of these and other intermarriages will see in these four biographies that there is much to discover. They will tell the life stories in a different and more complete way than I can.

Introduction

M ARY, A COAST SALISH WOMAN, slept beside her second husband, Chief Henry Kwina, in the darkness of a December morning in 1890 on Lummi Reservation in the northwest corner of Washington State. Not far away, her daughter Teresa Forsyth Finkbonner, along with her husband and five children, slumbered before the sunrise would wake them.[1]

A thousand miles east at Wounded Knee Creek in South Dakota, Colonel James Forsyth stood on a rise in the frigid winter morning, and watched as fire from four Hotchkiss mountain guns raked across the tepees of exhausted Sioux families below. It cut to pieces starving men, women, and children. Terrified mothers ran and crawled away with their little ones to seek shelter in ravines where scores died of wounds or froze to death in the following hours.

☙❧

When past historians scrutinized Forsyth's actions, their assessment of his character would have been better informed and perhaps more nuanced had they known about Mary and Teresa. The abandonment of his first family remained hidden for more than a century, except to Mary's descendants and local residents.

The lives of nearly all intermarried nineteenth century American indigenous women have long gone untold. Anyone who has read history or fiction about the westward movement has probably encountered the shadowy men on the edge of settlement who "went native" when they married across the cultural and racial line. Almost invariably, writers portrayed the couples as marginalized and rejected by the new communities. Alternately, writers portrayed Indian "princesses" as frequent fatalities in tragic romances with white men. Most striking has been the lack of interest in who the intermarried wives really were as individuals. Usually, local and regional histories, or biographies of the husbands, ignored indigenous wives, or if they were mentioned at all, they were nameless, stereotyped and unrecognized for their contributions to the new West.

The four women on whom this book focuses shared tenacity and personal courage as wives and mothers, bridging the cultural chasm between incoming settlers and the indigenous residents whose forebears had resided there for thousands of years. I call them "peace weavers," because they played a vital role in the establishment of peaceful ties between people and cultures. Within their own world, elders had already taught them to weave with wool and cedar bark fiber. Marriage brought "weaving" of a different kind.

Taken together, these biographies add complexity to the picture of life in Washington Territory during the second half of the nineteenth century after the first "pioneers" moved into lands of the Coast Salish people. There are undoubtedly other clusters of similar couples who helped their communities thrive in western places not yet recognized. Community history is the poorer for its focus on all-white "first" families that overlooks or ignores the real complexity of the time and the other family sagas taking place. As in the Forsyth anecdote above, a better knowledge of intermarried men and women can enhance our understanding of events and people.

These biographies may open the door to new consideration of the lives of average nineteenth-century intermarried Native American women and the legacies they left behind in future generations. The project started with a question posed by a long-time genealogy society volunteer who worked in county marriage records at the Washington State Archives branch in Bellingham, Washington. She asked: "Who were these Indian wives? Why don't we know who they were?" An early historian's list of more than sixty prominent intermarried settlers and military officers of the 1850s surfaced and revealed that local histories had made nearly all of their wives invisible. Though I was consistently told that the women were unknowable, I thought that new technology and increased archival sources might mean that their lives could be uncovered. They might take their rightful places among the founding mothers of Whatcom County.

My research included twenty-two women, gradually reduced to the four in this book. Generally born in the 1840s, they married in the 1850s, and lived into the twentieth century. Selection was based on varied lives and available information on both spouses. The narratives differ in emphasis and sources because of availability of information about one or the other. Neither party should be treated as if they dropped from the sky into the marriage or written history. It was vitally important to discover each man's past family history with indigenous people, and equally important to understand the wife's family history with whites before their daughter entered into the cross-cultural marriage.

Research for *Peace Weavers* integrated four broad types of resources rarely combined: (1) public and private archival collections; (2) research by professional historians; (3) work of independent historians and scholars, and (4) perfectionist family historians and genealogists. By accessing all of them, the *Peace Weavers* project took many years longer than expected, but yielded richer content than a short-term project with restricted sources.

The construction of a detailed timeline for each subject resulted in the discovery of surprising links between people and events. I added every date that appeared in the research to the timeline, whether it was personal, local, or national. Triggering, simultaneous, or resultant events appeared.

Stereotypes have prevented many researchers from investigating nineteenth century indigenous women's lives. They assumed that the intermarried women were of no significance beyond housekeeping, sex, and childbearing, and no conventional sources would reveal their lives. However, numerous undiscovered or unused primary and secondary sources provided a more even-handed approach to these bicultural pioneer couples' lives. For example, a white woman's diary revealed her indigenous neighbor's independent business.

Hundreds of descendants of these families still live in the region, too many to locate and individually interview. Those contacted were sometimes eager to share their own research and knowledge, eager to see "the grandmothers" at last given recognition, and others were not. Descendants often realized that modern interpretation of actions and events 150 years in the past is problematic, and our contemporary viewpoint offers only one explanation among many. This made finding long-ago interviews with the four women's children, relatives, or friends more important. Descendants less eager to share were protective because of past disrespect and patronizing portrayals of their ancestors. Some families knew little about the "Indian great-great-great-grandmother" they found while doing genealogy. In a mirror image, some families knew little about "that white guy" whose surname they might still carry.

I honored occasional family members' personal requests for anonymity as document donor or interviewee. Requests surrounding the use of the women's indigenous personal names have been honored. They are personal property with many implications, and the current owner has the right to decide who may share it publicly. In more recent publications about indigenous issues in Washington State, many names have been repeatedly published without permission. Younger individuals have also started to use their personal names publicly. Therefore, deciding when a name is so publicly known that control of its use by strangers has been lost became a difficult task. This was complicated by a frequent inability to find the name holder in the vast region occupied by Coast Salish people today.

Generally, I used someone's "white" name (usually a baptismal one) unless the personal name has been widely published or freely shared with earlier researchers. The use of personal names became a case-by-case decision and I take responsibility for them. If my use offends a family member, I sincerely apologize.

The geographical homeland of Salish culture in western Washington and southwestern British Columbia includes several languages and many local dialects. Geographical features have multiple names. Also, speakers and linguists may differ about spellings for the modern reader. Therefore, place names have been treated individually in what seemed the best language for that chapter and a spelling accessible to general readers.

The U.S.-Canada border presented differences in term usage. "First Nations" and "bands" are the preferred usages north of the line. As well, the term "country marriage" was associated only with Hudson's Bay Company marriages in all locations. Washington's Coast Salish people use "tribal custom marriage" to describe their culture's ceremonial union of two people. All the couples in this book had tribal custom marriages before they obtained "paper" ones via county or Christian officiants.

ᏰᏕᏞᎣ

While still teenagers, the four women in this volume crossed their own frontier to live between and within two cultures. I am not of their time, culture, or family history so have been reluctant to talk of their motives, emotions, and reactions to events and people unless they chose to share them with a contemporary. Similarly, the inner life of a nineteenth century man also existed in a different context, and is only hinted at by his personal history.

Unlike some areas in Coast Salish country, Whatcom County remained nearly void of strife between the two colliding groups in the mid-nineteenth century. I believe a primary reason for this tranquility has gone unrecognized. Intercultural in-law relationships dominated the county for its first two official decades and dampened the outcome of altercations. Talk prevailed over weaponry.

This text by Gretchen Bataille and Kathleen Sands embodies the lives of the four subjects of this book and the legacies they left behind: "Indian women have been forced to be flexible, resourceful, and tenacious in facing struggles for survival and growth in constantly shifting circumstances. They have drawn on the past for traditional values and spiritual stability. They have guarded the customs and ways of their ancestors and have passed them on to their children in measure they deemed appropriate in a changing society."[2]

Caroline, Mary, Clara, and Nellie served their communities as peace weavers.

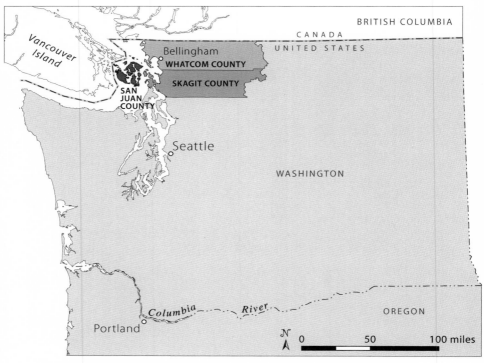

Map 1: Whatcom County, Washington 1854-1873. San Juan County formed in 1873 and Skagit separated in 1883. The extensive travel required by water and land exhausted early sheriffs James Kavanaugh and F.F. Lane, as well as deputy sheriffs Robert Davis and John Tennant. *Map by Chelsea Feeney.*

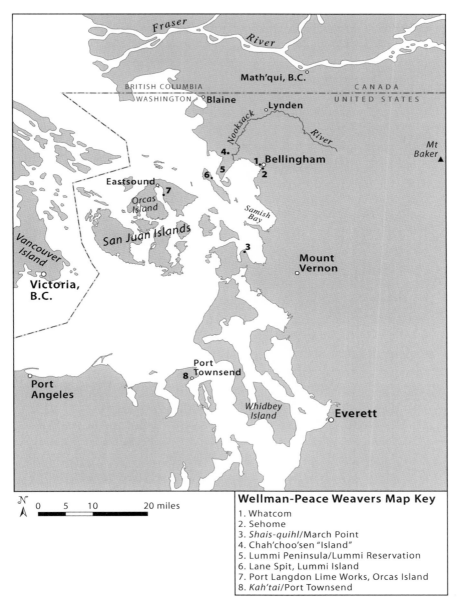

Map 2: The setting of *Peace Weavers*. *Map by Chelsea Feeney.*

Fraser River

Math'qui, B.C.

BRITISH COLUMBIA
WASHINGTON

CANADA
UNITED STATES

Blaine

Lynden

Nooksack

River

Mt Baker ▲

4.
5.
6.
1.
2. Bellingham

Eastsound

Orcas Island

7

San Juan Islands

Samish Bay

3

Mount Vernon

Vancouver Island

Victoria, B.C.

Port Townsend

8

Port Angeles

Whidbey Island

Everett

N
0   5   10   20 miles

Wellman-Peace Weavers Map Key
1. Whatcom
2. Sehome
3. *Shais-quihl*/March Point
4. Chah'choo'sen "Island"
5. Lummi Peninsula/Lummi Reservation
6. Lane Spit, Lummi Island
7. Port Langdon Lime Works, Orcas Island
8. *Kah'tai*/Port Townsend

Whatcom, August 1858. The sketch by S.F. Baker is the oldest known depiction of the mill settlement. Captain George E. Pickett's home is visible on the hill, surrounded by a stockade and with its own defensive blockhouse. The sketch did not fully represent thousands of prospectors camped on the beach waiting for the Fraser River to go down. A few Coast Salish canoes are visible at the left. *Hutchings California Magazine* 8/5/1858, page 52. *Courtesy of the California History Room, California State Library, Sacramento, California.*

CHAPTER 1

The Place, The Time, The Peoples

IT WASN'T LONG AFTER SPANISH FEET hit the sands of the New World that intermarriages began. The Catholic Church forbade Spanish marriage to non-Catholics so the intermarriages, by force or by free will, were what would be called in nineteenth century Pacific Northwest Coast Salish territory, "tribal custom." Few Spanish women cared to emigrate and move to the New World. Marriage to indigenous women among non-elite Spaniards produced the *mestizos* who founded Latin American families.

Some early English and French colonists in North America did the same, though the only indigenous wife most Americans hear about is "Princess" Pocahontas who legendarily saved one white man and married another from the Jamestown colony.

Thomas Jefferson and some contemporaries mulled the possibility of building a unique American ethnicity through wide-scale intermarriage and amalgamation. In 1784 Patrick Henry introduced a doomed bill in the Virginia legislature to encourage intermarriage and offered financial incentives. New Americans who maintained that European values defined "civilization" showed no interest in adopting their neighbors' culture or of living in a mixed community. The new states passed bills to prevent intermarriages. They were unaware that in the regions to the west of the new nation, solid French and Spanish mixed families had successfully blended expertise from both cultures to build fur trading and river mercantile empires.[1]

Eastern tribes showed little interest in abandoning their own cultures and spirituality to become faux Europeans, but never truly equal. To Americans' dismay, most of the tribal negotiators and rebellion leaders were the mixed-blood sons of traders who had taken up the cause of their mother's people. Cornplanter of the Seneca, Joseph

Brant of the Mohawk, Alex McGillivray of the Creek, Osceola of the Seminole—all were from cross-cultural families.

By the time of the 1830s Indian removals, Americans commonly believed that intermarrying was immoral and possibly a threat to the social and political order, particularly if it involved white women. Reinforced by literature and poetry that established negative stereo-types about Native Americans, the amalgamation idea died in favor of miscegenation laws.

As settlers pushed beyond the Appalachians, they encountered many intermarriages and some joined the practice common in French-dominated areas. The new nation absorbed a web of mixed communities started by intermarried fur trade and mercantile fami-lies linked by the great river systems: St. Louis, Detroit, Chicago, Kas-kaskia (Illinois), Green Bay and Prairie du Chien in Wisconsin, and Arkansas Post on the lower Mississippi. According to historian Anne Hyde, those communities were probably 80 percent biracial at the time of the Louisiana Purchase in 1803. Generations of the Choteau clan at St. Louis had already built a commercial empire upon their tribal in-law relationships when Lewis and Clark arrived to buy sup-plies for their Corps of Discovery. Some members of the corps were themselves mixed-blood and/or married Native women. As the U.S. army moved into the Southwest after the Mexican-American War, some officers and soldiers married indigenous women. They retired in new communities that joined established biracial towns such as San Antonio and Santa Fe.[2]

The opening of the wagon roads beyond Missouri brought more white women westward. As small towns grew into larger ones, Amer-icans largely excised the intermarried founders from their history. They trumpeted instead "the first white woman," even though her arrival was sometimes years after the true first families settled on the spot. The first all-white child became "the first baby" born in the community. Local historians and novelists cemented the myth of the nineteenth century pioneer woman.

She was a courageous sad-eyed wife or widow who left her home forever and walked beside a covered wagon across the continent to settle in a wilderness that, with her womanly efforts, became a real community.

Or, she was half of an improbable love story—the mail-order bride who braved the ocean's dangers to marry a virtual stranger and with him, build a community.

Or, she was the schoolmarm who brought culture to a dusty town. Perhaps she never married and dedicated her life to the town's children.

Or, she was the business-minded, satin and lace-clad saloon girl with a heart of gold whose for-sale femininity kept a settlement in the wilderness from devolving into violence and lawlessness until real ladies arrived.

And standing pugnaciously alone were Calamity Jane and Annie Oakley, symbols of fierce femininity equal to men in the face of the West's challenges.

Not memorialized were the young indigenous women who lived where forts were built and settlers staked claims that displaced native communities. High-born Native daughters sometimes wed army officers, merchants, and local officials whom the families considered of equal social status. The women played their own roles on a frontier that was cultural, not geographic.

Indigenous wives occupied a middle ground between people of alien cultures. Though settlers' white wives could almost never treat their Native neighbors as social equals, they often did become friends. White women praised their mothering, homemaking skills, and knowledge of natural medicines. Indian midwives delivered settlers' babies and taught them how to cook local foodstuffs. In times of conflict, the wives often mediated, as had happened since Spanish colonization started. Despite all that, when local histories were written, the best the indigenous wives usually got was "He married an Indian woman."

CRED

Most Americans assume that the Pacific Northwest's first female settlers were the wives of missionaries who arrived in the 1830s, followed by the intrepid women of the initial 1843 Oregon Trail party. The myth has them arrive in what had been an empty Eden waiting for other Americans to arrive. In truth, they were greeted in the Willamette Valley by indigenous wives at thriving Hudson's Bay Company

(HBC) communities of predominantly French-Canadian retirees living beside the Native survivors of imported diseases. If the new arrivals expected wilderness, what they found instead was the farming town of St. Paul preparing to build their new Catholic church, the first brick building north of San Francisco.[3]

Newcomers found these were not the transitory, exploitive sexual unions they might have expected. Rather, they were committed marriages and economic partnerships much like their own. Native American scholar Peggy Pascoe believed that an indigenous woman's value was judged only by how useful she could be to whites, but nineteenth century pioneers applied that same standard to all women. Both views minimized romantic love at the start of marriage, and emphasized the wife's economic contribution.[4]

North of the Columbia River in what would become Washington Territory, newcomers found a pleasant employee village beside the river at HBC Fort Vancouver, and other clusters of intermarried men and women wherever the company had a depot. Frenchtown near HBC Fort Walla Walla in the southeast already had at least a dozen couples farming when Marcus and Narcissa Whitman arrived in 1836. The Whitmans, New England Protestant missionaries, ignored these neighbors, perhaps, according to Frenchtown descendants, because the missionaries were deeply prejudiced against women who were not only Indians, but Catholics.[5]

Blended communities may have existed as early as the 1820s in the Colville Valley at Chewelah and remained behind at Kettle Falls when Fort Okanogan closed, while other families settled in the Okanogan Valley. Fort Spokane's closure left a cluster and another Frenchtown grew near today's Missoula, Montana. West of the Cascades other groups of mixed couples settled in today's Lewis and Pierce Counties on the prairies along the Cowlitz and Nisqually Rivers where the HBC ran herds of sheep and cattle.[6]

In British territory to the north, retired HBC men and their First Nations wives clustered and farmed on Vancouver Island. There, more of the wives came from Coast Salish families than in Oregon, where the retirees had often married farther east in Canada. In Victoria, James Douglas (the biracial son of a Caribbean relationship) ran the HBC and governed the new colony during the 1850s. He and his half-Cree wife Amelia and the families of other intermarried company officers lived an elegant lifestyle. Dinner on fine china in the Douglas home with French-speaking children was an eye opener to American guests new to the Northwest's unusual marriage culture.[7]

Starting in the 1850s, American clusters began to form on Hammersley Inlet in Mason County (then called Big Skookum Bay), at the mouth of the Snohomish River (Snohomish County), on March Point near today's Anacortes, Dungeness on the north shore of the Olympic Peninsula, and at Bellingham Bay.

ᚲᚱᛒᚲ

Just south of the Canadian border in the far northwest corner of the contiguous forty-eight states, an intermarriage cluster of wholly American origin started in 1853 on Bellingham Bay. Today that place is Whatcom County, Washington. Its largest city, Bellingham ("The City of Subdued Excitement"), finally blended several smaller bayside towns that had absorbed early Whatcom and Sehome. Where once there was a single oversized and water-centered county that exhausted early sheriffs, today there are three: Whatcom, Skagit (1883) to the south, and San Juan (1873) in the islands. (*See* Map 1.)

Spanish and British explorers met in Bellingham Bay during the summer of 1792. *Lhaq'temish* (today usually "Lummi") paddled out in their high-prowed carved cedar canoes to greet and judge the intentions of the strangers before they could land. Anyone who entered the circular bay on a sunny day from the great Salish Sea north of Puget Sound found themselves surrounded by views of islands on the west, jagged peaks on the northern horizon, and a nearly 11,000-foot volcanic peak emerging from green foothills on the east. The snow-covered living volcano thirty miles inland seemed to tower over the bay. Labeled Mount Baker by British Captain George Vancouver, the peak that dominated village horizons from many directions bore names in several indigenous languages. At sunrise or sunset, it turned ethereal pink, sometimes with a whiff of steam or smoke at the top. Around the bay to the northwest, Lummi Peninsula was home to the main village of interrelated Coast Salish families once mostly resident on the San Juan Islands. The dark humps of Lummi Island lay across the western edge of the bay, allowing entry from north and south, but shielding it from the largest storms. The great salmon river that wound from Mount Baker's glaciers across prairies and past *Nootsack* (today "Nooksack") villages emptied into the salt water beside Lummi Peninsula. In every direction from the beaches towered cedar and fir trees well over two hundred feet high and up to twelve feet in diameter. A stranger in the forest quickly found there was no view out, and the unfiltered light made it seem a dark and fragrant green prison.

Frequent rains spawned those enormous trees with their lush undergrowth of ferns and berry bushes. Weather could be instantly changeable since it was influenced by the mountain, winds from the Yukon that funneled down the Fraser River, occasional gales from the south, and the steady cold temperature of the saltwater from an ocean current that began in Japan. Rarely drenching, sometimes the gentle rain was interspersed minute to minute with sun and rainbows and it rarely got very cold or hot. The Coast Salish people who lived and worked along the beaches usually wore lightweight woven cedar fiber clothing and hats that shed rain and protected people from the sun. Although they adopted some European-style clothing from the HBC, it was never as practical or easily replaced. Leather boots rotted and wet dirty wool stank. (As did the white men who wore them.)

In the first half of the 1800s, unless a rare ship passed through, only the painted prows of Salish canoes cut the deep green waters of the bay and islands. Sometimes an orca pod's tall fins sliced through the water in pursuit of salmon headed for the rivers in schools so large they resembled a black or red cloud dancing underwater.

ଔଶ

The people who became the Coast Salish discovered Whatcom County's stunning scenery, abundant resources, and temperate climate and settled there at least 6,000 years ago. Euro-American settlement at Bellingham Bay began inauspiciously at the mouth of a salmon stream where a small waterfall tumbled. Henry Roeder and Russell Peabody received permission from a Lummi leader to build a small sawmill when they came looking for a suitable site in December 1852. The local dialect's sounds being foreign to their ears, the newcomers christened the site "Whatcom," an Anglicized version of the

Mount Baker as seen from Clara and John Tennant's lake which is now part of a public park. The volcanic peak was visible from homes of all four women in *Peace Weavers*. *Image #2012.0043.000168 by Mikhail Samoylenko. Whatcom Museum, Bellingham, Washington.*

word that loosely meant "noisy waters." Unlike the British and Spanish, who renamed every geographical feature, the Americans in Coast Salish territory adopted Native names most of the time.

The Lummi seem to have thought the invasion of their territory would be a temporary cooperative business relationship. It would integrate some "Boston" (American) men into their family economies to balance off the family networks to the north allied with the "King George" (British) men of the HBC. "Temporary" was not Roeder and Peabody's intention. After failing with their California gold rush businesses, they intended the mill and attendant settlement to make their fortunes.

As men arrived, cross-cultural marriages began. With no eligible Euro-American girls in the neighborhood, they quickly noticed the pretty girls from Lummi and other villages. The new mill engaged skilled workers Roeder hired in San Francisco, but only Edward Eldridge brought a wife. Hugging the beach and bluff, scattered cabins rose near a longhouse used by Lummi mill workers and families harvesting shellfish and salmon. A second settlement began

By Louie Brown (Mrs. John Brown) about 1880 – Ferndale, Wash.

"Trees so tall and straight you have to look twice to see the top, but the tall black stumps twenty feet high standing grimly around give it a wild desolate appearance." Letter home, April 19, 1880, and drawing by newly-arrived young wife Lou Nicholson Brown. *Lou Nicholson Brown Collection, Washington State Archives, Northwest Region. Bellingham, Washington.*

a year later a mile away around the shore at a new-found coal seam which immediately became a lucrative commercial and military asset. The mine manager married treaty-signer Seya'whom's daughter by tribal custom soon after he arrived, and named the settlement and mine "Sehome" for his father-in-law. Both Roeder and Peabody married indigenous women by tribal custom a few years apart, joined by a continuously growing group of cross-cultural couples.

Captain George Pickett, two lieutenants, and sixty soldiers of the Ninth Regiment arrived to build Fort Bellingham in 1856. The army officers saw the same intermarriage pattern they had already observed at Fort Steilacoom in the south Sound and Fort Vancouver. Nearby were many successful HBC intermarriages in the San Juan Islands with Tlingit and Tsimshian women from southeast Alaska. It wasn't long before Pickett and his lieutenants married young indigenous women.[8]

By 1858 only four white wives appear to have remained of six who had moved to the primitive outpost that boasted only a saloon and mine store. That year a fourth group of bachelors arrived. Approximately ten thousand men planned to pass through on their way to the new Fraser River gold rush. When spring water levels didn't drop, most camped all summer on the beach, while a few lucky early arrivals boarded with anyone who would take them in. Like most men who went from gold rush to gold rush, they saw their lives as an extended business trip from which they would go home and bankroll their futures with the profits. However, the Fraser rush was short-lived and some men either returned empty-handed to Bellingham Bay or ran out of money before they ever left. Some of those tired of the chase and decided they did not want to return home a failure. Whatcom County had much to recommend it. They cut their ties to the East or South and chose a home, a local indigenous wife, and a new future.

It is difficult to estimate the number of intermarried men at the bay by the time of the 1860 census because the United States did not count Indians. Many men seem to have used an official residence for the census though they lived elsewhere with their wives. Without specific marriage dates available, it cannot be said exactly how many of the fifty-five men at Whatcom and seventy-four at Sehome had already married indigenous women, but the evidence points to about 80-90 percent. The 1870 census did count Indian wives and children. Of 136 marriages counted in the region that became three counties, 89 were intermarriages plus at least six without the mother in the home, but the children were mixed blood. By that time, more white couples had arrived, particularly in the islands. The initial cluster at Whatcom and Sehome had expanded north and south as the first couples began to farm and others joined them.[9]

ᏃᏈ

With the exception of Captain Pickett's Alaskan native wife, the indigenous wives who moved to the fort and settlement were from Pacific Northwest groups who shared cohesive (though not identical) spiritual, family, technological, and creative lifeways. They belonged to vast interwoven extended families whose relationships stretched for hundreds of watery miles. People identified themselves by parents and villages, not as "tribes," which confused Americans, as did the lack of one authoritative "chief." Coast Salish culture during the women's childhoods centered around the abundant (but complex to obtain) resources of forest, river, and sea. They were, and are, people of the salmon and cedar. Women supplemented the fishing and hunting with a large array of wild food and medicinal plants available in short seasons. The women also practiced agriculture on prairies kept clear with fire. Elite women had their own wealth from their crops, intricate baskets, and the valuable white blankets they wove from the crimped hair of their (now-extinct) Coast Salish wool dogs. In the great cedar longhouses, carvings and decorations covered even the smallest practical item. To the whites, the most striking practice of the Northwest peoples was the unfamiliar "potlatch." The colonizers found it difficult to understand why reciprocal generosity on a grand scale was the critical way to elevate a family's prestige and status. Potlatches brought together families and friends from near and far to feast, celebrate life-changing events, and be gifted by the hosts. Because family and potlatch relationships crossed languages and dialects, the women of *Peace Weavers* commonly spoke several.

Most of Sehome and Whatcom's bachelors little understood that a ceremonial exchange of gifts and obligations was the wedding, and not the purchase of a companion, housekeeper, and sexual partner. Unless informed by another husband, the groom's gifts to the family seemed like payment to him, but the young woman's family saw a symbol of her value to them and her community. Though the father greatly influenced the choice of a husband for his daughter, the matrilineal society's mothers and grandmothers put strictures on who was genealogically eligible to marry into their lines. Most women married into another village, sometimes far distant. After a new wife moved to her husband's longhouse, her family did not see her regularly. Nor would she be gathering plants, cultivating her crops, or making cedar mats and baskets for the family's economy. A high-born woman would not be weaving the white blankets so important to her family's wealth and ceremonial regalia. Her new husband must replace her companionship and labor with gifts and an obligation to help his in-laws during the salmon runs or when they had other requests for assistance.

Not all prospective white husbands accepted the implications of their tribal custom marriage willingly, but no daughter of a good family was going to be allowed to "shack up" with anyone. The Coast Salish did not believe in premarital sex or pregnancy and good families chaperoned their virtuous daughters, as Captain Vancouver's crew noticed in 1792. Dr. Wayne Suttles, anthropologist and friend of the Coast Salish, summarized their view of marriage: "even [one] of short duration was still a marriage if some formal exchange of property had taken place and the intent to establish a bond had been announced. If it did not last it was merely a poor marriage."[10]

While the husband admittedly had practical advantages in mind and assumed that it was his right to decide if it was a real marriage or not, that probably diverted him from considering that the bride and her parents had their own agenda. Roeder and Peabody arrived just after new epidemics had apparently accelerated population decline, some power vacuums, village consolidation, and an imbalanced marriage pool. Marriage to a business, military, or government leader from the well-armed American invaders promised to benefit the family and its community. A daughter would live close by and her parents would have a son-in-law to mediate and influence the new authorities. A well-placed son-in-law might provide access to jobs and cash in the evolving economy. In the overwhelmingly male place, he would protect his wife in an unstable, possibly violent, atmosphere. In hindsight, the intermarriages took prominent, talented, intelligent young women out of the Coast Salish gene pool needed to rebuild the population.

CRINO

Even after the 1855 Treaty of Point Elliott cession of lands and the following Treaty War, life in Bellingham Bay's hamlets stayed largely one of peaceful cooperation and friendship with the Lummi and others, especially since so many were in-laws. Intermarried men may not have invited their brothers-in-law to an evening of cigars, whiskey, and poker, but friendly contact was frequent. Lummi and Nooksack families also ran the local canoe transportation business which was essential for any movement of civilians around the watery region. The Lummi had been largely Catholic since the early 1840s, but their missionaries ministered to all faiths if asked. Periodic priestly visits gathered everyone together for a week of church services, weddings, baptisms, and communal feasts. Reacting to mine manager E.C. Fitzhugh's pleas to the government for help, Fort Bellingham's mission was to protect the mine, settlers, and Native villages from the *Laich'wil'tach* ("unkillable ones") from Quadra and other islands off the north end of Vancouver Island, plus other "Northern raiders" from as far as southeast Alaska. Those raiders killed, plundered food supplies, and captured Coast Salish women and children to sell away forever. They killed occupants of canoes found in the bay and did not distinguish between settlers and Coast Salish. Cooperation enhanced everyone's ability to guard against and fight off the invaders in their fast-moving ocean canoes. It tied all residents tightly together.[11]

The few white women tended to overcome innate biases to form friendships with the indigenous wives who shared food and knowledge from the start. Irish lass Teresa Eldridge cooked for the mill crew while Lummi women babysat her red-haired toddler who soon spoke a second language. Cabin interior furnishings at first resembled those of a longhouse, with baskets, mats, and carved utensils and bowls obtained from the Lummi women. They shared recipes and cooking methods for unfamiliar foods: salmon for the white women, pies and cakes for the Native wives. All of them took in boarders, did laundry, nursed the sick or injured, and fed the bachelors. Everyday life tied women together.[12]

In what could have become a pattern, Roeder and Peabody's wives ended unhappily back with their own families. Several witnesses said later that Roeder hurriedly sent the high-born woman home with their two children when he received word that his Ohio fiancée would soon arrive. The children, and perhaps his wife, reportedly died within a few years. Peabody's wife went home after he left for California a few years later and sent his older children to a boarding home far to the south, where he expected they would be "civilized." Unlike Roeder, he provided for them with a gift of real estate before he left.[13]

The men's duplicity did not become the rule. In the first twenty years, in addition to Fort Bellingham's officers, sheriffs, justices of the peace, county commissioners, superintendents of schools, coal mine employees, county auditors, and the mine manager/territorial court justice—all married into indigenous families. They had the same unpredictable outcomes seen today: long-term unions, deaths, mutual divorce, men left, women left.

When Roeder's (white) daughter compiled the first comprehensive county history published in 1926, she omitted her father's first family so she could enshrine her mother and three other white women as the mothers of the community. Writers who followed dutifully covered the story up.[14]

CRSO

The nineteenth century American attitude toward all marriages was patriarchal. Legally, husbands controlled property and child custody. Laws disadvantaged women of any ethnicity and deemed them inherently inferior and less capable than men. After states and territories codified their marriage attitudes into regulations, they became the biased standard by which all other societies were judged. These attitudes probably typified those of most men at Bellingham Bay to a greater or lesser degree, something which often became apparent in the course of the marriage.

Mixed marriages had early presented legal dilemmas as American settlers moved into the regions where intermarriage was common. In 1824 a new judge arrived in Green Bay (Wisconsin), Michigan Territory. His first grand jury indicted thirty-six of the town's leading men for fornication. Most immediately got a "legal" wedding, but eight defied the court. It led to extended litigation against the indignant old men who refused to admit "immorality" in their long marriages to the mothers of their children. The case set a precedent for persecuting couples whose ceremonies did not fit the American idea of validity. Fifty years later, it echoed through Whatcom County.[15]

In 1854 Washington Territory's first legislature passed what the men probably thought was a boilerplate marriage law that included legitimizing common law marriages. They shortly realized it would include intermarriages and give indigenous wives inheritance rights to land claims. Less than a year later, they passed a defectively written amendment which confused everyone and appeared to both forbid and demand that men legally marry indigenous women. It voided intermarriages already solemnized, but if parties were together at the time of passage, they were to be left alone. None of it made any sense. Legislators imposed a $500 fine (over $13,000 in 2015) on anyone officiating at a mixed marriage.[16]

The new amendment revealed an unfamiliar problem for intermarried legislators who passed it. They saw that if the attempts to protect white culture became the final word, the law would disinherit their own mixed-blood children. The first Whatcom County marriage (a tribal custom one) was filed at the auditor's office after the fact, months before the new amendment went into effect, just to circumvent that reality. Thus began a chaotic succession of amendments over the next decade to limit intermarriages while at the same time keep those that existed legal and children legitimate heirs, but not cause undue trouble if someone did want to marry a Native woman.[17]

Anecdotal evidence exists that a priest and Justice of the Peace Russell Peabody officiated over intermarriages in Whatcom County during that period (*see* chapter 2). Whatcom County marriage records are absent from when the first amendment went into effect to after passage of the final one that paved the way for legal intermarriages. Though history records the missing records as lost in a windstorm or stolen, cash-strapped officiants may have avoided putting the weddings they performed in writing so they would not be subject to what was an enormous fine. The local intermarriages of that period do not appear in church records either.

The social environment of Whatcom County continued to be male-dominated until the 1870s. The mill burned in 1873 and the mine closed five years later, bringing the settlement's population down to a dozen families. However, the 1872 opening of the U.S. Land Office in Olympia and township surveys brought a wave of agricultural settlers. They homesteaded the traditional lands of the local Coast Salish which had been ceded in 1855. Soon outnumbering the "mossbacks," newcomers brought with them intolerant middle-class sensibilities about their intermarried neighbors and anyone living differently from themselves. If a mixed-marriage couple didn't have paper generated by civil or religious authority, the new moralists and their Protestant ministers saw the relationship as illegal concubinage. The new people also brought with them marriageable daughters, and a few teenage girls had by then grown up in Whatcom. Marriages of white men to full-blood Coast Salish women virtually ceased. Once the newcomers became a majority, they not only decried the ways of the "old settlers" with their Catholic wives, they began to pressure them (personally and in print) to conform to their stricter version of marital respectability. In the past, priests had not pressured their parishioners to have their tribal custom marriages blessed until the couple felt moved to do so. Now, some couples bowed under the social pressure and threats of new restrictive marriage legislation that would require civil unions. Most long-married tribal custom couples either re-married in civil or religious ceremonies, or they took out a license at the courthouse for documentation purposes but never followed up with another ceremony.[18]

"Local jealousies, selfish interests [and] political resentments" played a part in 1878 when criminal fornication indictments were brought in several Puget Sound counties against longtime intermarried men. A newspaper letter called the charges "frivolous and conceived in malice." In Whatcom County, Edward Eldridge (the much respected legislator and third settler) presided over a grand jury that included some legally intermarried men. They indicted nine "old settlers," all of whom knew most of the jurors and were in some cases friends, which makes racial prejudice doubtful as much of a factor in the indictments. Defendants included Henry Barkhousen, a former county auditor, legislator and election judge who had recently lodged an election procedure complaint against Eldridge.[19]

A recent decision by departing Third District Territorial Court Justice John Lewis (Appendix A) had invalidated the common-law marriage of a white couple and set a precedent against previously legal paperless marriages. The fornication defendants were generally prominent men in the early county whose marriages were decades-long. Eldridge and the jury probably intended to force the recalcitrants into line but the defendants maintained that their tribal custom marriages were just as legal as any other. Before the trials could take place, one of them died and seven others obtained the papers they had resisted. However, Henry Barkhousen loudly refused to dishonor his wife (daughter of treaty signer Seya'whom) and their seven children by taking the easy way out. Though defendant Charles Beale (on whose land claim Anacortes grew) and his wife had gone after the documentation, he asked for clarification of the term "marriage."[20]

Territorial Chief Justice Roger Greene took up the issue between sessions after Lewis left. Greene, well-known for his religiosity and uncommon belief in women's rights, thoughtfully considered the tangle of laws. He wrote an elegant legal opinion on the nature of marriage (Appendix B) that halted the divisive litigation and declared all tribal custom marriages valid. Greene saw marriage as a publicly declared and recognized contract between two people. He added his view that religious and civil ceremonies with their paper records were for the benefit of the government and church. Only the couple made the actual contract.

Greene concluded that if he ruled differently, by his own Christian-influenced reasoning, it would invalidate all contracts and other common law made after Adam and Eve, leading to legal chaos. Such a ruling would have also disrespected and failed to recognize marriages across the globe that took place within non-paper societies.

The question of tribal custom weddings' legal validity died for many decades before the legislature once again passed laws to regulate Washington State's marriages, including those on reservations.

CHAPTER 2

Caroline, The Widow Who Wasn't

CAROLINE KAVANAUGH, one of Skagit County's founding mothers, walked slowly along the six miles of country road between
Swinomish Reservation's Catholic Church and her aged cedar cabin
on *Shais-quihl*, now called March Point. Caroline's brown skin was
deeply wrinkled but her eyes still shone. She had spent nearly her
entire life on the three-mile long peninsula south of Bellingham Bay,
her homeland, her *illahee*. *Shais-quihl* held the story of her childhood,
most of her married life with two men, and thirty years of widow-
hood.

In the distance, she saw a motorcycle roaring toward her, dust
clouds billowing. The young rider easily recognized the tiny woman
whose long wavy hair reached almost to the ground when it wasn't in
her usual braid. Even in old age, her lifelong pride was still not fully
gray.

U.S. Navy sailor Lyman Kavanaugh braked his new machine to
a dusty halt and greeted his beloved grandmother. He kidded the
famously independent woman. "Grandma, don't you want a ride?"
Everyone knew how Caroline would bristle and reject offers of assistance.

The little woman surprised her grandson when she gathered her
long skirt and climbed up behind him without hesitation. Caroline
relished her ride home, hair flowing behind, brushed by the wind.[1]

CAROLINE

Writers have told the life of Caroline and her husbands within
accepted stereotypes. More than one called her a "princess" to fit
American beliefs about Native women when no such term existed
in her culture. In his time, her first husband, Robert Davis, was the
victim of regional assumptions about his famous family, though he

25

Caroline Davis Kavanaugh, daughter of Samish and Swinomish parents. The photograph was taken in 1913 for her interview in the *Anacortes American. Wallie Funk Collection, courtesy of Anacortes Museum, Anacortes, Washington.*

aspired to a much different life. Local historians lumped James Kavanaugh with Irish famine immigrants whose stories were actually much different from his own.[2]

In 1982 a writer said that Caroline had been adopted from a Cowichan war party when a raid collapsed. Nothing could be farther from the truth. Her parents came from neighboring Swinomish (*Swidabish*) and Samish (*Sam'sh*) villages south of Bellingham Bay. Daily life was nearly identical, yet less than ten miles of land and water formed an invisible line between two language groups who identified most with others who spoke their own. Their home and resource territories overlapped and as a child she frequented both of her parents' winter villages. The Samish clustered mostly on Samish Island, were small in number, spoke Straits Salish like the Lummi, and built their strongest ties to villages north and west across the islands to southern Vancouver Island. The Swinomish spoke Lushootseed and had close ties to villages south of them and in the Cascade Mountains watershed. Caroline was at minimum bilingual and perhaps spoke additional dialects of villages in the overlapping area. Unlike most Coast Salish wives who lived in villages distant from their birth families, her mother's home was just a short canoe ride away.[3]

Caroline said that her father Has'loch/Syalaxcut had led a major Samish winter village named for the blue camas flowers. The site of his and Caroline's birth was located on *Shais-quihl* peninsula of "Fidalgo" Island, separated from the mainland only by a winding slough. Camas abounded on the peninsula between the shallow tidal flats of two bountiful river-fed bays. His own Vancouver Island mother married into the Samish village, which was used only during seasonal harvests by the time of Caroline's birth there.[4]

Samish Island, the cultural seat and main winter village on the north side of Padilla Bay, was only three miles long and three-quarters of a mile wide. The Samish also had houses on Guemes Island just to the west. By the time of her birth, the only winter villages were probably on those two islands as epidemic-driven consolidation continued. Many astonished visitors in the 1850s described Samish longhouses over 1,200 feet long. During Caroline's childhood in-law relationships closely tied the Samish and upriver Lushootseed-speakers the Nuwhaha, who had retreated to their ancient home on Samish Island. Families there routinely spoke both languages.

Hundreds of years ago the Swinomish fortified their main village a few miles from *Shais-quihl* with ditches and ironwood stakes to protect it from unfriendlies who could reach it at high tide via its slough. Once the Lower Skagits were guarding the coastline, the Swinomish developed about twenty villages largely in peace, but after repeated epidemics, they abandoned most of them.[5]

Caroline's mother, Tsis'dias, probably came from the large village on winding Swinomish Slough between Fidalgo Island and the mainland. It provided a calm detour when storms brought gale-force winds to the open waters and village residents welcomed strangers who sought shelter. Most importantly, the slough hid the village from the view of passing hostile parties.

The tidal estuaries surrounding *Shais-quihl* produced a rich food environment that added to their fishing territories. Marital alliances with Lushootseed-speakers up the rivers also gave the Swinomish access to mountain resources unavailable at the edge of the saltwater. Swinomish and Samish resource territories overlapped on *Shais-quihl* where women burned the ferns and grass, and cultivated camas and potatoes in marked hereditary fields. Mothers passed their rights to daughters, so Caroline would inherit her *Shais-quihl* plots as well as any others her mother administered. Her Samish father had access to his own family's sites on the western side of the peninsula around his old village. The couple would have had use of other Samish and Swinomish resource places, and since there was a Vancouver Island grandmother, permission was probably granted to use more distant sites.[6]

Documents and census reports place Caroline's birth between 1836 and 1845. Based on Coast Salish average age at marriage and known facts of her life, the most likely time was 1840-1843, which made her fourteen to seventeen at the time of her first marriage, after her puberty seclusion and education in women's skills. Although she also owned the name Chelthkabaut, Caroline's grandchildren referred to her affectionately as "Stoly," short for her names Tol-asth (Swinomish) and Tol Stola (Samish), which she used as well as her baptismal name.[7]

Caroline never clearly identified the winter village she called home during her childhood. Observers reported a small Samish one at the base of *Shais-quihl*, but it was also abandoned at some point. Her father probably joined one of the large houses on nearby Samish Island where the water from four springs enabled it to support both the Samish and Nuwhaha. In her childhood, it was led by a S'Klallam man married to an important Samish woman. There, families held great feasts at the massive potlatch house on the southern edge of the island, near the salt marsh strip (a "tombolo") that connected it to the mainland at low tide.[8]

Caroline's daily life probably resembled that of other daughters from important families. She learned family history, etiquette and obligations, and to perfect her special gifts. Her family followed the seasonal movements, and attended distant potlatches and winter dancing gatherings. She certainly took part in the spring's First Salmon rite, in which children played a central role at the ritual feast that ushered in the harvest and assured future returns of the critical resource.

Intruding into the centuries-old routines, several circumstances in the 1840s led to major changes in Caroline's early life. First, Catholic missionaries arrived to convert the villagers of the northern Sound. Swinomish people who attended the first gathering at Whidbey Island were impressed by the priest's message and manner. They returned home with a "Catholic Ladder" banner that visually taught the basic tenets of Christianity without language. They soon built a simple church at Swinomish Slough after holding their first prayer meetings in a longhouse. The Swinomish adoption of Catholicism cemented the influence of Euro-American culture in the communities of the Skagit River.

Second, the *Laich'wil'tach* and other Northerners increased their seasonal raids after Fort Victoria was built in 1843. Despite their defenses, the Samish and Swinomish lost many men, women, and children to the raiders.

In 1848, when Caroline was a still a young child, measles spread to the Northwest from California and moved among hundreds of villages for ten months. Thousands died. It swept through her homeland in April when villagers were most physically vulnerable. Some tribes lost 50 percent of their people, which may have triggered the Nuwhaha move. In the winter of 1852-53, smallpox once again attacked the Samish and Swinomish, this time down the Skagit River from east of the Cascades. It left untouched those who had contracted it in the 1830s and anyone vaccinated by the Hudson's Bay Company (HBC) doctors or missionary priests. In later interviews, Caroline mentioned only her father and one sister (Annie or Alice) who were alive at the time of her marriage, so she may have lost her mother and some siblings that devastating winter. She inevitably lost extended family members at least. The Samish population dropped to 200 from the 2000 of the early 1840s.[9]

In the years before she met Lieutenant Robert Davis and moved to Fort Bellingham, Caroline and her family had already seen some local intermarriages, as well as those at HBC forts. The first white man known to settle in the area, "Blanket Bill" Jarman lived on Samish Island with his S'Klallam wife. And in 1855, George Richardson Hall married a Samish relative of Caroline's and took her to live in the tiny Sehome Mine community.[10]

ROBERT HUGH DAVIS

Lt. Robert Hugh Davis belonged to the most famous extended family in Mississippi. By the 1850s his uncle Jefferson Davis was Secretary of War and Uncle Joseph a wealthy and influential planter-lawyer. Jefferson would become president of the Confederate States of America at the onset of the Civil War. But Robert seems to be the most obscure (perhaps even deliberately so) member of the Davis family. The extensive official Davis family genealogy only records his birth and death years, an anomaly.[11]

Robert's father Samuel A. Davis migrated with his parents and nine other children after the Revolution to the "Dixie Frontier." They settled in Woodville near the great river in Mississippi where Robert's grandparents and others pursued an unwelcome toehold in the Choctaw and Chickasaw homeland. The senior Davis (Samuel E.) worked the fields beside his slaves and grew prosperous. The Davises instilled the value of higher education and a strong sense of duty in their children.

Robert's father Sam staked a claim one hundred miles upriver from the others at a long-time junction of indigenous trade routes, the place which became Vicksburg. He married Lucinda Throckmorton, daughter of another first settler, and in 1824 she gave birth to Robert Hugh, her fourth child of six. Life in general was uncomfortable and difficult. One settler wrote "If you wish to see splendid poverty, come to Mississippi. If you wish to see people worth millions living as they were not worth hundreds, come down here."[12]

Robert's grandfather died the same year he was born, and the way he died deeply affected Davis family dynamics. Debt had forced him to sell "Poplar Grove" to his eldest son Joseph for a pittance which left him nearly impoverished. Young Samuel A. and his father quarreled violently while working one day. Impulsively, Robert's grandfather took a few slaves on a flatboat and headed downriver to his son Isaac at Davis Bend. The feud and strenuous trip were too much for the aging man who died of a fever six days after landing. Robert's uncle Joseph became the family patriarch who would control the family and Robert's future.[13]

When Robert was seven, his own father died, leaving Lucinda with four children under twelve and great debts. She eventually lost her land to Joseph, who quit claimed it back so she and the children could stay in their home.[14]

Planter society and its laws did not consider women capable of running their own affairs, and slaveholding widows like Lucinda almost always turned over the management of their cotton fields to a relative or overseer. Robert and his brothers may have had large responsibilities at a young age. Joseph sent Benjamin, the eldest boy, to school in Memphis, and probably paid for Robert's private education since there were no public schools in Vicksburg.[15]

The slavery system that supported the Davis clan and the region's economy gave birth to the Vicksburg society of Robert's youth. Until the 1850s, his hometown featured only unpainted storefronts, dirt streets, roaming hogs, scavenger dogs, and roaches. Religion played little part and the river brought in gamblers and other miscreants. A distinctive feature of local culture was its fascination with dueling. It was a custom supported by the Davis clan that had even diminished their political influence for a time and that would pursue Robert to Bellingham Bay.

In this subrosa violent atmosphere, local culture encouraged Robert and his friends to pursue "manly" vices and entertainments: approved forms of aggression toward slaves, hunting, swearing, drinking, and "wenching" (forced sex with female slaves). This male subculture often produced "black sheep" among those who were not plantation heirs.

Twenty-two when the Mexican War began, Robert became a private in his Uncle Jefferson's "Vicksburg Southrons" company of the 1st Mississippi Volunteers, later renamed the "Mississippi Rifles." Congressman-turned-Colonel Davis insisted they carry the new rifled musket which gave Robert experience he called upon in the Northwest later. In the battle for Monterey, Robert's regiment lost the most men of 119 volunteer units, and was still first over the walls. The regimental surgeon declared Robert disabled after Monterey, either sick or wounded. He left for home at (or about) the same time as his uncle, and helped with Jefferson's successful campaign for the U.S. Senate.[16]

After Robert's older brother Benjamin left for the California gold rush in 1849, he had more responsibility at home. By 1850 Lucinda, Robert, and his younger brother lived near Jefferson's plantation at Woodville. The census listed the young men as "planters" and they may have been working for Jefferson, who had gone to Washington, D.C. Robert, still without a career path, without land or inheritance, was open to new possibilities.[17]

Benjamin permanently abandoned his privileged life when he went to California. By 1855 he co-owned a pack train business in the new gold rush boomtown Jacksonville, Oregon. Unusual evidence suggests that Robert visited to see if he wanted to join his brother in the West, where Benjamin became a lifetime gold-chaser and city father. The intriguing signature of witness "Robert Davis" appears on the January 22, 1855, Point Elliott Treaty. There is no evidence of any other "Robert Davis" in western Washington at that time, except the Secretary of War's nephew.[18]

The 1855 treaty was a business contract between sovereign nations, the U.S. government and the Puget Sound peoples (designated "tribes") from the Duwamish at Seattle north to British territory. It was not a surrender treaty, though the presence of the army with their guns was intimidating and made the signing less than voluntary. At the time, the new territory's legislature was trying to codify the legal position of Native and mixed-blood people regarding marriage, estates, legal conflicts, voting rights, etc. The settlers opposed removal of their in-laws, neighbors, and labor force, but wanted their land. Territorial Governor Isaac Stevens headed the federal commission to negotiate a binding treaty that would specify lands to be relinquished for remuneration in money and services, lands and rights reserved by the tribes, and behavior expected of both parties. Caroline's people believed that *Shais-quihl* would be a reservation because the treaty named it specifically. However, Article 7 gave the government the right to remove residents from any of the reservations in order to consolidate or to sell the land to homesteaders, making the reserved lands permanent only at the government's discretion. The U.S. Senate took four years to ratify the treaty, giving settlers like Robert Davis (and John Tennant, *see* chapter 4) time to move across the proposed boundaries, expecting to be left alone as had happened in other places. The Civil War and Reconstruction period occupied federal attention and funds, and *Shais-quihl* received nothing that would develop it as a reservation. It was ultimately ignored as if it had never been in the treaty at all.[19]

Jefferson Davis had a deep interest in the Pacific Northwest. He promoted all Senate bills that supported development of the Northwest, and did more after he became Secretary of War in 1853. He established two new infantry regiments for Washington Territory in 1855 to respond to entreaties for more defense, including against northern raiders attacking Bellingham Bay. If Robert was in the Pacific Northwest in January 1855, his uncle's interest in the region may have encouraged him to be in attendance at the treaty signing.[20]

It should not be surprising that Jefferson saw an opportunity to indulge his interest in the Northwest, and at the same time give his thirty-one-year-old nephew a chance at one of the few professions acceptable to planter society. Of the officers Davis selected for the new regiments, half were political appointments, and regular army officers used any political leverage they had. Young West Pointers coveted the rare chance at promotion in a new regiment because they languished behind old men refusing to retire. Robert's only military service had been his months in the "Mississippi Rifles" in Mexico. He never attended (or even applied to) West Point like the other officers of the company he joined, but he still secured the First Lieutenant position courtesy of his uncle. Jefferson appointed two West Pointers to Company D: Captain George Pickett from the Texas frontier and 2nd Lieutenant Hugh Fleming.[21]

Robert did not report in when the 9th Infantry organized in March, possibly because he was still on the way home from the Northwest. In May he met with Jefferson in Mississippi, who advised his nephew to take advantage of the career opportunity. In late August, Jefferson wrote to Joseph from the capital: "Robert arrived here this morning. As soon as he gets his outfit will proceed to his post at old Point Comfort. I gave him the new tactics, the text book of his regiment, giving him some 'good advice.' He has many high soldierly qualities and as he has never studied enough to test his mental power, I hope for more than you probably expect, if he can be stimulated to earnest exertion." Jefferson's description of Robert quite fits that of a directionless family "black sheep" who had entered his thirties without profession or marriage.²²

First Lieutenant Davis commanded Company D on their long sail to Fort Steilacoom because Pickett was on court martial duty. The new regiment boosted the number of army regulars in the Northwest to two thousand men charged with the protection of a vast territory stretching east into today's Montana. Nine companies left for service in the field, but Company D stayed behind to work on a ferry and blockhouse up the Puyallup River. In August, Robert sailed for Bellingham Bay.²³

On top of the usual frustrations associated with service at isolated western forts, political appointee Robert faced disrespect from fellow officers and enlisted men alike because of his lack of a West Point education or any service in the West. He took charge of teaching riflery to the untrained city boys and immigrants who were most of the privates, but whose weapon training had been largely neglected before they arrived.²⁴

CAROLINE AND ROBERT

Caroline never specified the place or occasion when she met her lieutenant, but others said it was at the "Eldridge" place on Little Squalicum Creek just north of Whatcom. That seems plausible since it lay on the crude road to the fort and Lt. Davis would have passed by frequently. Those sources assumed that meant the Edward Eldridge family's cabin, but when the couple met the only home there was Jim

Tse'wanamuck's longhouse. Edward Eldridge granted his surname to "Jim Eldridge" for the land claim, the sole transaction in which a settler offered a longhouse owner some kind of payment. Tse'wanamuck worked for Eldridge and continued to live in his home where he and his wife Katherine fostered children and sheltered many guests. She and Caroline may have been related through mutual Vancouver Island families and so Caroline and her sister would be welcome to stay there when at the bay, possibly for some time if their mother had died.[25]

Caroline described a meeting between her father and Robert Davis, and despite the 1913 Anacortes newspaper's romanticized version of an unrecorded conversation, the content is consistent with a wise Coast Salish father's thinking. She said her father viewed the alliance as one that would benefit their people by insuring cooperation with the military, easing tensions, and preventing future bloodshed. Caroline's father probably treated her marriage with the same agenda as with another native leader. She would be a "peace weaver." An army officer would be reluctant to attack his in-laws, and both parties would also mediate and transmit her father's point of view to the authorities at Fort Bellingham. Lieutenant James Forsyth may have met his Swinomish wife Mary about the same time. It is possible that the young women met the officers during heightened tensions when some native men allegedly killed a government surveyor on Whidbey Island. Davis and a detachment went to the Swinomish village looking for the suspects. This show of force by the heavily-armed competing authority in the area would have alerted area headmen to the implications of conflict.[26]

The two young officers had their own reasons for their unions with Caroline and Mary, which probably included convenient sex, housekeeping, and companionship. The 1913 article reported that Caroline said her marriage ceremony was attended by family and settlers. Either tribal or civil ceremony may well have been at the Eldridge land claim. Justice of the Peace Edward Eldridge had authority to marry them, though, as with Captain Pickett's and Forsyth's weddings, documenting that he united a mixed-race couple would bring an overwhelming fine. In the absence of a county marriage record, only Caroline's word (or what the writer said she said) evidenced there was a "Boston" (white) wedding to supplement the tribal custom one. Until she died, Caroline kept a large china platter the Eldridges gave her and Robert as a wedding gift, and remained close friends with Ed and Teresa.[27]

Robert's unlikely marriage to a non-white woman had its precedent in his family. Jefferson Davis contracted a tribal custom marriage to a young Menominee woman when he was a young army officer in Wisconsin. He probably never intended a permanent relationship despite many Menominee intermarriages among local friends and French-Canadian men. The young woman's family certainly expected the alliance to be a real marriage. Near the end of his service in Wisconsin, he fathered Joseph. During the Civil War, Jefferson's son fought under his tribal name (Ah-kah-kum-ahot) in a Union infantry unit composed almost entirely of Menominee men. After the war, one of Jefferson's prison guards on leave checked on the well-being of "Mrs. Davis" as everyone knew her in Wisconsin. Joseph Davis became the last living Civil War veteran in his county where whites and Indians alike publicly recognized him as the Confederate president's son.[28]

If Jefferson had ever shared his early Wisconsin intermarriage history with Robert, his nephew might have seen a parallel in his own situation 20 years later when he also was far away from Davis family control and expectations. Caroline moved into Robert's quarters at the fort. Frontier officer housing had advantages intended to make life as pleasant as possible. The Officers' Quarters contained four units with a covered walk in the middle. Caroline's home had a front and rear room that shared a fireplace with the next unit. Covered porches protected her from rain and summer sun. Handsome local sandstone walkways between buildings graced the fort. Soldiers painted the Officers' Quarters white and installed green "Venetian blinds." Although Captain Pickett lived in town with his Alaskan native wife, Lt. Forsyth (Fleming's replacement) and Dr. Robert O. Craig also lived in the quarters with their Coast Salish wives.[29]

Officers' wives were generally middle-class "ladies" who expected to have help with the tedious and difficult chores at frontier forts. In addition to the company laundresses, off-duty enlisted men ("strikers") often looked after horses and equipment, made fires, cleaned the homes and sometimes cooked. Like the white wives, Caroline had been raised to expect servants to free her from mundane chores. Fifty years later, she still remembered the army servants who helped in her home.[30]

The attention that the fort's men paid to her, which she long remembered, was likely a result of her own attractiveness as much as the small number of women at the fort. She never forgot her new clothes, most of which were certain to have felt constricting and bulky. The new style she had to adopt reminded soldiers of the girls at home. Caroline was young and pretty with a lively personality and as the first lieutenant's wife, she probably received much respectful attention from the lonely soldiers. Caroline also found a teacher in the missionary priest, Father Casimir Chirouse. He taught her to read and write English when he periodically visited Bellingham Bay. The lessons enabled her to enjoy newspapers and magazines until her death. Reading her Bible regularly contributed to her lifelong devotion to the Catholic Church.[31]

⁊⁊⁊

To Southern men, gambling had become a ritualized way to beat rivals without violence. Not to play when invited implied some level of cowardice as much as being antisocial. If a man cheated in this atmosphere of "friendly" rivalry, it was the highest disgrace. Less than a year after Robert arrived, Sehome Coal Mine manager Edmund C. Fitzhugh accused him of cheating in a card game at the mine saloon. Fitzhugh was a Virginian and an expert gambler whose company the locals enjoyed, but who they also knew to be deadly when angered. Only two months earlier he had killed Andrew Wilson, a drunken trespasser taking a shortcut home through Fitzhugh's back garden (*See* ch. 3).[32]

Both Davis and Fitzhugh often drank too much and were fearless by reputation. When whiskey-fueled gambling led to a quarrel about cheating, Caroline's husband risked his life when he challenged Fitzhugh to a duel.[33]

Captain Pickett intervened as soon as he heard about the impending duel, something already forbidden by the army, and convinced his friend Fitzhugh to decline the challenge. Davis argued with Pickett regarding his interference in this affair of personal honor. The heated argument ended with Robert's angry resignation on August 1, 1857. The Pacific Northwest offered civilian opportunities like those his older brother Benjamin had found in Oregon.[34]

Robert's men wrote an open letter to the Olympia newspaper two days after he resigned. They praised his competence, fairness, and "repeated acts of humanity" to men who were far from home. Perhaps believing that he would immediately leave for the South, the enlisted men wished him a "long and affectionate farewell." The paper printed the letter, unusual because officers and soldiers alike came and went. Their affection did not end there. Three days later, a more formal commendation from Robert's non-commissioned officers and privates (but not his fellow officers) appeared in the paper. They referred to his Mexican War heroism "to which conduct he undoubtedly owes his rank and station," and pointedly overlooked his political appointment.[35]

Perhaps to the surprise of everyone but Caroline, Robert did not leave town. He stayed with his wife, but Caroline's privileged lifestyle ended when they vacated their quarters abruptly. The same day the newspaper printed the first letter, the army advertised for bids on a contract to hunt and furnish meat to the Northwest Boundary Survey Commission and its military escort. Robert got the temporary job that a Mississippi marksman who grew up hunting for sport could do well.[36]

Soldiers who resigned often settled near their last post and started farms or businesses with savings. Robert purchased Assistant Indian Agent Charles Vail's half-interest in William Busey & Company. He became co-owner of a store, saloon, three lots, and a house. If Busey was unmarried (as seems the case), the three probably shared the house, and Caroline cooked, cleaned, and did laundry for both men. It's possible that Caroline baked bread for the store.[37]

Robert soon took an additional job when the county commission appointed him deputy sheriff. During his first month, he had a second confrontation with Pickett when the captain hosted a dignitaries' Christmas dinner. That day, soldiers beat local hunter Edward French when they suspected him of harboring deserters at his camp. Deputy Sheriff Davis brought assault charges against the soldiers and put up part of the accused's bond after his arrest. Pickett retaliated with a counter charge, putting Robert in the middle until the matter was resolved.[38]

Robert publicly opposed Fitzhugh again when he was the second man to sign a petition against the mine manager-lawyer's federal appointment to the territorial judiciary and the district that would include Whatcom County. It cited intimidation of voters, "autocratic and overbearing conduct" with the "poorer classes" that had alienated them, lack of qualifications, and the killing of Wilson. Davis was also on the witness list for Fitzhugh's murder trial, having seen the victim drinking at a saloon (probably his own) prior to the murder.[39]

Robert's business partner resigned from the county commission in mid-June 1858 to take over sheriff duties in the midst of the gold rush chaos, and Robert continued as deputy. Unlike that of the previous sheriffs and deputies in the county's four-year history, his frontier youth and military experience had equipped him with invaluable skills to handle the hordes of drunken rowdies and track suspects. The partners kept busy enforcing the law on the muddy streets and running their enterprises. One of their major tasks was separating indigenous women and men from incoming miners who did not see them as neighbors, friends, and family as the locals did. Enforcement of liquor, prostitution, and gambling laws was generally a losing effort and after Busey opened a store at Point Roberts near the Fraser River's mouth, Robert was left to keep the peace alone most of the time.[40]

Caroline could have already been pregnant when Robert left the army since she gave birth to Samuel sometime in 1858. The baby's name honored three men in Robert's family: his grandfather, father, and a deceased younger brother. For a planter-class Southerner, using that name for his son signaled Robert's intention to make the mixed-blood newborn boy his legal heir. The Whatcom County men who considered abandoning their family someday, and those that voluntarily did so, did not use that naming pattern.[41]

Caroline probably used her skills to make money from the thousands of miners camped on the beach and in the settlements like the other wives in the area. Most houses had boarders and women's ability to cook, launder, sew, and heal were in high demand by the

Whatcom, 1873. Taken five years after the 1868 forest fire that erased Unionville, the photograph clearly shows the damage to the forest as well as the town's lack of growth following the end of the 1858 gold rush. James and Caroline Kavanaugh, as well as John Tennant and other Nooksack River farmers, sold fresh produce and other foodstuffs at the settlement. Visible fourth from the left (under arrow) is the Whatcom County Territorial Courthouse, the oldest brick building in Washington State, and a remnant from the gold rush. *Unknown photographer, Image #1995.0001.008694. Whatcom Museum, Bellingham, Washington.*

stranded miners. With Caroline and his son, Robert threw his lot in with the Northwest's future like Benjamin had. He was on his way to an entirely new life far different from that of the directionless young man he had once been.

The following February, when the miners and most businesses were long gone, county commissioners ordered Sheriff Busey to turn in his liquor license money from Pt. Roberts, and the school tax collection records. With all the new businesses and townsite lot sales, there had been many more potential taxpayers in 1858 for a brief time. The money collected in flush times was critically important afterwards. A few weeks later, seeing no money or Busey, the commission confiscated his official bond, some of which Robert had put up. They decided that Busey had "absconded" with the county funds and appointed a new sheriff. Robert's association with Busey possibly put him under a cloud, though he continued as deputy until James Kavanaugh took over the position.[42]

A new opportunity opened just then with the intersection of the treaty ratification, Robert's acquaintance with some men open to new ventures, and Caroline's birthplace on *Shais-quihl*. Ratification of the Point Elliott Treaty in 1859 should have established what lands would be closed to white settlement permanently, but government negligence allowed the land-hungry to encroach on the peninsula once reserved for the native groups.

Robert went hunting on *Shais-quihl* with a party of newcomers. They liked the point's low fern prairie above the crab and clam beaches, with uplands in the middle where deer roamed. Though the old winter village stood abandoned, the extensive potato and camas fields were still obvious. Most important, a spring behind the village site could supply ample water for more than one cabin. Robert and the others found *Shais-quihl* immensely attractive for agriculture, though James Carr (*see* chapter 5) and another man from Whatcom had found it too inhospitable to stay. Robert's group ignored *Shais-quihl's* designation as future reservation land, just as John Tennant (*see* chapter 4) was doing within what were to be reserved Lummi lands at the same time. Robert and Charles Beale marked out "squatter" claims and built a makeshift cabin that straddled the proposed line between them.[43]

The two wandering Southerners from illustrious military families planted a small crop. According to Beale, they stayed at the cabin into the following winter when the snow was deep and food scarce. They hunted deer and canoed the meat to town for sale. In mid-winter they were joined by William Munks. When Robert moved Caroline and Sam to the cabin it allowed her to live much closer to her relatives, some of whom may have worked for them, as in most intermarriages. It was Caroline's family who understood how to grow crops on *Shais-quihl*. Most important for Robert's purposes, his wife doubled his claim to the land if the peninsula became part of the promised reservation. Beale, Munks, and the next few arrivals all married Samish, Swinomish, and Kikiallus (Lower Skagit) women who probably also had some hereditary resource claims there.[44]

Robert and the other husbands counted on the usual government leniency with "old settlers" whose claims intruded on the edges of reservation land. His claim to Caroline's land grew stronger when the Territorial Indian Agent announced after ratification that persons holding claims on Fidalgo Island would not be disturbed in their "possessory rights." The real message was that *Shais-quihl* would be taken out of any planned reservation and given over to the men.[45]

After two years of marriage, the Civil War disrupted the life Caroline and Robert were building with little Sam at the place where she was born. Mississippi seceded and a March 1861 newspaper headlined that Robert's uncle had been elected president of the Confederacy. Robert's visibility inevitably called attention to his politics and he could not avoid the increasingly virulent public attacks on the uncle who mentored him and had been a patron of the Northwest.[46]

Rhetoric increased. "The war spirit in the South is increasing. Jeff Davis declares that 75 times 75,000 of Lincoln's troops can't subdue the South…Davis says he will march to Washington and take it in 30 days." Possibly worse for Robert, the plan to suspend all mail to the South appeared in the paper. He would be completely cut off from his Mississippi family except for long-delayed news from Northern newspapers.[47]

Other Southerners in the region preferred money-making to serious interest in the war, except as it affected their distant families. The picture for Robert was more complicated. Evidence suggests that the long reach of the Davis family had already tried to disrupt his life with Caroline.

Published eyewitness accounts described Davis family actions, but often confused people and events, which led to decades of debate about Caroline and Robert's next months. For example, one version posited an alleged visit by Jefferson Davis, or family women from Mississippi, to convince Robert to go home. Jefferson never set foot west of the Mississippi after his Wisconsin years, and no respectable Davis woman would ever travel alone to Washington Territory to discuss Robert's "inappropriate" marriage.[48]

Yet, some things are plausible. According to William Munks' son, Jefferson wrote to Robert after one of the family women visited. The letter repeated her offer for Caroline to become a family ward whom the family would educate. The Davis men had done the same with some non-white children in the past. It was said to have made the couple so angry they had a priest marry them again. The offer would be consistent with the Davis brothers' habitual patriarchal control of the clans' younger members whose fathers had died. The offer was a way to separate a Davis from a non-white wife (not a mistress) who could never advance his career, military or otherwise, in the South.[49]

The family woman who visited would probably have been Pauline, Benjamin's wife, asked to convince Robert to adhere to family marriage "rules." Davis family women were as much influenced by the cultural line between "women" and "ladies" as the men. By their standards, Caroline was "common" and did not belong. She was an "unsuitable" wife. Not only that but little Sam, if a legal heir in Washington, might cause a legal fuss in Mississippi if his father died and Caroline sought support or a share of Robert's mother's estate.

The letter and visit point to the seriousness with which Robert had taken his marriage and his new home. He told the family, including the women, about his intermarriage with a non-white woman, which defied elite Southerners' social custom. When he could have left, he started a business and then a farm instead. Robert had given clear notice of his intent to stay in the West with his new family.

Robert had a dilemma, but he seems to have stayed with Caroline and Sam until mid-summer. As war overtook the nation, residents devoured the two bi-weekly territorial newspapers, though their news was weeks old. Given the increasingly vitriolic editorials about his uncle, Robert's local position was untenable by any standard. In July a small item appeared, almost buried in the delayed war news. One of Robert's cousins had enlisted in the Union army, and the paper noted that "he expresses great anxiety to put a ball through his traitorous relative." There is little doubt that Robert either read or heard about the item and given his enlistment in September, he probably left soon after the article appeared.[50]

In Caroline's paraphrased words in 1913, Robert explained that a war was starting and "honor called him to take up arms in defense of the land of his birth." Whether or not this was an accurate rendering of what she said, the statement's intent seems consistent with an effort to explain the situation in a way that she could understand. Caroline told her interviewer that she and three-year-old Sam accompanied Robert to Port Townsend where he caught a steamer bound for Portland and the month-long trip home. If a relative left with him, as she said, it was probably Benjamin going back to Jacksonville, Oregon, where Copperhead Southerners were forming a chapter of the Knights of the Golden Circle and a newspaper. Robert and Caroline might have been welcome there, but he chose differently.[51]

Charles Beale, the friend who settled next to Robert and Caroline, also reported that a Davis relative visited. Caroline's interview said one met him in Port Townsend to escort him back to Mississippi, but Benjamin never went south. More likely, he came from Oregon to discuss their situation as the Confederate president's nephews. The uncles (and maybe their mother) were probably pressuring both of them, and they discussed things in person before the mail service was cut off, as Caroline hinted later. Ben was 41 and had a house full of small children and another birth imminent. He stayed in Oregon. Robert was 37 with combat and officer experience.[52]

One of Caroline's friends said that Robert gave her two $20 gold pieces to help support his family while he was away at what everyone expected to be a short conflict. She fully expected him to return after he fought for his family's honor. After all, he had not taken her son from her and put him in a white home, as other departing fathers did. The money to take care of his family would be worth over $1000 today. Caroline, in her early twenties, stayed in the area, either with her family or in the cabin on *Shais-quihl* among friends, to prevent someone else taking the land. She said she received letters from Robert, but that is unlikely after the mails were cut off. Perhaps she received something from Benjamin.[53]

From Caroline's neighbor William Munks came a report that she had another visit from a Davis family member who asked her to release Robert from their marriage about a year after he left. If the report is true, it confirms that the couple had been legally married and also had a Catholic ceremony. Munks told his son that she rejected an offer of money.[54]

Caroline said her last letter arrived in 1863 during the Mississippi campaign and she told her 1913 interviewer it said "he was tired of life and longing to hear the laughter of his son on far off Puget Sound." The editor's rendition is questionable and the date for the letter and her remarriage and pregnancy were very close together. It would be unusual for a Confederacy letter to have gotten through. However, Robert's life did take an abrupt turn at that time. It is possible that a newspaper piece was read to her but remembered as a letter. She never knew what really happened.

The local status of young Samuel remained as the son and heir of a living Robert Davis until her second marriage. Because no one knew exactly what happened to his father, the probate court did not appoint a white male guardian for their son. Caroline retained control of her boy's future, something other Native wives lost if their husband died or left.

Robert

Whatever Robert's intentions were, they didn't last long once he was immersed in home, family, and war. If anyone wrote a letter to Caroline as late as 1863, his statement of longing was a lie.

He enlisted on September 6, 1861, in Vicksburg joining other relatives who took unit leadership roles. Robert gave his age as thirty-two (actually thirty-seven) and enlisted for the duration, not just three years. He organized the "Brierfield Defenders" (Co. G) in the 24th Mississippi Infantry, named in honor of Jefferson's home. As captain, he would walk with his men into the enemy guns.[55]

In December 1861, Captain Davis was still in Vicksburg and married nineteen-year-old Katherine Auter. Her older brother had joined Robert's unit and her father was a prosperous local riverboat owner-captain. Robert thus became a bigamist, in ethical truth if not in documentation.[56]

In November 1862 Robert returned to Vicksburg to find recruits. The Davis name was probably expected to win over some of the resistant farmers.[57]

By April 1863, hordes of troops were building more fortifications on the bluffs of a chaotic Vicksburg. General Ulysses Grant was determined to take the "Gibraltar of the Confederacy" and control all traffic on the Mississippi and the railroad lines shipping the town's ordnance production out.[58]

After 24,000 men started an overland assault, Robert may have switched to scouting as many officers did before a battle, operating alone and in civilian clothes. He knew the Mississippi's bottom lands, sloughs, and peninsulas very well.[59]

On May 18, 1863, Captain Robert Davis' location indicates he was apparently alone between the oncoming Union forces and the defenses of Vicksburg. Grant's forces nabbed him.[60]

After Vicksburg fell, 30,000 prisoners were exchanged, but it probably did not take long for Robert's captors to realize their prisoner was not just any Davis, but a *Davis*, who could be a valuable pawn. General Grant sent Robert and 701 other unrepentant officers to prison at Johnson's Island in Lake Erie. Robert became both a military and political prisoner.[61]

Back in Washington Territory, Caroline said his family wrote that he was dead. In November, the county commissioners dropped the lawsuit they had filed against him and Henry Roeder to recover the runaway Sheriff Busey's bond. If it was spurred by news that Davis was dead, missing, or imprisoned, accurate information never reached Caroline.[62]

Robert Davis suffered miserable conditions at the new Union prison where 2,500 pampered Southern officers refused to clean their barracks. That winter, temperatures dropped to -50 degrees and periodically rations were cut.[63]

Robert was no ordinary prisoner. At some point, authorities put him in "close confinement," a solitary cell in a special building, and records imply that he was shackled at least some of the time. Only one documentation of his daily life after August 1863 remains. He signed the autograph book presented by a prison staffer's young daughter and drew a delicately intricate circle around his signature.[64]

After an inspector reported seeing Robert in solitary in 1864, an effort was made to get him and others in poor condition out, but as no black prisoners were being released by the Confederacy, federal officials refused. In early January 1865, Lincoln's men hoped harsh conditions in the overcrowded prison would force the Confederacy to exchange black prisoners. Robert's diet became largely bread.[65]

After Robert's uncle and his government finally agreed to the Union conditions, exchanges could start, beginning with the sickest prisoners. Sixteen men captured at Vicksburg comprised the short list of longest imprisoned officers and included Captain Robert H. Davis, still in irons, sick, and in solitary confinement.[66]

Robert left Johnson's Island on January 27 for the huge tent camp at Camp Hamilton, Virginia. In his poor condition, he probably went straight to the 1,800-bed hospital.[67]

On February 2, General Grant ordered the disabled troops exchanged first and the register recorded Robert's release the same day "to await exchange." Confederate vessels under flag-of-truce took his group of 2,000 south to wait for their paperwork.[68]

The final document in Robert's service record is his "parole of honor," signed at Meridian, Mississippi, on May 9, after Appomattox. The small railroad junction, nearly destroyed, had turned into a center of hospitals for thousands of wounded Confederate soldiers, and of cemeteries. As Parolee #57, Robert was among the first to sign out by pledging to honor local laws and his parole. However, he never left Meridian.[69]

Robert Davis died in December, though no one seems to have recorded the date. Sometime after that, now-impoverished Kate Davis paid a stiff $100 (nearly $1,500 today) to Vicksburg's "society" funeral home for the disinterring and wrapping of his body in a fresh cloth, a casket, and the use of a wagon to take her husband home to Vicksburg. Robert does not lie in any Davis family cemetery, and investigation has led to the conclusion that she buried him in an unmarked grave within the iron fence of the Auter family plot.[70]

Kate Davis probably never knew that Robert left a young son in Washington Territory. She was one of Vicksburg's 1,300 fatalities in the 1878 yellow fever epidemic. The city hurriedly buried her for $5.00.[71]

James Kavanaugh

Caroline treasured Robert's memory into old age, never knowing that he had remarried. She and Sam led different lives by the time Robert actually died. Her second marriage provided another chance for her family to hold the land that was their ancestral village's territory.

Once she realized that she would never see Robert again, she found a future for herself and Sam with a man whose history unknowingly paralleled her own people's desperate efforts to keep their homeland, their *illahee*.[72]

The family history that infused James Kavanaugh's personality and relationship to his land began when the Kavanaugh clan became the kings of Leinster in eastern Ireland's post-Viking era. They made Enniscorthy, Wexford, their seat of power and it was there that James would be born centuries later. The clan always found ways to keep much of their homeland despite confiscations and elimination of many Catholic rights under later Protestant English kings.[73]

Kavanaugh country rebelled in 1798, armed only with pitchforks and scythes against 20,000 guns of the British Army who burned Enniscorthy and slaughtered hundreds. James Kavanaugh's thirteen-year-old father John (Jack) and his grandfather Murgaine survived, though other family members must certainly have perished before the British Act of Union eliminated their last remaining civil rights.[74]

The second of the adult Jack's six sons, James was born March 19, 1826 near Enniscorthy, still the clan's capital. He grew up in the fragile English-Irish cease-fire while the Protestant-Catholic rift grew ever wider and Loyalists celebrated their final defeat of his hometown in ways that terrified residents. Still, farmers like James' family grew prosperous with their diversified crops.[75]

By the time James was of school age, the government schools' curriculum relentlessly taught subservience, powerlessness, and shame for being Catholic. James Kavanaugh's knowledge of Latin and extraordinary level of literacy as a Whatcom County settler point to an education in a Catholic school (by then again permitted). That did not prevent James and everyone else in town from hearing the stories of free land and fertile soil in North America which the government teachers spread. When James was seventeen, some bold young Wexford men with dreams of a better life emigrated to Argentina where they quickly prospered. A window of escape had opened to those willing to cross the Atlantic.

Two years later, everything changed for James' family as well as for millions of others. Wexford had its first potato crop failure in 1845. Though it was a minority crop for Wexford farmers, Jack

Kavanaugh's family probably were already contemplating emigration because they had savings for travel and land purchase by the following early spring. They unknowingly started the family's emigration before the panic wrought by the following deadly potato blight of 1846. James' mother had died by then and a cousin cared for the house and younger children while the men looked for a new home in Canada. Jack, an elderly sixty-one, left with James (twenty), and probably John (seventeen) and his teenage wife. On April 2, the four took a ship across the Irish Sea for the port of Liverpool. The family left behind would shortly endure the famine whose effects touched even prosperous Enniscorthy.[76]

Three months later, the Kavanaughs landed near Quebec City and took up land near Vinton, Quebec, a haven for Irish Catholic farmers and tradesmen. The men started a farm and labored in the timber during winters for extra money to bring the others over. After four years, they sent James home. He found a devastated town.[77]

James returned to America with his married sister and her husband. They landed in New Orleans because a relative, Morgan Kavanaugh, and his family lived in Mississippi. Soon, two more of James' brothers arrived and settled in Robert Davis' home town of Vicksburg. It took James' father three more years to save the money to bring out the youngest son and the eldest, Morgahn and his large family, all of whom settled at Vinton. The family would be forever split between two countries.[78]

James Kavanaugh never returned to Quebec or Ireland. A wife and baby son died in Iowa. With the California Gold Rush in the news, in 1851 he boarded a sailing ship bound for San Francisco through treacherous Cape Horn seas.

For latecomers like James, conditions in California had changed greatly since 1849. Most prospectors' lives had become a quest for daily survival money because of the decline of individual-based placer mining and the increasing corporate control of gold extraction. Gold field society was riven with crime and brutality opposed only by vigilantes. James' partnership with Hiram March was established in this chaotic time. A man's "pardner" was often the only person who cared whether he lived or died and the friendship lasted for the rest of James' life. March's Vermont Yankee origins were very different,

and he nicknamed his Irish friend "Dub" (for Dublin). They stub-
bornly worked the Sacramento River tributaries, perhaps only for
wages, until spring 1858, when word spread of a new strike far north
on the Fraser River.[79]

James and Hiram arrived at Sehome on May 1 aboard Henry
Roeder's *General Harney*. They were among the thousands camped
on the beach that summer who Deputy Sheriff Robert Davis strained
to keep under control.[80]

The pair ended stuck in Whatcom with no money to leave.
Instead, they felled trees for the U.S. Boundary Commission during
the 1859 work season. The job was simple but life-endangering: cut
down every tree in a 20-foot-wide swath, including the giants over 30
feet around and 250 feet tall that rose from an impenetrable tangle of
undergrowth and stinging nettles. Swarms of voracious mosquitoes
made sleep at night impossible. It was an ordeal.[81]

The presence of other Irish in Sehome and Whatcom may have
encouraged James to settle down. The much-loved redhead Teresa
Eldridge had been joined by Mary Bird Tawes, coal miners and soldiers, even petty crook "Ragpicker" Johnson. The lilt of Irish-accented
English was everywhere. After the Survey job, James did construction and boat-building while March hunted deer for the mine and
fort. Having built a good reputation, James replaced Deputy Sheriff Robert Davis. James and Hiram may have also explored taking
claims on *Shais-quihl* near Robert and Caroline's unregistered claim,
but did not stay.[82]

March bought into a grocery and liquor store at the mine, called
in records "The Headquarters." Two months after William Busey
absconded, probably closing the competing Davis-Busey store and
saloon, James bought his friend March's business (though not the
land or building) for $300, a hefty sum when the bay's settler popula-
tion was only about one hundred. The purchase included two boats, as
well as a motley assemblage of wood, chickens, stoves, billiard table,
clock, guns and a bank scale—all useful at store or at home. Perhaps
not coincidentally, alcoholic militia veteran Oscar Olney had recently
tried to kill March. Perhaps he decided it was a good time to get out.
Deputy Sheriff Kavanaugh appointed a prior owner as manager and
bartender. At thirty-five, he had become a solid citizen.[83]

The lack of a re-sale indicates that James' business probably folded in the post-gold rush economic bust, but two years later on July 8, 1862, newly-elected Sheriff Kavanaugh took office. To the locals who had nicknamed him "The Parson," he stood out from the rowdy Irish coal miners with his continuing faith life, articulate speech, and peaceable demeanor.[84]

The job turned out to fit James' personality as poorly as it had his predecessor, the Quaker Tom Wynn. His first error was that he took on two related jobs. He became Deputy U.S. Marshal a few months after taking office. Then, the Indian Affairs Department hired him after hearing about his anger with liquor sellers who targeted native people, and his frustration getting courts to admit Indian testimony. The three positions meshed in the administratively isolated location, but he expressed frustration with the juries at Port Townsend very early: "There is always a goodly proportion of our juries made up of whiskey sellers and of those who hate the Indians and feel kindly to whiskey sellers. The greatest evil and stumbling block to justice lies in the jury box in this country."[85]

James started a personal diary of his official actions and other activities in 1863 on a day when the Sehome coal mine was on fire, a potential economic disaster. He kept his journal up for the next twenty-two years. It became regional residents' first look at what early day-to-day life was like after Caroline gave permission to publish most of it in 1913 to the *Anacortes American*. Those entries have been copied in many other books and articles. (See endnote regarding the two versions.)[86]

CAROLINE AND JAMES

Caroline Davis and James Kavanaugh lived in a community where quite literally everyone knew everyone else. She said they married while he was the marshal, and measured by her first childbirth and his diary entries, it was no later than March-April, 1863. By then, she had reconciled herself to the truth that Robert would never return. She and James began married life in Sehome where the mine saloon generated frequent trouble that required his official presence. Sehome was also his best jumping-off point to head south to the other bays or west into the San Juans, all within his responsibility.[87]

The last seven months of 1863 were typical of the Kavanaughs' unpredictable life while James held office. In July, the relative quiet on *Shais-quihl* ended when Northern raiders were suspected of killing O.V. Russell, a "quiet, peaceable, harmless old man." Russell was presently the only settler there other than William Munks and his Swinomish wife Lucy at the former Davis cabin. James was in the islands to collect taxes while a contingent of Lummi and two deputized men fruitlessly searched for the killers.[88]

Sheriff Kavanaugh served during the protracted aftermath of "The Pig War," an incident that nearly brought the British and Americans to war four decades after the War of 1812. For some time both the HBC and American settlers occupied San Juan Island. The border treaty in 1846 ignored the fact that two major channels surrounded the San Juan Islands, not one, and left ownership of the islands in dispute. When Whatcom County was organized, a taxation authority dispute led the national governments to authorize a boundary survey to conclusively set the border, finalized only in 1871. In June 1859 a wandering British pig ate an American settler's potatoes and paid for it with his life. Captain Pickett at Fort Bellingham rashly responded to pleas for help with an armed landing to keep the American from arrest by the British, triggering the arrival of three British warships and Royal Marines, as well as American reinforcements shortly after. When word reached cooler heads in Washington, D.C., and London in December, the governments avoided armed conflict by establishing joint military occupation at opposite ends of the island until the final channel decision. The British lived at English Camp on a lovely bay at the north end, and the Americans built their permanent quarters on the windswept barren south end. The forces lived peacefully and socialized. Whatcom County still claimed civil authority over the Americans.

James returned from his island trip livid about the arrogance of the army commander who had kept him from doing his job. Captain Lyman Bissell expected the sheriff to use his time picking up army deserters and James logically expected help with taxes or hunting killers in return, but was often blocked instead. He started a two-year letter-writing war with Bissell's superiors.[89]

Ten days after James returned, Lyman Cutlar (he of the Pig War's porcine assassination) arrived from San Juan's lime works to report a homicide during an alcohol-fueled fight at his house. James' long canoe trip back for an inquest required another extended absence from Caroline and Sam, plus another week would be required for the killer's trial in Port Townsend.[90]

However, Caroline was doing her own traveling. When James returned home from the inquest, his pregnant wife left for Victoria to attend a Songhees potlatch where many of the guests, and probably the hosts, were extended family. The 1863 wedding event was so large it attracted the attention of the Victoria newspaper after a flotilla of forty canoes arrived. Eighteen days after Caroline left home, the hosts gave out presents and food to thousands of departing guests. The *Colonist* reported that when everyone left, the canoes (including Caroline's) were "thickly dotting the water as far as the eye could reach."[91]

With Caroline and Sam at Victoria, James went hunting and when he returned, he found a new opportunity had appeared. Charles Richards (builder-owner of Whatcom's only brick building) had decided to quit his businesses and leave. Richards authorized James to care for his inactive small coal mine and in return, the Kavanaughs would have a free home at Unionville, the former Pattle Mine's small settlement. Vacant houses were a particular concern to absent owners as they were a scarce commodity and subject to squatters and vandals eager to appropriate free building materials. Caroline and James rented out their Sehome house with its rose bushes and thirteen recently planted willow trees, "with a view of by and by living in the shade." Caroline was very pregnant when they moved, and with a small son it could not have been easy for her.[92]

At the same time, James helped Hiram March disassemble a house and put it back together on the murdered Russell's vacant claim on the northeast tip of *Shais-quihl*. By that time, March and his Swinomish wife Anna had two sons. Caroline and James may have begun to discuss a move back to the place where she was born and lived with Robert Davis, though its status was still being argued. The fertile peninsula was almost wholly "vacant" of settlers, but nearby would be March and a woman who was at least a friend, if not Caroline's cousin.[93]

Caroline and James were at March's home on *Shais-quihl* when she went into labor on December 13, 1863, the fifth day of the year's first snowstorm that had started with "a screechin'" from the southeast. She gave birth to her second son, assisted by Anna. The terrible weather continued with a gale, deep snow, freezing rain, hail, and rising rivers that kept the Kavanaughs and their newborn there until the skies cleared ten days later. They were home in Unionville on New Year's Eve when their son died in the midst of another snowstorm. He had lived barely 18 days. Even as the snow piled higher in the winter darkness, the grieving sheriff was called away that day to deal with repeat liquor offender "Whiskey Bill" Smith, with whom he'd already had a fist fight.[94]

They buried Caroline's baby on New Year's Day in the mournful mist and fog. Willie Dickerson had lost infant twin boys and now he helped James dig the little grave in the back garden where the grieving and devout Catholic father probably led the prayers. It was not the tree burial Caroline's family would have done. She and James then carried on, as people did.[95]

The rest of James' term as sheriff was much the same as those seven months until he had to arrest and incarcerate his friend Willie Dickerson, who had killed a local Native man. Toward the end of James' term, the effort to get paid by federal and county bureaucracies became intolerable. It took three more years to be paid for his three years of duty as U.S. Marshal. When Fred Lane (*see* chapter 5) took over on June 7, 1866, James noted that he was "happily relieved of any further duties of that office."[96]

Caroline and her son Sarsfield (Kavanaugh) said years later that Fr. Chirouse married the Kavanaughs, both devout Catholics, in 1864. The ceremony, like others of the time, was illegal. The impoverished missionary again did not enter the marriage in his register.[97]

James had begun to plan for a permanent move to *Shais-quihl*. He and Hiram March harvested and sold wild hay from Swinomish Flats for quick cash, and caught dogfish and sold the oil to the Utsalady lumber mill. Apparently a novice with hogs and cattle, James copied a recipe for curing meat into his diary. He built a cedar board cabin on land that was not so far away from the Davis cabin, now occupied by William and Lucy Munks.[98]

One day when Caroline and Sam were at the *Shais-quihl* cabin and James was gone, she spotted a deer in the water off her beach. Taking advantage of its vulnerability as she had been taught, she ran into the frigid water and clubbed it to death. She hauled the carcass up from the beach, skinned and butchered it, and was cooking venison for dinner when James returned. In his journal that night, James expressed his astonishment at his tiny wife's solo accomplishment.[99]

Caroline gave birth to their baby girl on July 12, 1865, just before a heavy morning thunderstorm and hail assaulted their Unionville home. Eleven days later the little one died. She and James grieved the loss of their second child. It was time to move to *Shais-quihl* for a new beginning.[100]

⚮

Within two months of the baby's death Caroline and James moved permanently to their claim on the east beach across the peninsula from her land with Robert Davis on the west side. It was still treaty-

Munks Landing c. 1890. William Munks started his trading post in 1871 on the site of the former Samish village that was Caroline Kavanaugh's birthplace, as well as the squatter claim on which she lived with her first husband, Robert Hugh Davis. Caroline and James Kavanaugh's farm was behind the Munks land and a bit north on the other side of *Shais-quihl* (March Point). *Wallie Funk Collection, courtesy of Anacortes Museum, Anacortes, Washington.*

designated reservation land. Hiram and Anna March's house was only 50 yards north of the boundary between the old "pardners." William Munks, whom James and Hiram knew from the Boundary Survey crew, his Swinomish wife Lucy, and their son were on the former Davis place. Trails old and new connected the three Swinomish women. Two other intermarried couples lived nearby.[101]

The Kavanaugh claim included beach, prairie, and wooded uplands. Caroline was back home on the fern prairie with all its memories. Their new cabin was built of logs covered in cedar boards with a shake roof and rough floors, probably much like the one she had shared with Robert Davis. Making up for the poverty of a first cabin, her view was breathtaking. She looked east at Mount Baker above dark foothills beyond Padilla Bay. The burbling spring on the upland behind her cabin that nourished generations of her family now provided fresh water for new families.[102]

Whites began to call *Shais-quihl* "March Point," and it became a complex jigsaw puzzle of staked-out quarter sections that included both beach and upland. The community of mixed families there and near the peninsula continued to grow. Over a dozen more intermarried couples settled around the bays or on nearby Guemes and Cypress Islands. It is unlikely that James Kavanaugh or any of the other husbands were ignorant of the fact that their marriages constituted a back-up plan to keep their land, similar to what was happening on the lower Nooksack River's prairies with John Tennant (*see* chapter 4) and Thomas Wynn, both married to Lummi women.[103]

Like the community at Bellingham Bay, a symbiotic and friendly relationship between the in-laws developed at the March Point cluster. Swinomish oral history says that the white men needed them for companionship, as well as defense and hired hands at their isolated location. The small number of whites who lived in the Coast Salish-dominated place were accepted by the residents who made strong distinctions between "neighbor" and "stranger." Still believing that *Shais-quihl* would become their promised reservation, the Samish and Swinomish brought nearly all the newcomers into their family networks. They taught their new allies the expectations of trustworthiness, hospitality, and generosity. As at Bellingham Bay, women were the instruments through which peace flowed.[104]

Caroline was again pregnant during the first planting season, and James still served as sheriff. She and little Sam probably did most of the work getting a garden going, and caring for the baby fruit trees while James continued to fish. The season was "remarkably wet" and its effect on the first crops probably contributed to James' decision to go to Sehome and load coal at the mine for extra cash. The day after he started the "hard and disagreeable" job, the mine caught fire again, followed by more safety incidents. Someone broke into the Unionville house and stole the guns and money, as well as all of James' supplies, but he stuck it out until Caroline's baby came. They needed cash.[105]

Overworked and exhausted, Caroline gave birth to another little girl on September 20, 1866. The baby "ceased to live the instant it was born," wrote the father, grieving the loss of his third child. James stayed with Caroline for a month of harvest season before returning to the mine.[106]

Six days after James returned to the coal tunnels, a stubborn fire started that was quenched only by letting in the salt water after three days. He spent just one more stint in the coal, marred by another fatal accident. Perhaps he took that as a sign that he should stick to farming. He did just that.[107]

Through the hardships and tragedy of their first year on the farm, Caroline and James could turn to their shared religion. Only three months after their daughter's death, James wrote a heartfelt plea on New Year's Eve: "God be blessed and praised for His goodness and mercy to us and may it be His Divine will and pleasure to send us a Happy New year."[108]

Caroline gave birth to Sarsfield John (named for an Irish hero and James' father) on October 13, 1867, when James was at the Sehome Mine. It was only thirteen months after her daughter's stillbirth, but the child thrived and the couple rejoiced. James quickly sold a load of vegetables to the Utsalady mill to buy lumber for a kitchen addition for Caroline. He also built a flume from the spring to send fresh water into her kitchen and found small ways to bring in extra cash to support her and the two boys.[109]

Francis James was born in the middle of another wintry night on February 19, 1870, when Sarsfield was three and Sam twelve. A girl named Cecelia, recorded by the Church as the Kavanaughs' daughter, remains a puzzle because James' diary never mentioned her. She may have been a young relative of Caroline who was baptized along with Sam at "Swinomish house" in November 1874, two years after Sarsfield and Francis were baptized. One source reported that she died at seven of "inflammatory rheumatism" (rheumatic fever), a complication of strep throat that can cause fatal heart damage in children. If she was Caroline's chance to have an adopted daughter, it was another tragedy.[110]

When Sam and other neighbor children reached school age, James taught them before Sehome School teacher Almina Griffin moved to the point. The families quickly came up with a donated cabin schoolhouse for the students. James may have relished his short time as a teacher, as that profession was probably closer to his authentic self than any other job he held. He subscribed to the famously literate *New York Sun* and the *Phrenological Journal* that studied head bumps for many years, to which he added many other periodicals. The Kavanaugh children were exposed to learning at school and at home, unlike many farming families of the area. Though some intermarried parents sent their mixed-blood children away to Tulalip Boarding School, James and Caroline never did.[111]

James and other men farmed *Shais-quihl* with the uncertainty of keeping land without a title while investing money in development. James' soil on the east side was less fertile and harbored more rocks than the black loam of the fern prairie. The farm's value in 1870 was $1,000, one fifth of Munks' west side farm where Caroline and Robert Davis had lived. James' young orchard yielded only $10 that year. He did not produce lucrative meat or grain, but instead repeatedly planted potatoes, beans, and peas, the crops that had worked in Wexford, which kept his income low for years.[112]

Caroline's role in the farm's survival is clearly visible. Nearly one-third of the farm's 1870 income was earned by the market garden. The Kavanaughs wholesaled produce to the Sehome Mine store and Whatcom until a trading post opened at the new settlement of LaConner on nearby Swinomish Slough. They traded Caroline's butter, strawberries, and wild currants there for cash or credit well into the decade. When Munks built a small store at "Fidalgo" (his landing), Caroline became one of his major suppliers. She sold him as many as twenty-nine dozen eggs at a time, and seventy-seven baskets of berries. The market garden produced 475 pounds of cabbage in 1875 that they held for December sale so they could pay off their account and buy toys for Christmas.[113]

The close-knit neighborhood began to change with heavier white in-migration onto reservation land still left only proposed and unsurveyed. By then officials advocated selling the small Swinomish Reservation on the channel and sending the people to Tulalip. That caused Swinomish reluctance to move there and they remained scattered, probably including some of Caroline's relatives. Local agents admitted that the Swinomish were being harmed but were unable to handle the "vicious whites" bent on taking advantage of the situation.[114]

The Samish situation was different, and if anything even worse for Caroline's family. They believed they were promised *Shais-quihl* for their reservation, but by the early 1870s, they could see it had filled with white settlers, even if most were in-laws. They had mostly continued their traditional lives at their usual locations, but on Samish Island, Daniel Dingwall's Cowichan intermarriage seems to have given him entrée to the village complex on the east end, most likely because his wife also had Samish connections. He treated it like a private fiefdom once he established a land claim there and built a store and hotel rather than farmed. No government entity tried to stop him from doing so right where the village was. Other men followed, some with Native wives and some without. They staked out most of the rest of the island. The pressure upon the Samish village was unrelenting after Dingwall started a logging camp. Very shortly, the Samish families were also in deep debt to his store and he had the leverage to force them to leave the center of their lives.[115]

Caroline's Samish family began to abandon their beloved island, its burial places, and potlatch house. Some tried to move to *Shais-quihl* where the Samish wives lived, but white newcomers, who uniformly had white wives, had no history with the intermarried families and little respect for them. They drove the Samish relatives away. The Samish consolidated at a new village on Guemes Island to the northwest after two Samish men obtained U.S. homesteads. This allowed nine family heads to build a five-hundred-foot-long communal longhouse on the line between the two properties. "New Guemes" enabled Caroline's kin to continue their traditional life with little interference for several decades.[116]

In 1871 officials asserted that the "temporary" Swinomish Reservation map, which by then included *Shais-quihl*, was incorrect. Their new survey put it permanently outside and did not make it a Samish reservation as promised, either. They would give title preference to the "old settlers," which confirmed possession by the Kavanaughs and their intermarried neighbors. The Samish dream of a separate reservation died. Authorities and settlers drove away the remnants trying to hang on to seasonal camps or living singly on the point. Some settlers (probably intermarried couples) allowed the elders to remain on their homesteads but expected younger generations to leave.[117]

Caroline's father may not have lived to see the final outcome of his daughter's marriages to the army officer and the county sheriff, but her settlement back on her *illahee* kept Samish land in Samish hands. Most of *Shais-quihl* stayed in the hands of Samish and Swinomish-affiliated women for the time being, but not all intermarried husbands behaved as well as Kavanaugh. Munks sent his Swinomish family away after the final survey was done, married a white woman, and began to expand his "Munks Landing" businesses. Hiram March did the same and married his white wife Kate in Seattle. While the two men tried to rewrite their personal history and "forget" to mention their first wives, the names carried forward through their Swinomish sons. One family carries the story that Anna March was so heartbroken when he sent her away that she walked to the end of the lane and died.[118]

In an echo of Ireland, Caroline and James Kavanaugh's land battles began and spanned decades. When James went to the new U.S. Land Office in Olympia to apply for his patent, he and neighbor George Becker decided to buy and split 40 adjacent acres. Becker put up the cash, and James found a friend in a nearby saloon who loaned him the money to pay Becker a deposit on his half. After months of avoiding completion of the transaction, Becker admitted that he sold the land to someone else, but kept James' money. Like his ancestors, James tenaciously fought to get justice and filed both civil and criminal charges. Witnesses overwhelmingly supported James and a jury found in his favor, but only for his $25, not the land. Nevertheless, James triumphantly wrote "Lawsuit came off and I beat him." Becker fled to avoid the criminal fraud charge.[119]

Though their homestead seemed safely in Kavanaugh hands, the fight over land would begin again in a few years. It lasted for the rest of James' life, and nearly all of Caroline's.

Twenty years after Caroline and Robert Davis moved to *Shais-quihl*, the cultural and geographic separation of settlers from their native in-laws and neighbors was hardening. Of the mixed families that nearly filled *Shais-quihl* in the beginning, only a few remained. Frontier intimacy ended once the new all-white families dominated. No longer did people see each other within extended family contexts, nor were they familiar with each other's ways. The spheres of the two small groups moved farther apart until business and employment provided most interactions. A young diarist nearly ignored the presence of the Kavanaughs because her family's friendships included only other white families.[120]

When Whatcom County indicted nine "old settlers" in tribal custom marriages on charges of fornication in late 1878, James was not among the defendants but neighbors were. Former Sheriff Kavanaugh's presence on that grand jury probably accounts for his escape from prosecution. It seems likely that jury foreman Edward Eldridge knew that he and Caroline were officially married even if there was no paperwork. Even if not, their union would shortly be made legal by Justice Greene's decision (*see* Appendix A and B).[121]

The Kavanaughs and their three boys remained a close family trying to get ahead. James accumulated enough money to spend $30 on a new-fangled stove for Caroline. He repeatedly told his diary that he'd never seen weather so bad and made it the reason for bad crops. His furious complaints may have actually masked the onset of severe arthritis. By 1880 he was fifty-four and only three years away from terminal heart disease. Sam had left home, so "Sass" and Francis probably shouldered much of the farming burden. In ten years, the farm value had not increased one dollar and production had actually dropped. During a time of harsh winters that reduced production of his unvarying crops, Caroline's contribution of 130 pounds of butter was critical.[122]

James, his long slender fingers increasingly crippled by arthritis and his eyesight deteriorating, did not completely stop working, but his diary entries became brief and infrequent. Instead, he wrote several lengthy letters to the local paper airing his complaints with the court system that had persecuted the old settlers while it ignored other problems.[123]

Caroline and her children remained involved in still-vibrant tribal life. When five thousand Coast Salish gathered at the new Guemes longhouse, the local editor called the week-long potlatch the largest ever known on Puget Sound. Local stores even opened stands on the potlatch grounds, though it demonstrated how much Euro-American culture had infiltrated a traditional gathering. There are hints that James, though ailing, stayed involved in Caroline's family to some degree.[124]

Another land dispute began when James applied for his patent. The Kavanaughs finally received Land Patent #1280 in January 1882 for their 144.4 acres, though they had lived there since 1865. They owned the water rights, plus those to ditches and reservoirs on their land, something which seemed obvious at the time, but which would haunt the family. His land was Lots #3, 4, and 5 of Section 28. He and his friend of thirty years, Hiram March, had informally shared March's Lot #2 and Kavanaugh's Lot #3, each using part of both. After James applied for his patent, he told March that he planned to take sole possession of #3 and improve it. March said he would "hold it in spite of me and *also water* on said lot." March immediately built a shanty on lot #3, the location of the Samish spring whose waters neighbors had always shared. After the men cooled down, they divided their lots to give each one the portion they actually occupied. The dispute seemed settled. James was supposed to obtain and register a county deed, but he never did. That omission would bedevil Caroline later.[125]

SAM DAVIS

Sam Davis left home when he reached eighteen in 1876. Caroline's sons with James would inherit the farm, so Sam had to find a different path. James noted in his diary that Sam left with two friends for "parts to us yet unknown." Apparently, the young man told his mother goodbye with no particular destination in mind. He returned home later and worked as a Lushootseed interpreter for a grand jury session, but soon was off with March's half-Swinomish son William and other friends to a logging camp near Seattle.[126]

By twenty-five Sam had begun a marine career. Captain Fritz Dibbern (another intermarried man) employed him as fireman on the *Josephine*, a small steam sternwheeler that hauled grain and freight on the Skagit River. By steps, it expanded the reach of steam navigation seventy miles inland and was the chief means of communication for the upriver settlers. People at homesteads, logging camps, and mines enthusiastically welcomed the vessel wherever it landed. Despite its importance, the five-year-old *Josephine* was a bit of a hard luck boat, having lost a deckhand overboard on one trip, and sinking after striking a river snag on another trip. Sam's job below decks loading the boiler with coal was a brutally strenuous job, but it was a start on an important boat.[127]

On January 16, 1883, passengers on the *Josephine* were sitting down to their noon dinner, despite the winds that assaulted the vessel as it steamed north out of Seattle. When the captain shoved the safety valve down hard to make more headway, a massive explosion split the hull in two. It blew the boiler entirely out of the boat and that half of the hull sank in thirty feet of icy cold waters of Port Susan Bay (near today's city of Everett). Survivors clung to the overturned half kept afloat by its cargo of wood. Residents of the Snohomish village on Tulalip Reservation canoed a mile out to the wreck and picked up battered and injured survivors, as did the *Politovsky*, a large steamer. Fireman "Sam Kavanaugh" was not among the seventeen people rescued.[128]

By the next day, word of the catastrophe reached Caroline and James. He noted what little he knew in his diary, that "eight or nine persons disappeared forever, among them my stepson Sam." Searchers never found his body.[129]

An official inquiry concluded that the explosion was not caused by contraband explosives as had been rumored. Instead, though the gauges showed enough water in the boiler, there was not. A careless inspector had failed to discover the defect that took Sam Davis' life.[130]

Caroline had lost four children, perhaps five if Cecelia had been her adopted daughter.

CAROLINE AND JAMES

Coincidentally the same day that the LaConner paper provided more details about Sam's death, it printed one of James' letters to the editor. James was responding to a call for the formation of a pioneer society, and his communication touched off a very public argument between long-time residents about what year of settlement divided "old settlers" from newcomers. James was angry about the attitude of many comparative newcomers who disparaged the lifestyle of old settlers who they thought had not improved their land enough nor laid down "carpets for the new civilizers to walk upon." His letter revealed the deep anger of the intermarried families who, instead of being lauded for their role in the founding of the new Skagit County, were looked down upon for not living "white" enough.[131]

Shortly after James helped start a March Point debating society in early 1885, the Anacortes paper noted that he was expected to die at any time from heart disease. James had already made out his will, giving Caroline and his boys equal shares in the land despite there being no legal requirement to do so. He appointed her the executor, then lived for another two months under her care. In his last diary entry ten days before he died, James returned to his concern for the integrity of the Kavanaugh land, now his *illahee* too. He noted that the county surveyor had run the lines around Lots 2 and 3, the same shared lots in the previous dispute with March. Something was wrong again and James made sure to note the survey, knowing that Caroline would soon inherit the issue.[132]

James Kavanaugh died on June 19, 1885, at age fifty-nine. Given his faith, it is puzzling why he did not have a Catholic funeral. The reason may have been a simple one: the absence of a priest in the area at the time. Caroline's family and neighbors buried him at the new Pleasant Ridge Cemetery near LaConner.[133]

Though three newspapers printed an obituary, none of them gave Caroline's name or mentioned the children. In a condescending tone, one described Caroline as "an intelligent Indian woman."[134]

No suggestion has ever been made that James was anything other than a loving and kind man to Caroline, his stepson Sam, and his own children. He had even defended his lack of full commitment to a "white" way of life in public letters. He never lost his faith and his writings indicate that kindness to others was a major drive, though his newspaper letters and courtroom appearances exhibited a capacity for righteous anger. James Kavanaugh prayed often for his neighbors, health, and a good life for his family. He knew how to give thanks for what he had even when times were bad. His religion taught him social justice and kindness, and he found a wife in Caroline who shared his religion and goals. He practiced fairness to the end when he gave his wife an equal inheritance in the farm.

Caroline

Caroline was a healthy, smart, and still beautiful woman in her forties. The boys, eighteen and fifteen, were adults by rural standards. In addition to keeping the farm afloat with her sons, Caroline developed a new business of her own in addition to the eggs and butter she usually sold.

In the past twenty years, the once-feared Northern tribes from British Columbia had undergone their own cultural changes and become an integral part of the burgeoning hop industry in Washington. The ocean canoes once manned by seventy warriors sported sails and rudders and carried entire families, many of whose children had the light hair of their white fathers. The Northerners used March Point's beaches and Swinomish Slough's banks to rest overnight as they traveled south in August and returned in October. At least twenty canoes passed every day during their journeys and on some evenings fifty to sixty canoes pulled up on the point's beaches. Caroline sold her own products to the families before they could reach LaConner's stores, including her hot apple cider and wine from her currant bushes.[135]

Caroline had embraced life in white society, and Sarsfield said she liked the new ways. She told others that she was proud that she had mediated between the two cultures and fulfilled her father's goals. The family grew closer to the world of her birth after James' death. She had taught the boys her language and ways in addition to the English literature they had read with their father. Caroline brought them further into her world where they were a "chief's family," and the boys formed indelible memories of the respect and courtesy that status brought the family. They also absorbed the obligations that went along with such respect. As a widow, she made frequent visits to her sister at "Cowichan" (Duncan, B.C.) on Vancouver Island, as well as to other friends and cousins, including Jenny (Mrs. Thomas) Wynn at Ferndale. At the same time, she continued James' magazine subscriptions that brought new knowledge into her home from his culture. Both parents educated their boys beyond the level agricultural settlers usually thought necessary, so her sons approached adulthood with a duality of natures and educations. A writer who interviewed Sarsfield concluded that the combination of both parents' affirmation of their cultures was the force that created his "unassuming, gentlemanly bearing."[136]

Though newcomers to March Point found it easy to ignore the Samish woman and her sons living at the north end, Caroline remained connected to the remaining "old settlers." She handed out cookies when neighbor children visited. She "sat with" Kate March, who had separated from Hiram a few months after James died. Kate had been frightened of all indigenous people at first, but Caroline charmed her into a close friendship. Kate's son Fred talked about Caroline's warm personality and intelligence, and how she took the time to teach the boys Chinook jargon at a time when few white children had the chance or desire to learn it. He thought her teaching through conversation was better than reading a book a dozen times.[137]

As James had anticipated, Caroline confronted new legal challenges soon after he died. The disputes divided old friends Munks, March, and the Kavanaughs. Vindictiveness over some legal cases in which the Kavanaughs played a small part led to vengeful litigation against Caroline.

The first cases pulled the family into William Munks' affairs. The year James died, March Point men celebrated Christmas with drinking at Munks' Store as usual, but this time someone reported he sold liquor without a license. Caroline was one of the grand jury witnesses. After Munks was indicted and arrested, the case dragged on until it was dismissed after a year. Her neighbor may have held a grudge against her.[138]

Second, two local men were charged with a criminal conspiracy that started at a logging camp where Sarsfield worked. A drunken crowd of gamblers that included "Sass" went to Munks' Store and threatened to force him to expel his Chinese cook.[139]

The third case involved both Munks and March, two old men fighting over water rights to Caroline's spring and an irrigation ditch that crossed one property to water the other. Munks decided that March should pay him for the water that had always been free when it crossed his land. Both men questioned Sarsfield in court, including about how the survey had affected his family's possession of the land and a statement that March had made about moving the fence between him and the Kavanaughs. Sass had to confirm that the ditch was on Munks' land, thereby antagonizing March.[140]

Perhaps driven by anger at Sarsfield's testimony that favored Munks in another minor criminal case, March sued the family. He had delayed filing the 1881 title changes that settled the dispute over adjoining lots, and now he claimed he had recently noticed a mistake that transposed the words "west" and "east" in laying out who got what. He claimed to feel compelled to sue the widow and sons of his friend of over thirty years because they refused to comply with his demand to change the title and change the spring's ownership. He wanted his separated wife Kate to join him but she refused to help sue her friend, so he sued her too. She had been deeded a piece of the land in question when they parted ways.[141]

The Kavanaughs hired Virginia-educated lawyer and future congressman J. Hamilton Lewis. He asserted that the statute of limitations had run out and the deed was correct as written. March hired Cornelius Hanford, soon-to-be Territorial Chief Justice. He asserted that James purposely did not register the deed, that he spotted the mistake and kept it secret because he liked the land he got in the trade-off.

Sarsfield found a witness who would testify that March said he was "playing a good joke on old woman Kavanaugh" by moving the stakes to give himself more land. A second would add that March said "he had got the old woman." Michael Sullivan, a regionally prominent early settler, would swear that March knew there was no mistake. Sarsfield didn't realize that he would need the men in court immediately until he got there and it was too late to summon them. He concluded his own testimony by facetiously calling himself "an uneducated boy." He called his mother "an Indian woman and an ignorant and unlearned woman, who could supply no facts" that would help him build a case. Neither statement was true, but Sass and the lawyer seem to have cleverly taken advantage of white stereotypes to build sympathy for the family in the absence of their witnesses.

The case dragged on for a year before the attorneys worked out a settlement and revised the deed. While they waited for court approval, Sarsfield's brother Francis mortgaged his floating saloon, probably to pay the attorney fees. The court awarded no damages to anyone and made March pay all costs. That told him the suit was frivolous and he had unjustly accused James of hiding the truth.[142]

Hiram March was not through with Caroline and the boys. He hired future governor Henry McBride to again dispute events surrounding Lots 2 and 3. He apparently could not abandon his claim that he "had got...old woman Kavanaugh." This time he claimed they kicked him off three of his own acres. He wanted the land, damages, and lost rents and profits. Caroline's new lawyer asserted that James and Caroline had owned them for fifteen years. Water rights again seem to be March's underlying goal, given his original dispute with Munks over access to his drainage ditch that supplied both a boundary line and irrigation water. The jury awarded March the three acres and six cents. Caroline and the boys still owned the precious spring of her birth village, but they were ordered to pay court costs.[143]

The Kavanaughs tried to pay the large court bill, but even with loans, they failed. The judge ordered their farm sold in April 1892. Despite the judge's rejection of an appeal to modify the order, the county sheriff chose to postpone the sale of a predecessor's land four times. Finally, Hiram March paid $160 for most of the beachfront homestead that bordered his own and ended all arguments over the field that he and James had once amicably shared. The court received its fees, and Caroline was left with her original cabin, the house, and about twenty acres to support her family, none of which included her clam beach. However, she still owned the spring.[144]

THE KAVANAUGH BOYS

Days after the judge ordered the land sold, Francis married a widow from Munks' townsite who brought Caroline two instant grandchildren. The twenty acres could not support everyone, but Skagit County held new options for a strong, ambitious man.[145]

Francis learned blacksmithing and went to work in logging camps, especially that of mixed-blood Thomas Williams, who also grew up on March Point. He ran a successful operation on and off the Swinomish Reservation that employed many Swinomish men. A photo of Francis with the crew shows a stocky, confident mustachioed man with his mother's dark skin and his father's poor eyesight and long fingers. His broad-brimmed hat is pushed back over a shock of wavy black hair and he wears a white dress shirt and vest which identify him as a skilled mechanic rather than a laborer.[146]

Francis' marriage did not last. When they divorced, Martha pleaded poverty and asked the court to require him to take the children they had together. His descendants believed that she did not want her mixed-blood children with her if she re-married. After Francis remarried a half-Wisconsin Tribe woman (Alice), he enrolled his children in both Samish and Swinomish tribes before they moved on to other timber towns. Unlike his parents, he sent all four of his children to Indian boarding schools and at least one bore emotional scars.[147]

Using a life lease, Sarsfield assured Caroline a home for the rest of her life. It gave her ten acres and buildings, but subject to the "rights of the owner of adjoining land to the flowage of water from the spring on the premises." She controlled the land that held *Shais-quihl's* life-giving spring, except that she could not prevent the man who had gleefully taken her land, or any other adjoining landowner, from using her water. Her original cedar cabin sat fifty yards south of the boundary with her tormentor, but her friend Kate March lived close. Caroline moved back to the cedar cabin that held so many memories though her small acreage may not have included the graves of her children.[148]

March Point was moving into the future. Munks Landing became the short-lived village of Fidalgo. Caroline outlived Munks, March, and other original settlers. She grew from her family's "Grandma Stoly" into the larger Skagit County community's "Grandma Kavanaugh." She still put cookies into the hands of small visitors. She bought a telephone. She started to collect postcards that gave her a new view into the wider world.

Unlike Francis, Sarsfield was small like his mother, but looked like his father, slender with light skin and hair. He had James' long fingers and bad eyesight, like Francis. He interpreted at court occasionally and continued to self-educate with his father's books and magazines. He never married, but farmed the ten acres and cared for his mother during her last years.[149]

Sarsfield inherited the Irish Kavanaugh clan's determination to protect his homeland beyond the family farm he had fought for—his *illahee*. He turned the larger world view he developed, in the home of a politically aware father and as defendant with Caroline in the lawsuits, into a passionate defense of Samish and Swinomish treaty rights. The man who listened to his mother proudly talk about her role in bringing understanding and friendship to both her communities now sought to bring his extended family and others out of the supplicant role outsiders had foisted upon them.[150]

"Sass" became one of the first of a new generation of far-sighted, educated tribal leaders who were ready to pursue the treaty's unfulfilled promises. These men included others from intermarriages who brought useful knowledge and confidence to actively confront the government. All of them had a growing sense of Indian identity within the American one that had overwhelmed the Northwest. They understood the treaty's importance as an instrument to distinguish themselves from whites whether they lived on or off the reservations, and as the basis for future tribal relationships with the whites.[151]

In 1913/1914, Thomas Bishop, son of an early Clallam County legislator and his S'Klallam wife, initiated the first effective organized response. The Northwest Federation of American Indians (NFAI) planned to press the government to enroll and provide the promised allotments to all landless Indians. Sarsfield soon founded the small Anacortes branch, mainly to represent Samish and Nuwhaha interests. The NFAI developed a cooperative and unified political voice.[152]

Sarsfield became the popularly chosen chief of the Samish, which since 1900 had no organized presence or place to call home. Members recognized his abilities, connection to his roots, status as the grandson of an earlier leader, and son of Caroline, a respected Samish elder. He would speak for them to the new power structure.[153]

CAROLINE

It was Sarsfield's sudden regional prominence that probably called the attention of the *Anacortes American* editor to his elderly mother in 1913. J. M. Post interviewed Caroline and photographed her sitting on the front porch in her rocking chair. For the occasion, she dressed in her best black jacket and plaid skirt. Her wavy hair, freed from braids, showed only partially gray beneath a scarf. Loose, it hung below her waist. The formal portrait appeared with the article, but the editor also took one out in the field where Caroline held her husband's old musket, nearly as long as she was tall, tight in her hands. The slight smile on her lips betrayed the sprightly personality only hinted at in the formal photo.[154]

Caroline starred in a front page article entitled "Swinomish Princess was Sister-in-Law of Jefferson Davis." The subtitle read "Aged Woman, Spending Evening of Life at Home on Padilla Bay Was Wife of Dashing West Pointer More Than Half Century Ago–Tells Interesting Story of Pioneer Life in Skagit County." Starting with the title's "facts," many details taken at face value by later writers were seriously incorrect, if not outright fabrications, in the name of exciting journalism to fit white stereotypes. They continue to make determination of her actual remarks a challenge.[155]

Someone mentioned Caroline's most prized possession to the editor: her husband's *Record of Current Events* that is known today as "the Kavanaugh Diary." The *American* wanted to publish excerpts from more than twenty years of entries because they were the earliest and longest private account of life in Whatcom and Skagit counties. The diary had never been out of her hands and the editor had to use "considerable influence" to convince her to allow its publication. Caroline had to trust a stranger to care for and return the journal and that was difficult for her. J. M. Post recognized the historical importance of the diary and a few years later wrote to a Seattle history buff that it "should be in one of our historical libraries." Post tried to get the diary away from Caroline for the University of Washington. He summarized his results succinctly: "Unsuccessful."[156]

Caroline Davis Kavanaugh died Sunday afternoon, February 9, 1919. She had continued to read her Bible every day after rheumatism made it impossible to attend Mass at the reservation church. In her final years she worked on her little farm, chatted on her telephone, continued her hobbies, and rode on her grandson's new motorcycle. She lived long enough to see Sarsfield carry on her father's leadership role. Though she was left out of articles about her husband's death, she received headlines when she died. She had usually declared her birthdate more and more recent until she would have been age 5 at marriage, but the obituary made her older than she was. It named her "Much beloved Grandma Katherine Kavanaugh," getting her name wrong as well as other facts. One of Bellingham's papers reprinted much of the obituary, but the other ignored her death completely.[157]

Old friend Rev. Horace Taylor conducted Caroline's crowded home funeral, inexplicable today for a devout Catholic. None of the pallbearers were from pioneer families. Her grandson Lyman did not attend because he was in the U.S. Navy, even though indigenous Americans were still not citizens. They did not bury her next to James. The stone on her grave at Fern Hill Cemetery reads "Wife of James Kavanaugh, Princess Tol Stola."[158]

The Anacortes editor added his (probably embroidered) version of something she said to him in 1913, but had not published. Though it seems clearly paraphrased, her feelings about the transitions she saw during her lifetime were clear.

"Isn't life a funny state of affairs? I started in as a little Indian girl, living the wild outdoor life of our tribeswomen. Then I became the wife of a member of an illustrious white family and did not have to cook, but had servants to wait on me and make my clothes for me. Then I became the wife of a farmer, and had to do all my housework. Isn't life a funny proposition?"

THE KAVANAUGH BOYS

Caroline left little material wealth behind, but as many Coast Salish prefer, she left much personal wealth in her friends and especially in her sons.

Sarsfield sold the remaining land, worked as a carpenter in Anacortes, and got more involved in the NFAI. Authorities started to equate the chapters with "tribes" in the absence of formal tribal government. As their popularly chosen chief, Sass represented the landless and scattered Samish when they dealt with the Bureau of Indian Affairs from 1921 to 1926, as well as in the NFAI where men had begun to formulate treaty-based claims against the government.[159]

The NFAI elected Sarsfield their president in 1923, despite the small size of his local chapter, and re-elected him the following two years. He presided over annual conventions that moved the goal of treaty rights and more allotments forward. The Samish authorized him to sign documents with the government on their behalf as they started their own quest for federal recognition.[160]

Sass led the NFAI's critical and successful fight to hire and control its own attorney for the claims case. The NFAI planned to use *Duwamish, et al. v U.S.* to air all their grievances about the treaty promises as well as tell history from their own point of view. President Kavanaugh and other leaders met at Swinomish to develop rebuttals to the government's case, which he continued to work on after his presidency.[161]

In 1927, the Federal Claims Commission convened at Suquamish Reservation. By then, Sass had led the Samish for twelve to fourteen years. Holding James Kavanaugh's diary for reference, he testified about the government's promise that March Point would be part of the Samish Reservation. He told of visiting the immense Guemes longhouse with his mother where he witnessed the superiority of communal ownership.[162]

When the commissioner announced his decision, the tribes got little more than an admission that though wrong had been done, the cost of services offset the claims value. There would be no additional land for allotment or promises kept.

After working for the U.S. Fish Commission in Alaska for some time, Sarsfield died in 1943 at seventy-six. The newspaper portrayed him as "the oldest living white person born on Fidalgo Island." The paper ignored his Indianness completely, as it did his mother.[163]

Lyman Kavanaugh, the military veteran, then took up his uncle's cause, though he had been living entirely in the white world for many years. Francis' family had kept their Samish membership and subtle identification with Caroline's people, but they had become progressively less involved in the lives of their relatives. The short man whose looks so mimicked those of his beloved grandmother began to chart his own path to help relatives with treaty activism after Sarsfield died, keeping a Kavanaugh tradition intact. In the Samish fight for recognition, he advocated for a cash settlement that could be used to buy land since the prospects for getting a reservation were dismal, even though it was an unpopular position. He also enrolled at Swinomish after World War II, and returned to the reservation for tribal meetings. He developed a reputation for asking hard questions few others were willing to ask during the fight against a federal tribal termination policy. Lyman put himself on the front lines in the 1960s to secure fishing rights. Like others who defied state regulations, he was arrested.[164]

Later generations of Kavanaughs maintained their Samish enrollment, though they became only minimally active. Though factually accurate memories of Caroline and James faded, the pride of heritage in being their descendants and their part in early Northwest history did not.

Today, Caroline's home on *Shais-quihl* at the end of Kavanaugh Road is marked by the huge plumes of steam or a gas flare from the oil refinery that sits on the land she protected all of her life.

CHAPTER 3

Mary, Daughter of the Strong People

T HE SPRINGLESS WAGON CREAKED and moaned through muddy
ruts and over rocks in the crude approach road to Washington
Territory's new prison.

Rough-looking men in dirty suits and dirtier boots swung the
gates open and the wagon rolled through the unfinished stockade
that smelled of newly cut logs. The horses halted before the two-
story prison building whose glassless windows stared at the wagon's
occupants.

Mary Phillips struggled down from the wagon, hampered by iron
manacles. Convicted of killing her alcoholic and abusive fourth husband on Christmas day nine months earlier, she would call the prison
"home" for the next two years.

Though the prison confined no other women prisoners, nor had
even a single female guard, Mary was not alone.

Also in the wagon were Mary's infant son and three-year-old
daughter. Prison records called the little ones "boarders," but in fact,
they would also be prisoners in the brutal institution.

MARY

The court system well-documented the worst moments of Mary
Fitzhugh Lear Phillips' life. With those records, writers used the
former wife of a Territorial Supreme Court justice to exemplify how
badly a cross-cultural marriage could end. Mary's family says that
whites have presented her only as a misguided victim of the white
men she married. Her descendants do not see her that way. She was
S'Klallam, a daughter of "The Strong People." Her story is that of
a survivor, as well as of the unusual husbands and sons whose lives
intertwined with hers.[1]

❦

Uncounted generations of Mary's ancestors developed their ways of being for perhaps 14,000 years on the Olympic Peninsula's north shore around its river mouths and two large spits. Their necklace of S'Klallam villages spread from Makah territory at the stormy, rocky tip of the most northwestern place in the continental United States, eighty-five miles east to Puget Sound's entrance. On a sunny day, Mary's people could see the traces of smoke from longhouse fires on Vancouver Island twelve miles across the rough and windy Strait of Juan de Fuca. Waters flowing from the towering Olympic Mountains behind the narrow lowland tumbled to the salt water where four-foot-long salmon began their journey upstream to spawn.

Unlike sheltered Puget Sound villages, most of the S'Klallam longhouses sat exposed along the shoreline. Peaceful relations and marriages prevailed with neighboring groups, while less friendly ones and fewer marriages were the norm with distant villages whose families spoke less related languages. To others, *S'Klallam* meant intimidation and ruthlessness against those who harmed their families or villages. They usually sought reparations for a death caused by someone from another village, but if negotiations failed, retaliation could be ferocious. Like others, they built defensive strongholds in the forest to guard against Northern raiders.

Spanish explorers landed at the Dungeness River village in 1790 where the people greeted them with fish, venison, blankets, and baskets. S'Klallam copper and iron, buttons, and knives showed the Spanish that trade networks were already long and ended any expectation of wonderment at European goods. Two years later the S'Klallam, clothed in their fine blanket and skin garments and with faces painted just as Londoners did, surprised British explorer Captain George Vancouver. They seemed rather indifferent to his distinguished self, clad in British Navy finery. Vancouver and his crew recognized the message of enemy heads mounted on poles. Unlike many other indigenous people the British had encountered, the S'Klallam did not make their daughters available and most oddly, rejected their "gift" of liquor.[2]

The young man who would become Mary's father boarded a ship and tried the sand-like sugar and drank the hot black liquid that was coffee. Whey'ux left the ship when his people suspected it was a kidnap. He explained that but for the color of their skin and eyes, the newcomers were humans and the food would not kill them. The S'Klallam adopted useful European technology, excluding bar soap which made a mess in a salt water shampoo. Though raw flour tasted terrible, women adopted bread-making, as they soon did chicken and potatoes.[3]

Despite friendly trade, the British and S'Klallam did not understand each other's assumptions about authority and dominance. After some guides felt mistreated, the S'Klallam killed five Hudson's Bay Company (HBC) men in 1828. In retaliation, the British killed close to three dozen people and burned villages. Trade resumed, but the S'Klallam deeply distrusted the British for years and the way opened for Americans.[4]

The upheaval and change that began scarcely forty years before Mary was born about 1835 continued beyond her childhood in the 1840s. The population declined to half of what it was before the epidemics came. By the 1840s, it had dropped to 1,485 and then to 926 in 1855. Despite that, when she was small, the S'Klallam were clearly the most powerful group living on Puget Sound and the Salish Sea. Prosperous from their strength and dominance of trade, they owned over two hundred canoes when most groups had fewer than one hundred, and they owned five times as many guns.[5]

Mary's extended family dominated the coastal S'Klallam villages in Vancouver's time and beyond, beginning with her grandfather Ste'tee'thlum, who is said to have married a Cowichan leader's daughter from mid-Vancouver Island. Their seven sons and a daughter enlarged the family's network with their marriages. Mary's father was the sixth child and as an adult, his winter longhouse was near today's Port Townsend at *Kah'tai* (Kaw-tie) where a brother also lived. One of the brothers married a Lummi woman, which gave Mary's family a tie to Bellingham Bay.[6]

Kah'tai's position where the Strait's waters sweeping in from the Pacific met the more placid ones of Puget Sound, made it important. *Kah'tai* ("pass through") referred to the little valley through which travelers portaged canoes in rough weather and water. The geography was gentler than that of the villages sited below the mountain fronts

and Mary spent her childhood surrounded by a riot of life. Wildflow-
ers and rhododendrons bloomed wherever wet places gave way to dry,
and a lagoon sheltered thousands of waterfowl. Behind the beach's
longhouses, a bluff rose to a plateau rich with deer and bear.

Mary's mostly traditional Coast Salish childhood diet was supplemented by sea gull eggs S'Klallam women collected from nests on
steep cliff faces. The dangerous job sometimes exposed them to sudden storms and the Northern raiders. S'Klallam men left the North
Pacific whaling to the Makah, but when whales happened by, they
quickly took to their canoes. Women processed enormous whale car-
casses and wasted nothing, including the skeleton. Like other Coast
Salish cooks, S'Klallam women combined their foods in ways that
became the foundation of today's "Northwest cuisine," such as halibut or salmon paired with steamed potatoes, or roasted flounder with
berries and sprouts.[7]

Mary could lead a traditional childhood before Port Townsend
grew nearby. Children bathed in fresh water before breakfast, cleans-
ing themselves physically and spiritually. They learned to use a duck
quill to clean their teeth and rinsed after their sunset meal. Woven
conical hats protected their heads from sun and drizzle, and girls
wore soft woven cedar bark skirts for everyday work and play. Mothers painted children's faces with ochre (red clay pigment) for spiritual protection after age six. Mary and other girls played a variety of
games, put on performances, and kept pets. They learned the skills
wives and mothers needed. High-born girls like Mary learned how
to care for the family women's purebred wool dogs and shear their
crinkly "wool" undercoat. Grandmothers most often taught them
how to turn the white hair into yarn and then weave.[8]

At the end of the day, elders told stories to the children around
the fire before bedtime. Every S'Klallam child knew about Slapu the
witch who snatched children who didn't follow directions. The place
in Sequim Bay where the story said she drowned continues to bubble
today, perhaps from the tidal changes on a barely concealed shoal...
or perhaps not.[9]

Mary's relative Alice married "Blanket Bill" Jarman, probably the
first white man permitted to live among the region's Coast Salish,
and they also settled at *Kah'tai*. Other settlers invaded in 1850. At

first the bachelors married S'Klallam women and their families permitted the men to log or farm on S'Klallam prairies. The white men
did not always recognize it was the goodwill of their wives' families
that allowed them to settle there. Some introduced a constant supply
of liquor, engaged in smuggling, and generally brought a new type
of disorder. It wasn't long before the settlement near the Dungeness
Spit village became known as "Whiskey Flats." Many Ste'tee'thlum
family granddaughters married settlers, for better or worse.[10]

When Mary was a teenager, *Kah'tai*'s strategic location and abundant food resources proved to be irresistible attractions for moneyed
white businessmen. In a short time, the U.S. Army found the high plateau equally attractive for a fort to defend Puget Sound's new towns.
Kah'tai and "the Strong People's" territory were under full attack by
a different kind of enemy. Mary's *Kah'tai* cousin Cheech'ma'ham
(Chetzemoka) stepped up and managed S'Klallam relations with the
settler invasion next to her village.[11]

Mary probably wed her first husband between 1850 and 1853,
because she remarried in 1854. No details have survived about who
he was except that he was indigenous, probably from another Coast
Salish village. Some later governmental records used "Clax" as her
surname, but that could as well be a clerk's corruption of her father
Whey'ux's name. Family history says only that he and their son died,
perhaps during the early 1853 smallpox epidemic that killed hundreds.[12]

The young widow needed support because she was a member of
her husband's longhouse only by virtue of the marriage. As a Coast
Salish woman, her lifelong ties remained to her birth family's house.
If a widow had children, her in-laws might arrange a "levirate" marriage to her brother-in-law to keep the deceased man's offspring
part of their father's house, and multiple wives were common for
the prosperous men. However, without children a widow like Mary
usually went home. And the epidemic had killed many prospective
husbands.[13]

Mary's parents may have died (or her husband could have been
Samish), because she went to her brother Seya'whom's longhouse on
Samish Island. By then, her S'Klallam brother was the de facto leader
of the legendary 1,200-foot-long cedar house there. For a variety of

reasons, Coast Salish men sometimes left their family longhouse and moved to another village without losing status. Seya'whom moved to his wife's longhouse when he married, thought to be spurred by an epidemic-caused power vacuum on Samish Island. Perhaps because his own family had a number of capable leaders, Seya'whom took that role in his wife's village. His wife Emily was the daughter of the last war chief of the Nuwhaha, the group so decimated it had joined the Samish village despite speaking a different language, and Seya'whom may have also had Samish connections. The move cemented an alliance with *Kah'tai* which provided both groups with hospitality and protection. Emily was a woman known for her compassion toward people in need. She and Seya'whom welcomed Mary into the longhouse.[14]

The young widow probably converted to Catholicism after she moved into Seya'whom's longhouse since no missionaries converted the S'Klallam villages until several decades later. Most villages in the Salish Sea converted in the 1840s. Later, many whites as well as family knew Mary by her personal S'Klallam name and her baptismal name, which was unusual.[15]

Mary was a petite seventeen- or eighteen-year-old teenaged widow with high cheekbones, large eyes, and a mouth made for smiling. She was a high-born beauty. Circumstances now sent her into the home of her second husband, a Virginian of treacherous charm, with consummate ability to manipulate and intimidate.[16]

EDMUND CLARE FITZHUGH

A "First Family of Virginia" scion, Edmund Clare Fitzhugh came from Falmouth, a town founded by a noble Piscataway daughter and her colonist husband in 1657. After lawyer William Fitzhugh's 1670 arrival, he amassed 54,000 acres to enrich future Fitzhugh generations. His time in the House of Burgesses established the family political tradition. One hundred fifty years later, Dr. Alexander Fitzhugh's wife Elizabeth Clare gave birth to Edmund at "Boscobel," his family's ridge-top mansion a few miles upstream from their friends, the Washingtons. Their first son entered the world of 1820 as a "Fitzhugh of Stafford County," one of the oldest, richest, and most influential Virginia families. They would expect much of Edmund.[17]

Ever since "William the Immigrant" married a wealthy eleven-year-old girl, Fitzhugh men consolidated and expanded their wealth and influence through marriage. Each of Edmund's four marriages would benefit him, but be a disaster for the wives and children, starting with Mary.[18]

Edmund's father graduated from the University of Pennsylvania Medical School. After service in the War of 1812, he lost his inheritance right to "Boscobel" when he failed to repay debts to his father for medical school and a house. He spent nearly forty years as Falmouth's doctor, local magistrate, and legislator. Of Alexander and Elizabeth's ten children, only Edmund and four sisters reached adulthood.[19]

Falmouth lay at the Rappahannock River's head of navigation

Edmund Clare Fitzhugh. The Virginia lawyer managed the coal mine's construction and was appointed a territorial justice while under indictment for murder. The photo is probably his official court portrait. *Unknown photographer, Military Records Collection. Washington State Archives, Olympia, Washington.*

where Appalachian water dropped over picturesque rock outcroppings full of fishing and swimming holes. It was once a major commercial hub, but by Edmund's time its silted-up landing sent vessels to Fredericksburg just across the river. Dr. Fitzhugh's Falmouth practice stagnated in the sleepy "rough" backwater village, though such economic distress mattered little to the Fitzhughs' social position.[20]

Sixteen-year-old Edmund was in Washington, D.C., when his mother died in childbirth. The year before, he had entered the Jesuits' prep school at Georgetown College. It promised a rigorous liberal arts education in a sophisticated atmosphere of internationalism and religious pluralism. Many of Edmund's classmates came from the diplomatic corps. Alexander's first bill included a charge for his son's engraved silver spoon.[21]

Two years at Georgetown finished the prep course, and seven earned a classical university degree. Until summer vacation, Edmund could leave only once a month and only to visit his local married sister. The restrictive atmosphere sharply contrasted with his indulgent life at home. He lasted two and a half years before Georgetown dismissed him in March 1838.[22]

Alexander was a new member of the House of Delegates and he went to work to get his only son into West Point. Perhaps discipline would benefit a smart, over-indulged, and unmotivated son's life. After he called upon his connections, West Point admitted nineteen-year-old "E.C." two years later for the Class of 1844. After one semester, they dismissed him for "deficiency in studies." It was a disgrace Fitzhugh hid from his friends when he lived in Washington Territory.[23]

Faced with pressure to find a profession acceptable to his family and social peers, Edmund studied law at a local office and started his practice in 1843 at age twenty-three. He followed his father and dozens of Fitzhughs into Democratic Republican politics, first by getting out the vote, and then following his father into the House of Delegates for a single term during the Mexican War instead of enlisting. During his term, he met Fayette McMullen, a colleague he would meet under very different circumstances ten years later in the Pacific Northwest.[24]

When Alexander began sending the family's forty-five slaves to a Richmond slave dealer, Edmund took a look at his father's finances. He discovered that Alexander had misappropriated his children's inheritance from their mother's brother two decades before. The five siblings recorded a "deed" that gave Edmund permission to sell everything, reimburse them, and only then pay Alexander's personal bills. When he died two months later, his dishonesty left a poor example for personal integrity to his son.[25]

Edmund sold the family home and as new patriarch, settled his three unmarried sisters at a Fitzhugh family "big house," where they would be taken care of. At age twenty-nine, he joined the great rush to California in 1849. Young lawyers and other professionals like him went to provide lucrative services to the gold seekers, not dig in the dirt. Virginians were becoming part of a new California-American elite, including the first governor. It was a place where Fitzhugh could work his personal connections. And as a Fitzhugh, he had a lot of connections.[26]

The booming city of San Francisco was a fascinating eyesore with every form of indulgence and entertainment Edmund might seek. Observed contemporary historian H.H. Bancroft: "Fugitives from trouble and dishonor had been lured to California, graceless scions of respectable families and never-do-wells, men of wavering virtue and frail piety, withering before temptation."[27]

Gold rush California was a lawyer's utopia according to one who described the "most cheering and exhilarating prospects of fussing, quarrelling, murdering, violation of contracts, and the whole catalogue of crimen falsi…what country could boast more largely of its crimes. What more splendid role of felonies! What more terrific murders! What more gorgeous bank robberies! What more magnificent operations in the land offices!"[28]

In 1853 Edmund partnered with his third cousin's husband, U.S. Attorney Calhoun Benham, a nephew of former Vice President John C. Calhoun, and brother-in-law of California land baron Charlie Fairfax from Virginia. He also practiced with a future U.S. Secretary of State, Virginia blueblood Edmund Randolph. Benham and Randolph were operatives in the Democratic Party and resisters against the Vigilante Committee. Fitzhugh continued his political activism with these two men, as well as with William Gwin, once President Andrew Jackson's personal secretary. All had much to teach a young politico about opportunism and using the system for personal gain. All were pro-slavery in a politically corrupt new state subject to open bribery and without secret ballots.[29]

Edmund's career took a sharp turn when Benham offered him a job that promised prosperity and a significant role in the development of the northern Pacific Coast. On February 13, 1854, during Washington Territory's wettest, most depressing month, he slogged across Bellingham Bay's mud flats in his polished gentleman's boots to establish the Bellingham Bay Coal Company mine.

Two of Henry Roeder's men had stumbled upon coal beneath the roots of an overturned cedar tree on the fringe of Roeder's land claim. After a sample arrived in San Francisco, Calhoun Benham formed a syndicate to obtain the land claim and finance a mine. It consisted of some of San Francisco's most powerful men: Collector of Customs R. P. Hammond; U.S. District Attorney William Inge; soon-to-be treasurer of the new U.S. Mint and legislator Jacob R. Snyder; and Charles Minturn, owner of the Contra Costa Steam Navigation Company on the river route to the mines. All were active Democrats and flush with gold rush funds to invest.[30]

Fitzhugh would become the land claim settler of record after Roeder moved to another claim. Evidence suggests that the syndicate sent him north for reasons as much political as business. He was a known quantity for pro-slavery party leaders who wanted to extend the Democrats' influence into newly-formed Washington Territory. They hoped to form a future pro-slavery Pacific Coast voting block in Congress.

Edmund Fitzhugh was unlike any other arrival at the Whatcom mill settlement. When Elizabeth Roeder described him to her daughter, she betrayed the fascination and charisma of the man: "A born fighter, quick to take offense, absolutely without fear, something of a roisterer, imperious and self-willed, following his code of honor without thought of consequences, but withal a man of superior intellect and many kindly impulses. Generous, hospitable, impulsive, self-indulgent, honest and brave."[31]

He landed weeks before a small group of men finished organizing Whatcom County. They elected him county auditor because of his "varied intelligence and practical business knowledge." He gained control over land transactions and the flow of county money, including the final say on the taxable value assessment of his mine. His first actions included recording the land claim transfer to himself and exchanging "his" mineral rights for stock in the syndicate.[32]

Fitzhugh would control the U.S. Navy's only American coaling station north of San Francisco just forty years after the War of 1812, because Britain owned the coal mine on Vancouver Island. Within months he was the territory's largest employer, bringing him instant political influence in the territorial government.

MARY AND EDMUND FITZHUGH

Edmund Fitzhugh saw the disadvantage in bachelor living and decided that he needed a female touch in his cabin. He went looking for a suitable young woman at the nearest Lummi village.

According to Seya'whom's daughter Ruth Sehome Shelton, he asked the Lummi headmen for a young woman of status (i.e., one of their daughters). The union would follow the Fitzhugh tradition of young wives from families of wealth and power. They told him there were no unmarried girls available. It was probably untrue. More likely Tsi'lixw, Sea'nult, and others were put off by his arrogant and patronizing manner.[33]

The men told Fitzhugh that Seya'whom had a marriageable daughter, so he hired two Lummi sub-chiefs to take him to Samish Island. Their presence, Ruth believed, made her father erroneously think Fitzhugh was worthy of his trust. Seya'whom saw the mine superintendent as an influential equal and it would be to his family's advantage to ally with him. Ruth thought her father also wanted to keep his family safe in a changing world. His teenaged daughter Julia cried because she did not want to marry the strange white man, to no avail. Given Fitzhugh's background and personality, it is unlikely that he ever saw himself truly married when he went through the tribal custom marriage ceremony. Even so, he named the mine and his settlement "Sehome" after his father-in-law. Others treated Julia as Mrs. Fitzhugh.[34]

Julia grieved for her family, more so after she quickly became pregnant. Her desolation was unusual since she would normally have been prepared to move away to her husband's village. "She cried and cried over the turn of events which brought her to him," wrote Ruth. Julia's tears may have resulted from Fitzhugh's abusive blows and his demands on a pregnant teenager who knew nothing about the cooking and housekeeping ways he expected. He even wanted the coffee pot in a precise spot on the dinner table. A Southerner like Edmund Fitzhugh would never treat a non-white teenaged bride half his age as much more than a servant.[35]

Toward the end of Julia's pregnancy, Seya'whom sent Mary to his daughter (Mary's niece). She became Edmund's secondary wife,

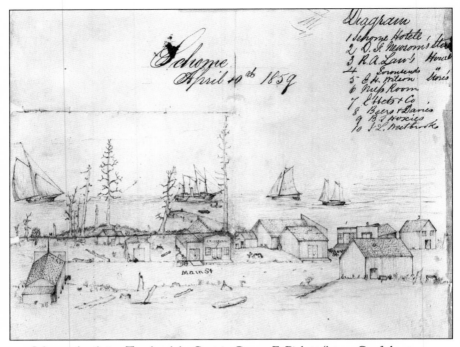

Sehome, April 1859. The sketch by Captain George E. Pickett (later a Confederate general) from the hill in back of the coal mine settlement shows the only wharf on the bay, as well as several different types of vessels and specific businesses along a stump-filled path. The E.C. Fitzhugh home is not pictured. *Image #1957.0005.000001, Whatcom Museum, Bellingham, Washington.*

whether that was the initial plan or not. Under her circumstances, she may have agreed to it as a variation on the custom that usually provided for the support of widows. In Seya'whom's eyes, Fitzhugh was a wealthy upper-class man, and in his tradition, allowed to have multiple wives. Responding to Julia's despair, her father also moved the immediate family to a longhouse near the mine. It was Lummi territory, but he took advantage of his family connections to obtain permission to dwell there, possibly in common with Lummi mine and mill workers.[36]

Julia gave birth to Julianne on October 6, 1854, and Mary gave birth to Charles Mason (named for the territorial secretary) on June 7, 1855. The co-wives were close in age and could look forward to raising their babies together. The Fitzhugh family moved into a new white two-story house at the end of the mine settlement nearest Whatcom. It was surrounded by garden and orchard, and "tastefully laid out, expressive of comfort and convenience."[37]

Soon, Mary and Julia lived among a mixed community of Irish, English, Chinese, and Coast Salish miners as well as other indigenous wives, and their own family. Caroline Davis (*see* chapter 2) was probably Julia's cousin and moved to Sehome in 1857. Other strangers arrived on board vessels that docked at the mine, including military and government men who stayed at the Fitzhugh house. If Edmund sent Mary and Julia from their home when visitors arrived, as one employee claimed, they were not without welcoming places to go to.[38]

In the five years after Mary moved to Edmund and Julia's house, he was in constant motion and frequently left the women alone with their children. When the Treaty War broke out farther south in 1855, he became "Colonel Fitzhugh," military aide to Governor Isaac Stevens. He learned to speak at least one Coast Salish language fluently which led to an appointment the next year as interpreter and then special Indian agent for the Bellingham Bay region, including the Samish villages. Stevens forced hundreds of villagers from the north Sound into quarantine on Whidbey Island to prevent them from entering the war. Edmund checked on them but did little to ameliorate their suffering and rumored mass (food?) poisoning. The man they called "Mistuh Pichuh" did, however, reassure Stevens that the Indians were "entirely" under his control and took unwarranted credit for their lack of interest in joining the war. A more important reason may have been the employment of Lummi men (and probably his Samish in-laws) at the mine and mill, as well as the family bonds between settlers and Indians. To Fitzhugh's credit, he began a long campaign to get the destructive liquor trade to the Indians stopped. He also focused on getting the army to protect settlers, Indians, and the mine from the Northern raiders and happily welcomed Captain Pickett's troops at his dock in August 1856.[39]

Edmund Fitzhugh found ways to accumulate more power. His simultaneous paid positions enabled him to become one of the region's unofficial bankers. He garnered obligations and loyalties during a decade when lending money was one of the quickest way to wealth. He continued to rise in the Democratic Party hierarchy, even threatening his employees with dismissal or getting their "head(s) knocked off" to get the open ballots cast as he and Gov. Stevens wanted. In May 1857, the Territorial Democratic Convention unanimously elected him the chairman.[40]

Though Edmund had used his legal training since arrival on the West Coast, territorial records do not show his admission to the bar. He obtained appointment in 1855 as District Court Commissioner courtesy of Territorial Justice Frank Chenoweth, which made him the region's judicial authority when Chenoweth was gone. After the war, Governor Stevens rewarded Fitzhugh's militia service and personal loyalty with a nomination for Territorial Justice to replace his benefactor Chenoweth. It meant a good salary for three, three-week sessions and a seat on the Territorial Supreme Court once a year. Frank Chenoweth was a fine justice, but he stood in the way of the Virginian's ambitions.[41]

Nominees Obadiah McFadden and William Strong had superior legal educations and territorial judicial experience. Though their nominations moved along smoothly, Edmund's was endangered by an incident five hundred feet from where Mary and Julia were probably cooking his dinner, babies underfoot. Even New York City newspapers noticed. National readers heard about Mary and Julia.

∝≫∞

Sunshine lingered into the evening on May 30, 1857. Edmund, with Francis Cooty and his son, walked from Whatcom along the curve of the bay toward the Fitzhugh home and the row of small mine employee houses beyond. It was nearly seven o'clock on Saturday night, the end of the work week. Some men arrived home from the mine saloon sober, and many arrived inebriated before wives and landladies served dinner.[42]

The walkers drew up to Richard Williams watering his garden near the Fitzhugh home. Obviously drunk, Andrew Wilson swayed in the dirt street loudly talking to him. The stout, short man was known to be quarrelsome and a fighter when he drank. Edmund told him to move along and get away from the path by his house, but Wilson claimed it was public road and he would go where he liked.

Edmund replied that the public road was back of his garden or he could go along the beach, but he had to get off the mine's property and away from his home. Wilson ignored him. He started down Fitzhugh's path to the beach, then threw his bundle down and went back. He said "If you want anything out of me, come on."

Fitzhugh's response was typical of his Virginian gentry culture: if stranger, neighbor, or even kin invaded one's property without permission, some level of violence could be expected. It was a question of honor and patriarchal responsibility to protect family and property.[43]

When Wilson grabbed his employer around the waist, the two wrestled over Fitzhugh's pocket pistol. The other men couldn't move fast enough to prevent the shot that hit Wilson in the groin, but they grabbed the pistol from Fitzhugh's powder-burned hand.

Late that night, Fitzhugh and others asked the dying man why he had been so foolish as to come back and grab the gun. Wilson had no answer.

Said Fitzhugh: "I did not mean to harm the poor devil. He shot himself."

Before Wilson died, he accused Fitzhugh of following him to the beach trail and shooting him there. At 10 a.m. the next day, Mary's husband faced a hasty inquest and a possible charge of assault with attempt to kill. The territorial justice nominee angrily demanded that his accusers produce evidence to sustain such a charge.

Before the grand jury could meet, Fitzhugh nearly got into a duel while gambling with Lt. Robert Davis, even though the two may have married cousins. Captain Pickett's determined intervention hints at the mismatch in abilities and Fitzhugh's willingness to kill. The territorial justice position was further jeopardized.

When Fitzhugh's Virginia legislature acquaintance and new territorial governor Fayette McMullen arrived, he took control of the nomination. In view of recent events, McMullen supported keeping Chenoweth on the bench over the man he knew. Most Third District voters signed a flurry of petitions to the U.S. Attorney General opposing Fitzhugh's appointment. They were countered by his friends, new Congressional Delegate Isaac Stevens and California Senator William Gwin working in the capital on his behalf.[44]

When the grand jury prosecution witnesses did not appear at court in Port Townsend for five days, Fitzhugh took to his canoe in disgust, thinking that Justice Chenoweth would take no action. As soon as he left, Chenoweth issued the indictment without the witnesses or Fitzhugh's intimidating presence.[45]

Mary and Julia probably knew there was controversy over Wilson's mortal wounding in their garden, but their husband carried on while waiting for trial and confirmation of his appointment. The doctor's son dealt with the winter epidemic in the longhouses that probably killed Pickett's wife in her home uphill. By summer the Fraser River gold rush's unruly thousands were camped on his beach and most of Fitzhugh's mine crew had deserted. On August 7, 1858, Whatcom's *Northern Light* announced the confirmation.

Not long after Fitzhugh took his oath of office and left his Indian agent post, the sheriff finally came calling to arrest him, though "His Honor" was quickly released on bail. At the end of the last day of his first court term, he granted himself a change of venue to Olympia. The scandal of a judge who took the bench while indicted for murder grew. The *New York Daily Tribune* printed a letter from Whatcom whose writer called Wilson's death "cold-blooded murder" and claimed the victim was denied justice because of Fitzhugh's connections.[46]

The anonymous writer attacked Edmund's marriages to Julia and Mary, saying they disgusted town families (presumably the all-white families, of whom there were less than half a dozen). He called it "the keeping in a public manner a harem supplied with Indian girls… There are two certain that I have often seen at his house, at different times, for the last three or four years, by both of whom he has children." Local anger at the public letter in one of the nation's largest newspapers, which made the whole territory look bad, prompted a legislator's speech excoriating Fitzhugh. Whatcom Representative John Tennant replied with a long, admiring defense of his employer and legal studies mentor.[47]

By then nearly two years had passed since Andrew Wilson's death. His Lummi widow Lucy and son John had returned home.[48]

Justice Fitzhugh stood trial for the hanging offense on March 14, 1859, before his colleague, Justice Obadiah McFadden. Before witnesses could testify, the prosecutor moved that the court acquit him for lack of evidence to support the murder charge. Everyone may have concluded that if Fitzhugh were to be convicted, the complications and appeals would happen in a vacuum of precedent. More scandal would descend upon the young territory and its Democrats.[49]

The jury rendered a verdict of "not guilty" in ninety seconds.

Edmund went home to Mary, Julia, and his children, and resumed his life as though the trial never happened. The year was promising. The syndicate invested more money in mine improvements and sent in professional operators to work under him, which allowed more absences. He entertained General William Harney at their home, and took out a loan to enlarge the mine store. While Edmund traveled on judicial and party business, he left the women alone more and more, and they spent time with their relatives and friends.[50]

When in Olympia, Edmund was part of an indulgent, self-centered culture of men with money to spend. This caught up with Justices Fitzhugh and Strong at the end of 1859. They frequently played "hazards," an illegal fourteenth-century game like "craps." Fitzhugh's murder trial prosecutor Butler P. Anderson indicted the two sitting judges and five others. With the Democratic Party beginning to split over states' rights and slavery, politics may have played a role in his choice to indict a party leader. Once a "Stevens Democrat," Anderson had joined forces with the national "Douglas Democrats."[51]

Fitzhugh and Strong claimed that the grand jury was defective, but Justice McFadden overruled their motion. Then they tried unsuccessfully to get charges dismissed because they had bet nothing of any value, probably meaning they were wagering liquor, cigars, or an oyster supper. A verdict was hard to come by, and more than one jury heard the case before Anderson decided to drop the whole thing. Fitzhugh slipped through his own judicial net once again.[52]

ొళ౮౦

The personal fortunes of Mary's husband declined further. His murder and gambling trials brought negative publicity to the territory and his town. The mine expanded under the management of professionals and his position fell to "resident agent." The community may also have disapproved of his treatment of Julia and Mary, who were relatives of many other local wives. One hundred fifty years later, Mary's descendants still remembered her description of him as "mean."⁵³

Still, Justice Fitzhugh was a good justice. He wrote literate, informed opinions that were occasionally appealed to the Supreme Court (of which he was also a member), but people usually did not quibble about the wisdom of his decisions. Although Mary's husband was on the bench when it was illegal to accept testimony from "non-citizen" Indians against whites, he did it anyway and no one stopped him. It may be too much to suppose his family associations informed his conscience, but there is no evidence to explain why he took such an innovative attitude. That included treating a land claim as community property for a tribal custom couple's divorce in which he awarded the S'Klallam wife substantial support. Lucy Madison may have been Mary's cousin, but no one accused the judge of conflict of interest. His decision stood in the Supreme Court appeal, with only a reduction in award.⁵⁴

He controlled boisterous court sessions, where sometimes a man was a juror in the morning and defendant in the afternoon. For every man who could get away to Port Townsend, each court term meant three weeks away from home combining court business with politicking, financial deals, gambling, and socializing in the evenings.

Fitzhugh's actions during the 1859 election did little for his personal reputation in town. He swaggered about Sehome and Whatcom with intimidating armed guards, delivering every vote against what he called "the damn murderous Black Republicans." Territory-wide dissatisfaction with the heavy-handed, Southern-dominated Democratic organization and the slavery issue led many dissidents to join the tiny Republican Party.⁵⁵

The next year, when the Democratic Party split over states' rights, Isaac Stevens chaired the "Peace Democrats" Breckinridge campaign for president. The Washington Democrats sent Mary's husband east to make sure Stevens, the congressional delegate, didn't forget his territory's interests. Edmund was probably also motivated by personal ambition to succeed Stevens.

Edmund Fitzhugh took Julianne (nearly six) and Mason (just five) from their mothers before he left on June 11. He sent (or took) the children to southern Puget Sound where several other mixed-blood Whatcom County children lived in homes with people who would raise them "white." One account says that Mary and Julia went berry-picking and when they came home, the children were gone, but it was unlikely that Mary and Julia would have left the children behind under their father's sole care. Mary's descendants carried the story that he directed the women to speak English around the children and when he arrived home one day, they were speaking their own language with visiting family. He angrily grabbed the children and took them away despite the women's pleas. Julia's family said that he took them away because he wanted them to learn better English in an all-white family. All versions demonstrate the women's trauma that never left family memory.[56]

The women discussed the situation with Seya'whom and Emily, though the decision of what to do was left to Mary and Julia. The two mothers may have beaten the cruel and unfeeling man before they left Sehome and never returned to him, as another family account says. They did not know how or where to find their lost children. Seya'whom moved the rest of the family back to Samish Island.[57]

The nineteenth century was still mired in patriarchal rights over families and property. In Washington Territory, when an intermarriage broke up, a white father always retained custody unless he decided to let a child go with its mother. Henry Roeder sent his children with their mother to Lummi, while Russell Peabody sent his older ones to foster homes down the Sound. White fathers "owned" their children's future in Washington Territory. It matched perfectly with a Virginia Fitzhugh's way of parenting.

A century later, Mary's grandniece Harriet Dover attached a personal note to her mother Ruth Sehome (Seya'whom) Shelton's account of what happened. The women's anguish still echoes. "I have shrieked to high heaven every time I hear this story of Fitzhugh and my aunts. I vow I'll look for him and beat his head off by bits— tear him to shreds—and my mother smiles, and says, 'Why he must have died long ago.' And I say I'll tear his grave apart and kick his head to bits anyway. I wonder where he came from? And where did he go? … Life is so fascinating—even while your heart aches for the people who get hurt in it."[58]

CR&O

Fitzhugh returned from the 1860 campaign embittered and suffering from "Panama fever" (malaria). He went back to his house, now empty of Mary and Julia's soft voices and of Mason and Julianne's boisterous activity.[59]

"Lame duck" Justice Fitzhugh faced a different political world when he presided over court in early 1861. His party was in shambles and new leaders did not welcome "Copperheads" who had worked to elect Breckinridge. Most of Fitzhugh's old friends were new Republicans hoping to keep their federal jobs. The Civil War loomed.

Fitzhugh left for Virginia shortly after his court term ended. He could have gone to Victoria where some Southerners clustered at the St. Nicholas Hotel. Many belonged to the secretive Knights of the Golden Circle that included many Fitzhugh associates in California. Edmund, however, was a Unionist and Virginia's secession convention voted to stay in as long as the government did not use force against them. He and fellow Virginian and friend Captain Pickett were of similar mind, but Edmund was first to return east.[60]

Scarcely six weeks after he left Sehome, he married Cora Weems Bowie in Maryland. Her family, like all those with whom Fitzhugh men allied, had wielded political and financial power since the Revolution. Cora cared for her widowed father and was far into the social death of a spinster at 31. She may have been willing to marry a man with great flaws rather than never marry at all. She probably believed she was Edmund's first wife, but she was in effect his third. With the uproar in the East about his "harem," she may have heard about Mary and Julia and accepted his explanation, or in a long tradition shut her ears to the whispers.[61]

Maryland stayed in the union and Virginia seceded the same month they married. The pair's political situation in either state was problematic and federal troops soon used Falmouth as a camp. Though Fitzhugh at forty-one could still avoid Confederate service, the newlyweds were back in Washington Territory within two months of their marriage. A few months later, his California friends Calhoun Benham and William Gwin were arrested on the way to Cuba to buy arms for the Confederacy.[62]

Mary's former husband needed a new source of income. Years earlier, he loaned money to a former Whatcom County commissioner who put up his land claim as collateral. Though others succeeded on Whidbey Island's most fertile prairie, William Cullen had not. Fitzhugh foreclosed, but did not add Cora's name to the new deed. He had never lived on nor worked a farm, but he and Cora moved there. There is no record of him practicing law, but he was never going to be a successful farmer.[63]

Edmund is not known to have reached out to Mason or Julianne, though his letters to their foster parents after the war suggest he may have sent payments for their care while he lived on Whidbey Island.

In less than two years, Cora Weems Bowie Fitzhugh was dead.[64]

Fitzhugh owed money to friends who, in the habit of Southern gentry, tied themselves together in a web of financial obligation and rarely worried about quick repayment. His old loans with a one-day repayment deadline were probably gambling debts. As soon as he buried Cora, his old friends pounced and filed suit. Evidence suggests that they may have been outraged by Cora's fate, or though they had known Fitzhugh for many years, he was no longer popular. The short gap between her death and the lawsuit may point to the end of friendships and the desire to strike back at the Copperhead who they believed was about to sell the farm and run before they got their money with hefty interest. The sheriff nailed a notice to his door, attached the homestead, and valued it at much less than when he had taken it a year earlier. Three days later, Fitzhugh signed over his farm.[65]

Edmund Fitzhugh left for Virginia and a war he could no longer avoid. In his pocket, he carried a copy of Whatcom's 1858 *Northern Light*'s first issue, a reminder of his happiest days. It would be many years before anyone in Washington Territory saw him again. Mary and Julia rebuilt their shattered lives, and his children suffered.

Julia married County Auditor Henry Barkhousen, a kind and honest man who had lived his own tragedies. He moved his petite, vivacious wife to a homestead at the base of March Point, not far from Caroline and James Kavanaugh. Henry called Julia "the happy whirlwind" during their long and successful marriage. Julianne Fitzhugh found her way back to her mother only years later after her own marriage.[66]

MARY AND WILLIAM KING LEAR

Mary's life in the early 1860s is undocumented until she married slender, sandy-haired William King Lear in 1864/65. She may have returned to Bellingham Bay to work because she probably met her next husband there. Her financial and protective needs may have figured larger in her choice of a new spouse than her wants. Still pretty and with a quiet nature, had she fully known Lear's past and been able to see his future, she might have married a different man. Lear was ambitious like Fitzhugh, and his life with women was similarly dysfunctional.[67]

Lear's father, Major William W. Lear, accomplished the unheard-of feat of moving from volunteer private in the War of 1812 into the small permanent army's commissioned officer ranks within six years, and without a West Point education. His wife gave birth in 1826 to William King Lear. Major Lear's thirty-four-year career ended when he was fatally wounded in the Mexican War. Though William K.'s brother Clinton was a decorated hero in that same war, William K. first appeared in army records when he went to work for the Fort Gibson post sutler on the 1853 Arkansas frontier next to Indian Territory.[68]

The government charged Lear with trying to smuggle liquor into Cherokee Nation. Military prosecutors thought he was deaf before he ran to Texas. A year later, apparently uninformed army recruiters there examined the twenty-seven-year-old for a commissioned officer rank. They thought he was nearly mute, with little command of English grammar, but they also suspected him of deception. Despite these drawbacks, Lear received a second lieutenancy, possibly due to his father's and brother's heroic reputations. In early 1856 his unit transferred to Fort Dalles, Oregon, during the Treaty War. Despite having resigned, he went with them and rescinded the paperwork after arrival.[69]

Lear transferred across the Columbia River to Fort Cascades near the village of the late Chief Welawa (Chenoweth), a Lewis and Clark peace medal recipient who had recently been hanged by the army in a tragic and unjust error. Soon after arrival, Lear married Welawa's daughter Taswatha (Ellen), left the army, and moved to her village above the river. He worked as the Indian agent on that side of the river, and as a civilian packer for the army moving supplies for Forts Walla Walla and Simcoe. Ellen gave birth to Lear's daughter Isabella, but before she was a year old, he abandoned them. Finding a better man, Ellen married Amos Underwood and they founded the town of Underwood, Washington.[70]

In early 1858 Lear joined the gold rush crowd at Whatcom. He opened a store at Semiahmoo, south of the Fraser River's mouth near the U.S. Boundary Survey Commission headquarters. Expecting a permanent gold rush route to develop, Lear started selling lots in his "Semiahmoo City" on the spit across Drayton Harbor, though he had no deed or registered pre-emption claim. When the gold rush ended, so did his real estate sales. The store went bankrupt.[71]

Two years later, Lear had been hired as the abandoned Fort Bellingham's caretaker. He ran a small store there. When Mary wed Lear and moved to the fort, her new home provided many advantages, including housing in the officers quarters, an orchard, pasture, and garden. She gave birth to their son Billy (William K. Lear Jr.) in 1866. When Billy was two, Lear abandoned Mary, just as he had Ellen. According to family, he told Mary he had to return to the East because a relative had died. If that is so, he lied. His own destructive pattern with women—abandoning them when they had a baby—was set.[72]

In July 1868 the United States had finalized its purchase of Alaska from Russia and the army moved into Fort Wrangel, including Lear, this time as a "non-com" and then post sutler. He purchased the fort's buildings when the army left in 1871 and ran a trading post, making him one of the town of Wrangell's founders. Lear married a Tlingit woman and fathered two children before he abandoned them, too. He married again, but he didn't stay with Matilda either. He died of "senility" at the Washington State Soldiers Home in Seattle in 1910. The family believes that Mary never saw him again.[73]

MASON

The Fitzhugh children disappeared from records until they emerged in the 1869 diary of John Campbell, a settler at Kamilche Inlet off

southern Puget Sound. They lived not far from the inlet where
George Pickett's mixed-blood son lived with his informal adoptive
parents Catherine and Aaron Collins. Accounts by Julianne and her
aunt Ruth Shelton agreed that wherever the children were sent first,
the wife put them out on the street when her husband died. Before
the Campbells took them in, life had been a daily struggle. With the
Campbell's four children, the two Fitzhughs and occasional other
boarders, the home was crowded and chores numerous, but it was
a home where people cared. Mary Campbell trained Julianne to be
a nurse and it was Fitzhugh's daughter who cared for the adoptive
father of George Pickett's son in his last illness.[74]

Mason Fitzhugh at fourteen grew restless and ran away from the
farm several times. The Campbells would find him a day's journey
away in Olympia, at least once at renowned restaurateur Rebecca
Howard's home. The African-American woman and her husband
had adopted the abandoned mixed-blood grandson of the late Snoqualmie Chief Patkanim. Mason and young Frank Howard may have
been friends or Rebecca, who surely knew Fitzhugh in his Olympia days, understood Mason's problems and took him in until John
Campbell arrived.[75]

The Campbell diaries reveal a genuine fondness for, and commitment to, the Fitzhugh teenagers. They chased away a stalker who
repeatedly harassed and frightened Julianne, then hosted a large
wedding for her and logger Reuben Reid. According to Campbell,
Mason's flights seemed largely driven by a desire to attend school,
which was not yet possible on Kamilche Inlet. To solve the problem,
the couple allowed him to live on Oyster Bay with C. C. Simmons
(son of Michael Simmons, the first territorial Indian agent) and
attend school as he wanted to do.[76]

MARY AND GEORGE PHILLIPS

While Mason was safe with the Campbells in the late 1860s, William Lear's abandonment left Mary once more vulnerable, and
without support for herself and Billy. If she moved home, a court-
appointed guardian could legally take Billy away, and she would lose
her remaining son. Where she went at that time is not clear: Guemes or Samish Island, Julia's farm, or to work for a family in town.

She had hard decisions to make in order to balance her desire for personal safety and even the material goods she was used to, against her limited choices in mates at her age, with her marital history and a toddler. Without speculating about Mary's emotional life, another intermarriage may have been Mary's most practical strategy during a period of rapid societal change.[77]

Within months of Lear's departure Mary met George Phillips, an immigrant Welsh cooper from Orcas Island's Port Langdon lime works. She may have been visiting family at one of the island's longhouses or the small village just along the beach from the lime kiln settlement. Phillips was only twenty-four and Mary in her thirties when they wed by tribal custom in late 1868. For a third marriage, the exchange of gifts and obligations that formed the ceremony of a first marriage did not have to apply. She moved to the cooper's cabin near the forge. Nearly all the settlers and lime workers on Orcas had married Coast Salish or HBC women, including the lime kiln owner and many workers whose wives spoke one of Mary's languages. When she walked the path along East Sound the one-and-a-half miles to "Eastsound," Charles Shattuck's Coast Salish wife Jenny greeted her at the store.[78]

Port Langdon, Orcas Island. The lime works settlement was the location of Mary Fitzhugh Lear Phillips and her husband George Phillips' home. *Courtesy of Orcas Island Historical Museum. All Rights Reserved. Photo by James Theodore Geoghegan, August, 1914.*

The Port Langdon cooper's job was hard. Phillips had to be strong enough to make about sixty-five barrels per day to keep up. When new owners added a second kiln, they demanded even more barrels. George Phillips was big. He was strong. He was tough. And a mean drunk.[79]

Mary gave birth to her third son the year after they married by tribal custom. Four years later, Fr. Casimir Chirouse officiated at their Catholic wedding ceremony at Lummi Reservation's St. Joachim's Church in February 1873. The date puts them among the many intermarried couples reacting to the new pressures toward government-sanctioned ceremonies to regularize their union. She gave birth to Thomas, her fourth son, the following year.[80]

Mary and the babies went to Lummi at Christmas 1875 and stayed six months. Mason, her niece Sarah, and other relatives were in the area and she was away from her abusive husband during the winter hiatus at the lime works. While she was there, violence entered Mason's life as it had his father's. At age twenty-one he was living and working at Sehome when he was seriously wounded in a fight. When the running altercation reached Lummi Reservation, it caused jurisdictional problems for Chief Henry Kwina and county law enforcement. Both authorities determined that Mason shared responsibility and decided to abandon the case and avoid the legal authority issue.[81]

Mason's temperament and appearance may have been contributors to the argument over an unnamed woman. He had grown into a light-haired, blue-eyed handsome man who little resembled his father or his mother. Sometimes he used his looks for an advantage in the white community. Though he kept up his S'Klallam and Samish connections the rest of his life, he listed himself as "white" in the U.S. Census. Even his death certificate said "white." Later generations of Fitzhugh descendants claim that a peppery and controlling temperament run in the family.[82]

Edmund Fitzhugh

During the years that Mary linked her life to Lear and then Phillips, Edmund Fitzhugh's life took its own turns before it intersected with

Mason again in 1874. When he arrived back in Virginia, probably in January 1863, Falmouth and Fredericksburg lay in ruins and "Boscobel" was Union General Daniel Sickles' headquarters. Even at nearly forty-three, Fitzhugh had little choice but to join the Confederate cause and seek a good assignment before a wider draft turned him into cannon fodder.[83]

He had plenty of connections to call upon, particularly through General Robert E. Lee's Fitzhugh mother and George Pickett. Plus, his resume included service as a militia staff aide and the federal judiciary. Everything pointed toward an assistant adjutant general (AAG) appointment. A staff AAG wrote official orders, was the correspondence conduit between officers, handled the paperwork flow, and did miscellaneous tasks like distribute mail. In battle, he often fought.[84]

General Lee appointed him to Pickett's Division, after his Whatcom friend requested him. A brigade inspector at first, he replaced Brigadier General Eppa Hunton's dead AAG in 1864. Hunton's father-in-law was a Fitzhugh.

That Christmas, Fitzhugh married his first cousin, Ann ("Nannie") Fitzhugh Grayson. Like Cora Bowie, she was of impeccable social lines and an aging spinster at 35 who was a companion for her aunt Elizabeth Grayson Carter near Hunton's home. Once again, he saw advantages in marrying within the small elite marriage pool that made first cousin marriage acceptable.[85]

During those last frantic days in April 1865, a minie ball struck Captain Fitzhugh in the forehead at the Battle of Sayler's Creek while he ran through the woods with the 56th Virginia in the midst of hand-to-hand brutality. "Poor Fitz! Forward, Boys!" exclaimed Hunton, who thought the unconscious man dead when he saw the wound. Ten minutes later, forty-five-year-old Fitzhugh caught up. At the end, with Hunton captured and the brigade decimated, Fitzhugh and one other officer kept the consolidated regiment's last twenty-six men together on the final march to Appomattox.[86]

On the final day of the Civil War, Fitzhugh still had his issue of Whatcom's *Northern Light* with him.[87]

Old friend General George Pickett signed his parole, and the wounded veteran with his exhausted horse reached home and Nannie at "Oatlands" ten days later. After a brief convalescence, Fitzhugh walked fifty miles to Washington, D.C., "to see how things lay." No job offers from old Northwest friends in federal positions resulted from his trip and the pair stayed at "Oatlands."[88]

That fall, Fitzhugh fell off his horse and was badly injured for the second time in six months. Ann was pregnant for the first time at thirty-seven and after a difficult pregnancy gave birth to "a very fine large daughter" on May 16, 1866. Fitzhugh named her Cora Bowie Fitzhugh, turning their baby into a memorial to his dead wife.[89]

Fitzhugh never found a new job in Republican and military-run Virginia. He probably gave up after a second trip to the capital to testify in an old HBC lawsuit against Washington Territory. He saw James Tilton and other old friends but none had a job for the Confederate officer and Copperhead. He was reduced to working the fields with "Oatland's" former slaves.[90]

One avenue lay open to the old veteran who was growing mentally impaired after two injuries, and with a heavy drinking habit. That was booming Fort Dodge, Iowa, where Ann's brother Ben sold real estate. Edmund practiced law in Fort Dodge and the aging "Nannie" gave birth to three more children in the next five years.[91]

The fresh start didn't last. Fitzhugh's drinking habits and injuries took an increasing toll on the brilliant jurist's mind and personal behavior. In 1873 a rumor circulated back in Whatcom County that he had gone insane, which his friend John Tennant (apparently in touch) quickly refuted in print. However, the next year Fitzhugh abandoned the genteel Virginia belle and their four small children in Iowa, or Ann threw him out. She went home to Virginia. He headed for Whatcom.[92]

Mary's former husband arrived at Bellingham Bay in early December 1874, where he had once been at the top. He presented the *Bellingham Bay Mail* editor with his precious tattered copy of the *Northern Light,* a gift whose meaning may not have been fully appreciated. The editor reminded readers of the former mine manager's generosity to the often destitute prospectors camped on his beach in 1858. He noted that "the present outlook at this point does not offer sufficient inducement for the location among us of the Judge's well-known energy and enterprise." Having found the mill and the mine both closed by flood and fire and few people around, Fitzhugh saw no future in the town where he had once been so powerful.[93]

Fitzhugh had another visit in mind before he left town. He had not seen his oldest son in about fourteen years and the boy had endured many hardships after being torn from his mother. He found Mason living and working in Sehome and asked his son to go to California with him.[94]

Mason replied, "Go to Hell."[95]

Fitzhugh found a different San Francisco, a grown-up city of 150,000. Many of his old associates were dead, and though syndicate member Calhoun Benham was back practicing law, and R.P. Hammond was president of a railroad, neither offered him a position. George Mendell, once Fort Bellingham's topographical engineer, was in charge of major port and fortification improvements and gave him a job as a "clerk" on the sea wall project. In late 1880, Fitzhugh was again practicing law, but his life was closing down. He moved from boarding house to boarding house and the 1883 city directory listed the former Territorial Supreme Court justice as having "no profession."[96]

The seedy What Cheer Hotel had been gold rush San Francisco's premier lodging. By 1883, it sported a sign that patrons could take a bath and a liquor store was next door. Hotel staff found Edmund Fitzhugh in his room dead of a stroke on the morning of November 24, 1883. The *Evening Bulletin* announced his death at 63 and noted that Fitzhugh, in "failing health," didn't know the whereabouts of his family. A week later in the Northwest, the *Washington Standard* hailed his accomplishments, as did the *New York Times* which touted his contributions to Washington Territory. Neither named any family. Perhaps Mary heard he was dead. Perhaps not. His burial at the Masonic Cemetery was short-lived before he was moved with hundreds of others to the cemetery city of Colma.[97]

MARY AND GEORGE PHILLIPS

All women found life on the fringes of settlement to be fragile. Infant and maternal death at childbirth were frequent. Epidemics swept the vulnerable away and the specter of accidental death hovered. Some women were abused. Husbands died, and left widows to fend for themselves. Sometimes the husbands just left—a "poor man's divorce." Some women suffered from depression or breakdowns under the harsh personal conditions away from their own family's support.[98]

The worst dangers caught up with Mary Fitzhugh Lear Phillips on the first of May, 1877.

In the two months prior, Mary had given birth to her first daughter Marguerite (Maggie), and she was probably busy while the little Phillips boys (three and eight) played outside. They found the door to the lime works storehouse unlocked. Slipping inside, they discovered an open half keg of gunpowder. The boys knew about its combustibility, but did not understand the immensity of the danger when they found some matches, lit one and tossed it into the keg. The blast somehow left the building nearly untouched while it concentrated damage on the two small boys who inhaled the flames. They lived only a few terrible hours during which the eldest was able to tell his distraught parents what happened. Mary and George and the East Sound community buried the boys at the informal cemetery. Madrona trees with their distinctive peeling sunset-colored bark gave their name to the small rocky peninsula that jutted into East Sound not far from the Shattuck store. Not only did it hold graves of the new settlers, but was also an ancient sacred burial site for Lummi and other groups. When word of the tragedy reached Whatcom, the newspaper offered the town's sympathy for Mary and George's terrible loss.[99]

Mary Fitzhugh Lear Phillips was never the same after the horrifying deaths of her little ones. George just drank.[100]

Mary's mental health deteriorated. Memories of her boys' final agonized hours and her last sight of them probably haunted her. Now in her forties, she carried on, taking care of George and Maggie, even churning and selling butter during another pregnancy. George was abusive and alcoholic but she stayed with him, perhaps in part because as Catholics, divorce was not an option. Perhaps she was unable to see how life might be better without him.[101]

By 1878 Edmund Fitzhugh was in San Francisco, William King Lear was in Alaska, and Mason had moved to Orcas where he lived at the lime works learning the cooperage trade from his stepfather. Mary seemed to be fine some days, but at other times, according to court testimony, was "insane," "out of her head," and "not in her right mind." She began to tell people that her boys' deaths were a plot and George told at least one person that he was afraid of her.[102]

The highlight of the boring, rainy winters on Orcas Island was always Christmas Eve, when everyone who could escape their isolation celebrated Christmas together. James Tulloch, a self-righteous bachelor new on the island, maintained that his moral principles would never allow him to attend a party with racially mixed couples. So, absent only Tulloch and a few others, Orcas pioneers looked forward to an all-nighter of drinking, dancing, and feasting at Shattuck's store in 1878.[103]

As usual, former Whatcom County Sheriff Enoch May took his boat through wintry seas to Victoria to buy the rum supply. On Christmas Eve, the Phillips family rowed to the head of East Sound and left their canoe at Shattuck's dock on Madrona Point, mere feet from the graves of Mary's boys. Some of the island's Coast Salish longhouse residents, probably in-laws of some settlers, also attended the party. The dancing would go on all night at the schoolhouse.[104]

Mary and her husband started to drink. She was about seven months pregnant. George laughed and sang in holiday high spirits, and began to dance with a young widow. Mary grew jealous as she watched him dance with the much younger, prettier woman. The couple traded accusations of infidelity and their voices grew louder. Before the argument ended, guests heard Mary say that she would "fix" George when they got home. When Mary tired, she left to sleep in a little room off the Shattuck kitchen while George danced the night away.[105]

After Christmas Day breakfast, exhausted party guests filtered slowly out to take canoe or trail home. George was still drunk and Mary had trouble getting him to leave. When they finally departed in mid-afternoon, she feared he was still too drunk to pull the canoe oars. If the trip took too long, they would be caught in December darkness, tides, and weather. Her niece, Sarah Seya'whom Pearson, sent eleven-year-old John to help with the oars.[106]

The party's canoe with Mary and little Maggie in the stern and the two males toward the front started toward Port Langdon. Those on shore could hear Mary "growling" at George as the canoe pulled away. They began to quarrel over where Mary was when George went looking for her at the party. Names were called. He took an oar and struck Mary on the side of her head and knocked her out. When she recovered, she told Johnny to watch out for George and he hit her again, this time in her side. Mary protectively grabbed Maggie as the canoe rocked. She called George an "old dog" and asked him if he knew she was pregnant. Her husband shot back that he didn't care if he killed her because he could get another woman.[107]

Mary admitted later that she vowed to pay George back. He could have killed her unborn child. She asked for an oar to steer since she was having trouble with the rudder, but when he handed one over, she hit him on the head twice, and his hat flew into the water. They argued over going back for the hat, but the fight seemed to have died out by the time James Tulloch saw the canoe pass by his beach.[108]

After landing at the lime kiln wharf, the group walked to the Phillips cabin where George demanded the key from Mary. When she didn't give it to him fast enough, he grabbed an axe and broke in the door. He took down the two shotguns hanging over the fireplace, set Mason's by the door and started loading his own.[109]

Mary ran. Behind her, Phillips yelled that he would kill her.

Outside the cabin, Mary wanted Johnny to go after Mason at the old cookhouse, but the boy didn't know where it was, so they went together. When she woke Mason up, he saw his mother's bleeding and bruised face. Still, Fitzhugh's son thought his stepfather would sober up soon enough. By the time he dressed, George arrived with Maggie in tow and a stick in his hand instead of his gun. Johnny Pearson ran for the trail home.

After a few more hot words, the enraged drunk yelled at Mary to get her things and get out, to go to the "siwashes," by which he meant the Indians at the longhouses. Mary left for home with Maggie tied on her back while the two men stayed at the cookhouse to get cleaned up for Christmas dinner. They assumed that she was going home to cook despite what George said, but when Mary arrived home, she saw both guns beside the ruined door. She believed George's threat that he would kill her. She picked up Mason's shotgun, the shot and powder, and started toward the cookhouse.

When Mary got to lime kiln owner Robert Caines' house, she saw Mason coming her way, followed by George. With Maggie on her back, she crouched in the brush across the trail from the root house. When Maggie called out "Papa!" George stopped and saw his wife hiding. She stood up and fired the shotgun through the underbrush from about fifteen feet away. George was struck with full force in the left side of his neck.[110]

George Phillips staggered backward. "Mason, come here. I'm shot. You're the only friend I've got." Mary's son grabbed the gun from her hands and threw it down before he went to George's aid. Perhaps in his last moments, George had realized how few would miss him.[111]

Mary later lied that she and George wrestled over the gun in the bushes until it went off, but Mason corroborated nearly everything else she said. According to trial testimony, Mason looked over at Mary and said either "What have you done now?" or "Now see what you have done!" No one said whether he spoke in sadness, or in anger. Mary replied in broken Chinook and English: "Bym bye he'd kill me."[112]

Mason helped his stepfather walk about twenty steps before George collapsed and said he was dying. Mason did not want the settlers' free-roaming hogs to get at the mortally wounded man, so he tried to drag him inside the Caines' picket fence. The Caines family was still gone and George was too heavy so Mason put a block of wood under his head and ran for help.[113]

Reaching Tulloch's cabin, Mason asked him to hurry down to where George lay on the trail before the hogs found him. Mason had no time for questions and ran on.[114]

George was dead. Tulloch ran to the Phillips house. He met Mary coming out the door, distraught and grieving, yet oddly still doing her chores. He led her back to George and they managed to carry the body home. Tulloch asked her twice who killed her husband. She answered in Chinook, but the island newcomer did not understand the jargon.[115]

Mason ran on in the Christmas darkness, seeking help but finding only empty cabins. He ran across the island to Enoch May's place. His wife was S'Klallam and might have been helpful, but they were gone, too. On the way back to the scene, he met former-Sheriff May and H. M. Stone on the trail and they spotted the gun lying where Mason threw it. When they reached the cabin, they saw that Tulloch and Mary had laid out the corpse.[116]

Both of Mason's parents had killed someone before he was twenty-five.

More help was needed for such an unusual homicide, so Tulloch and Stone left to find the justice of the peace for a coroner's inquest the next day. Enoch May and Mason went to pin down the relative positions of everyone at the crime scene. Though the sheriff's job when May filled the office was very informal, he knew enough to make detailed observations by lantern light and ask pointed questions. He had known Mary for over 20 years and spoke her language, so he stayed with her after they returned to the house.[117]

The next day, Mary testified at length at the hastily organized inquest, with Enoch May interpreting. Justice of the Peace W.H. Gifford had never presided over an inquest for murder before and hoped he was doing things right. The gun stayed with him.[118]

They buried George Phillips on Madrona Point near his little boys.[119]

MARY

Mary had to be arrested and jailed, even in advanced pregnancy, but there was no suitable jail for a woman in the islands. After he placed her under arrest, the sheriff and Mary boated to the Port Townsend jail. Though San Juan County's probate judge quickly appointed Enoch May as Maggie's guardian, the two-year-old did not go home with him. She went to jail with her mother.[120]

Newspaper coverage demonstrated the case's uncertainties. On December 28, the *Bellingham Bay Mail* printed an anonymous letter from one of the witnesses under the headline "Murder at Orcas Island." The editor pointed out that George Phillips was well-known to be a "hard case" and that Mary "no doubt" had provocation. However, Port Townsend's *Puget Sound Argus* printed Enoch May's letter under the headline "A Disciple of Lucretia Borgia." His letter was not sympathetic and he asserted, as he had at the inquest, that Phillips was "generally well liked."

Seattle and Olympia papers took the angle that Mary was the former "mistress" and "common law wife" of Judge Fitzhugh, and noted Mason's paternity. Long-time Washingtonians remembered the controversial justice and he was still newsworthy if a scandal involved his ex-wife. Their tone reflected the ongoing social and legal assault upon intermarried couples. It was the same year of the fornication indictments against intermarried settlers, including Julia Fitzhugh Barkhousen's husband. The articles didn't mention the fact that Mary and George were legally married.[121]

The grand jury foreman inspected the jail while Mary waited for her court date. He suggested better discipline, and to prohibit visitors without the sheriff's written permission. He never mentioned Mary by name, but his report hints at lax discipline where the Phillips family was concerned. Mary's first cousin Chetzemoka (Cheech'ma'ham) still owned a nearby longhouse, though whites had burned *Kah'tai*, and family members may have paid impromptu visits. Emma Balch (Lummi wife of Mary's cousin Solomon) visited and thought Mary's "room" was comfortable and the people kind.[122]

Mary and Maggie waited in jail nearly two months because Territorial Chief Justice Roger Sherman Greene heard his district court term's criminal cases last. His background gave his approach to criminal trials a different flavor. Grandson of a Declaration of Independence signer, son of a minister and Dartmouth graduate, in the Civil War he suffered wounds commanding a U.S. Colored Infantry unit. He was willing to hold unpopular opinions, including a longtime advocacy of equal rights. Within months, he would issue an opinion that legitimized tribal custom marriages. [*See* Appendix B.] The hawk-nosed Greene's religious beliefs informed his jury instructions and underlay his reputation for fairness. He often issued severe sentences, but sympathized with those who had gone wrong.[123]

Mary's lead attorney, New Yorker Charles Bradshaw, was Clallam County's first sheriff and studied law while farming his Dungeness land claim. Like nearly every other early settler there, he had married a S'Klallam woman. It's possible that Mary was even his wife's cousin and he certainly knew Edmund Fitzhugh from the legislature. After Bradshaw opened his Port Townsend practice in 1867, he married a white woman. His mixed-blood daughter was with a nearby foster family, but her mother's fate is unknown. He served four years as 3rd District prosecutor, which was valuable experience to defend Mary.[124]

Bradshaw's junior partner William Inman's background was very different. Born in Alabama to a Unionist family, he worked for the Freedman's Bureau after the Civil War. Columbia University-educated, he joined Bradshaw's practice after working for the prosecutor briefly.[125]

Irving Ballard, the newly-elected prosecutor, was no Ivy-Leaguer. His father founded the town of Auburn, Washington. Irving taught while he read law, then finished his education in a Portland law office. If he succeeded with the grand jury, Mary's criminal indictment would be a hanging offense.[126]

When the grand jury met on February 25, 1879, some reluctance to indict Mary for murder might have been expected. Sam Gross had a native wife and some jurors knew Fitzhugh from the old days when Mary was with him. However, they indicted Mary and described the homicide as the result of "deliberate and premeditated malice." They concluded that Phillips died "instantly," though Mason told them he had not.[127]

Justice Greene read the indictment to Mary with the help of an interpreter. Her lack of English fluency and unfamiliarity with concepts of American criminal law would keep her from understanding the nuances and implications. She had until the next day to enter her plea.

Bradshaw entered Mary's deposition that she was close to delivery and did not want to go to trial immediately. She was afraid that she would go into labor and was "much annoyed at being brought forward as a public spectacle." Though nothing appeared in the newspaper to support her accusation against the citizens of Port Townsend, a crowd could watch the proceedings anytime and many would be eager to see the pregnant former judge's woman now accused of murder.[128]

The next day, Mary pleaded "not guilty." A legal plea of self-defense against long-term domestic abuse or an insanity plea, as they are known today, did not exist. Greene continued her case until the next term of court.[129]

Mary gave birth in jail sometime after February 26. She named her son Thomas Frank Phillips after the little boy lost in the explosion. The sheriff hired a nurse on April 10, so there may have been some problems with Mary's recovery or the infant's health. The little family waited in jail for Mary's trial five months away.[130]

In September 1879 Mary came to trial. After her lawyers rejected seventeen prospective jurors, it was a short trial on the sixteenth. Interpreter Elizabeth McAlmond had lived among intermarried S'Klallam women at Dungeness for decades and spoke their language well. Jurors heard testimony until noon, including Mason's. When everyone returned at 1:30, the prosecution and defense presented their arguments and requests for jury instructions.

Prosecutor Ballard wanted instructions that assumed sanity unless the evidence was overwhelming for partial insanity. He requested a specific instruction that said the danger to Mary from George had to have been "eminently perilous."

Bradshaw's most important request was that if there was "any evidence" showing that Mary was *not aware* at the time, then the prosecution must show that she was *sane beyond a doubt*. Second, if the jury believed that George attacked her with the intention of killing her baby, and they met suddenly in a way in which she was in his power and unable to contend with him physically, then she could reasonably take his life if she feared he was about to renew the attack. He also wanted the jury to take George's character and general conduct toward Mary into consideration.

The jury's decision might send Washington's first woman to the gallows. Greene used Bradshaw's instructions about sanity, which allowed the jury to find every possible reason why Mary might have legitimately shot her husband.

The jury did not deliberate long. When foreman Rufus Calhoun read the verdict, Mary was "not guilty of murder" but "guilty of manslaughter." Most important, the jury recommended mercy. Calhoun, a pioneering mariner, certainly knew Fitzhugh. Clearly, he and the others understood that there were psychological and situational mitigating circumstances, and they wanted the religious judge to use his discretion. Short of complete vindication, it was the best that Mary's lawyers could have hoped for. Sheriff Miller took her back to jail.

The next day Mary returned to court for sentencing. She did not want to make a final statement. Greene sentenced her to "hard labor" for two years at the territorial prison. He ordered her to pay the cost of prosecution, $1,098, an impossible sum. She would be the first woman to enter Seatco (see-at-co) Prison, built only for men and staffed only by men.

A small notice in the LaConner paper that served the islands and Whatcom County reported that "an Indian woman" had been convicted and sentenced. The editor seemed unaware of Mary's story or of the significance of her conviction. The Port Townsend paper oddly took no notice at all.[131]

More than one of Mary's friends believed that the whites would have hung her if she hadn't been pregnant.[132]

If anything indicated that Greene and the jury believed the complicated situation that surrounded George Phillips' death, it was Mary's sentence. It exemplified the contradictory attitude of punishment mixed with sympathy seen across the West for the few women felons. Without any women's prisons, little sentence uniformity existed. Oregon's Charity Lamb went to the men's prison for life after killing her husband under nearly identical circumstances to Mary's. Unlike Mary's jury, Charity's thought her cowardly for not facing her husband down or leaving. Mary and Charity acted alike toward their abusers when they suddenly had had enough. After eight years in the men's prison, Charity Lamb was deemed psychotic and spent the rest of her life in Oregon's mental hospital. Mary faced the same possibility.[133]

c3&o

The Lushootseed word *tsi-at-co*, from which the prison's name was derived, meant 'devil' or 'ghost place.' What must Mary have thought if she knew that word?[134]

She had no preparation for the alien world that was Oliver Shead's contract prison, far south of Puget Sound. Inmates were rented out or put to work at his sawmill 600 feet away, a form of legalized slavery. With minimal financial outlay or oversight, Washington Territory made money from the year-old institution. Like others, it was both a system and buildings constructed by men for men—a violent masculine community. The nonverbal threat of sudden attack by fellow inmates or guards was ever-present. The legislature had not yet defined what "hard labor" meant or what constituted allowable discipline, not for men and certainly not for women.[135]

When Justice Greene sent Mary Phillips to Seatco, thirty-eight prisoners were at work finishing the stockade. The 150-foot-long main building was a maze of iron. Planks had been laid flat and spiked at five-inch intervals with sixty tons of eight-inch nails. One exterior staircase led to the second floor main hall, kitchen, and small rooms for shoe repair and tailoring. Those also served as a doctor-less "hospital" if needed, and Shead intended them to house a female inmate, if one was ever incarcerated in his prison.[136]

Thirty-six unheated cells with barred and glassless windows sat at ground level, reached only by a single inside staircase down from the second floor. Guards living on the second floor had an outside staircase but they and the prisoners below feared fire. They knew that the inmates would burn alive if the inside staircase was blocked. Inexplicably, flammable kerosene and paint were stored at the top of the stairs.

Evidently neither Maggie's guardian Enoch May nor Mason was willing or able to care for her and the baby, so they stayed with Mary as "boarders." On September 23, 1879, after a long journey from Port Townsend, officials registered Inmate #56. They thought she looked 50, though she was in her early forties. If they housed her and the children in the makeshift female cell, it was only temporary. Superintendent John McCallister had a "shanty" built in the yard for them.[137]

Mary and her two children began what her fellow prisoner George France called "a pilgrimage through hell."[138]

Her daily life began. One account suggested that women at Seatco did not work. If she did, Mary's "hard labor" probably consisted of mending or other "women's work" that she could do without leaving her children. McCallister may have allowed her to wear her own clothes, as a few men did, instead of the thick denim uniform with pant legs of different colors. Possibly, they allowed her to go without the heavy padded shackles around her ankles and connected by a chain. The children's presence would likely be enough to keep Mary from trying to escape.[139]

Oliver Shead and his partners completely controlled their prisoners with minimal government interference. That situation usually led to corruption and brutality in western contract prisons where heavily armed guards were often heavy drinkers, as they were at Seatco. Only a single guard was on duty overnight and he was frequently drunk or asleep. Seatco was a place of sexually deprived men, both inmates and the guards who lived there. Mary was only the first woman to feel the terror of darkness as her head lay on the straw-stuffed grain sack. George France said that one unnamed female prisoner did not go to bed at night for months because of her fears of assault.[140]

No female matron or medical help was available, leaving Mary to cope if she or the children got seriously hurt or sick. After Mary's first year, convicted abortion doctor Charlie Betts arrived and was the only possible medical assistance for the remainder of her incarceration. Rules prohibited visits from family or friends, so neither of her older sons nor any other relatives could check on the well-being of the little family living in the shed.[141]

Under these conditions, Mary had to find ways to survive as well as provide a home for Maggie and Tommy. Her interaction with the children may have saved her sanity. They gave her focus and meaningful everyday tasks to occupy her hours, days, weeks, and months. The children's minimally edible prison food had to fit within the sixty cents per day that Oliver Shead received for boarding them. Mary began to lose weight, perhaps because she sacrificed some of her own rations even while she nursed the baby.[142]

A year after the Phillips family arrived, Whatcom County's Susan Clark passed through the prison gates with a manslaughter sentence three years longer than Mary's. Also an emotionally fragile woman, Clark had ordered her eleven-year-old son to shoot their neighbor Michael Padden in a homestead boundary dispute and the boy obeyed.[143]

Women sent to territorial prisons often set aside racial and social differences to bond because of their gender and terrible isolation in the midst of violent men. Mary was probably excited and relieved to see the Irish mother. Both had small children and no experience with the judicial system. Unlike Mary's children, Susan's youngest stayed with her husband, with no hope of a visit.

One mental factor was different for the two women prisoners—what historian Anne Butler called "critical grit." Formerly private, respectable women like Mary and Susan were usually stunned by prison, and their health and spirit deteriorated quickly. They had to find a way to survive. It could be stoic endurance, rebellion, or cooperation with anything a guard asked for. For two years, Mary successfully found ways to keep herself and her vulnerable children alive in an inherently unhealthy situation. Housed in the main building over the cellblock, Susan Clark did not find such a way. Inmate George France below could hear her "heartrending moanings for her children." Susan walked the floor day and night in a "frenzy of grief and despair."[144]

Just two weeks after she arrived, Susan heard that her toddler had nearly been gored to death by the family cow. She took a bedsheet and hung herself.[145]

No other woman was incarcerated at Seatco before Mary's release. Hers was the only female voice ever heard in the prison. She received no clemency or pardon, only a one-week reduction in her two-year sentence.

On September 23, 1881, the *Puget Sound Argus* noted that "Mrs. Mary Phillips" had served out her sentence and returned to her house on Orcas Island. The paragraph appeared exactly two years from the day Mary had entered the prison with her toddler and five-month-old baby. While Susan Clark survived only two weeks of the "pilgrimage through hell," Mary persevered and endured the inhumane conditions so she could walk out with her children.[146]

Years later, law-abiding Tommy told his children that he had been born in a jail, and he would never die in one. When he left the prison at age two, he spoke no English and had never seen beyond the walls. Seatco was the only home he had ever known, his mother the only woman in his world. He had never seen his brothers.[147]

∞

Mary and the children returned to Orcas. Perhaps Mason, or Julia and Henry Barkhousen, took them home. But "home" was no longer at Port Langdon. As Maggie and Tommy's legal guardian, Enoch

May had sold all the Phillips' belongings to pay Mary's fine and her lawyers. Any assets in George Phillips' estate were long gone.[148]

Mason had married in January 1880 during his mother's imprisonment. His bride was Sarah Seya'whom Pearson's daughter Mary, the older sister of the boy in the canoe. They offered his mother a refuge where she could recover from her ordeal and start over with her young children. Billy Lear was never mentioned in Mary's case file, but the teenager reappeared after his mother's release. One family account said he had been in Wrangell with his father and attended school for some years.[149]

There were new roles for Mary Phillips while she lived with Mason on his rented farm. He still worked as a cooper at the lime kiln, which left many chores to be done by the two Marys and Billy after he returned. Like many other farm women, Mary Phillips even saved feathers and sold them to the Lummi trading post. And Mary's daughter-in-law gave birth to her first grandchild, Laurinda.[150]

In the months after her release, Mary renewed ties to her relatives and friends. One day Emma Balch (her pre-trial jail visitor) saw a woman at Lummi whose face she didn't recognize. A companion reminded her that it was Mary Phillips. The lovely, round-faced, and plump woman Emma had known was gaunt and thin. Emma found out that Mary had eaten little of the unfamiliar prison food for two years. One clue to her physical condition may be the "old age shoes" that she bought at Bernard McDonough's store, a singular sale in his records.[151]

Despite the prison's soulless atmosphere, Mary's Catholic faith had remained strong. Maggie had been baptized five months after her birth, but no priest could visit Seatco to baptize Tommy. Mary had her toddler receive the sacrament three months after their release.[152]

Mary still had no legal control over Maggie and Tommy, with Enoch May their guardian until Mason took over a year after their release. Either May or Mason sent Maggie to the Tulalip Reservation boarding school, a long way from her mother. Mary's only daughter could have attended the Eastsound school, but was sent away instead. Mary's niece Ruth Seya'whom Shelton lived close to the school, offering at least some family support.

After spending two of her five years alone with her mother and brother, Maggie probably spoke mostly S'Klallam when they emerged from Seatco. In little time, she went from one institution built on obedience and regimentation to another. Having also witnessed the shooting of her father, Maggie's short life had unquestionably been immersed in psychological trauma. Just as had happened to Mason, men took her from her Native mother.[153]

The Sisters of Charity ran the girls' section. Their mandate was to produce English-speaking literate Christian girls with American homemaking skills they could share upon returning home. Today the Coast Salish refer to this practice as cultural genocide.[154]

Indian boarding schools harbored influenza, tuberculosis, and homesickness so severe that children, especially the youngest, died of it. Mary never saw her only daughter again. The kindly Father J.B. Boulet, who would be Mary's priest for many years at Lummi, buried little five-year-old Maggie in the Tulalip Cemetery. It can be assumed that he presided over a funeral mass for the little soul, perhaps attended by the student body as was customary at many schools. Only one of Mary's children with George Phillips survived.[155]

The allotment survey of Lummi Reservation also occurred in 1883. Eighteen-year-old Billy Lear received one that became Mary's home for the rest of her life. His allotment meant that unlike Mason, who planted roots among the mixed families of Orcas who were mostly "living white," Billy's descendants would join Lummi Nation. Billy began the backbreaking work of developing a farm. Other S'Klallam-connected people were doing the same at Lummi, including Mary's sister-in-law Emily, Seya'whom's widow. She lived with her daughter Sarah, now married to John Oshan, a high-born Lummi.[156]

Mary could live out her life in peace among family and friends.

CRBO

Every August, Chief Henry Kwina recruited, led, and supervised the large Lummi hop picking crew that traveled to the Puyallup River Valley. Mary's family joined them.[157]

The broad Puyallup Valley in the shadow of Mount Rainier had two thousand acres of hop vines. Their sticky yellow cones had to be picked during a three- to four-week window that required at least four thousand workers. Willing Coast Salish families and First Nations families from Canada dominated the lucrative seasonal venture. Working together, a family filled two to three fifteen-bushel boxes a day at $1.00 per box.[158]

The tent and cedar mat temporary city not only housed families for the grueling harvest, but also provided a venue for dances, sports, gambling, and an occasional fistfight. Women and children picked while men did the heavy work, and some hunted and fished in the foothills to supply food to their crew. It was little different from the traditional fishing camps.[159]

During the years that Mary and Billy went to the fields, city folk began to journey out to observe the "colorful spectacle" and tribal families took advantage. They put on cultural shows, guided hunting and fishing trips, and sold carvings. Perhaps Mary was one of the women who made baskets that sold for $3.00, equal to three days wages in the field.[160]

Billy met his wife one season. Eighteen-year-old Rosalie Nix was the mixed-blood daughter of one of the valley's first pioneers, Ronimus Nix and his first wife. Rosalie's maternal grandparents were a French-Canadian HBC trapper and a Puyallup leader's daughter. Nix prospered with his large hop operation where the town of Puyallup is today. Mary and Billy were probably working at the Nix farm when Rosalie met the young man, who looked much like a darker version of his handsome brother Mason. They married about 1889 and by the next year, the couple and baby Celina lived in one house on the allotment, while Mary and Tommy lived in another. Six more children arrived.[161]

Mary Fitzhugh Lear Phillips lived into her 90s, a testimony to the endurance and survival skills of a daughter of "The Strong People." By her death between 1920 and 1922, she had outlived all four of her husbands, the parental kidnapping of one child, the deaths of four children and some of her grandchildren, as well as imprisonment. She saw her three surviving sons marry and give her grandchildren. She remained a devout Catholic her entire life and is most likely buried with Lear family members at Lummi Reservation Cemetery, though Madrona Point on Orcas beside her sons is a possibility.[162]

MASON FITZHUGH

After Mary left Orcas to live with Billy, Mason and his wife bought part of the Shattuck homestead and continued to farm while he worked as a cooper. The neighbors again were mostly intermarried couples, some with ties to Bellingham Bay.[163]

Mason Fitzhugh, the oldest son of Mary Fitzhugh Lear Phillips. As an adult, he farmed and commercially fished in the territory and tradition of his S'Klallam relatives. *E.A. Hegg, photographer. Howard Buswell Collection, #0052. Center for Pacific Northwest Studies, Western Libraries Heritage Resources. Western Washington University, Bellingham, Washington.*

Mason and Mary had four children before she died of breast cancer at age twenty-five in 1889, an event that came between Mason and his half-sister Julianne. The experienced nurse had a large and growing family in Port Townsend when Mason asked her to come and care for his terminally ill wife. She turned him down. By then a modest Victorian woman, Julianne didn't want to tell her brother that she was pregnant. In his despair, Mason thought she just didn't want to help out and never spoke to her again. One of his children had died before his wife, and sons Russell and Tracy passed away in the following year at eight and three. Only Laurinda survived, just six when her last sibling died.[164]

Mason remained a single father for eleven years. He farmed and fished with his mother's S'Klallam relatives at their traditional sites and the pair stayed close to Julia Barkhousen and her family near LaConner. Mason and Laurinda lived in a mixed community growing ever more "white" on Orcas, but she married widower Richard

Squi'Qui, grandson of a Lower Skagit treaty signer. The couple moved to Lummi Reservation, near her grandmother Mary Phillips.[165]

Mason remarried on his fifty-sixth birthday. Thirty-two-year-old widow Maggie Anderson's maternal grandfather was famed S'Klallam fisherman Yakship. Her father Tom She'kle'malt owned the only U.S. Indian homestead in the San Juan Islands. His land on Speiden Channel at the north end of San Juan Island had been a Coast Salish village site for several thousand years and occupied by his wife's family for a very long time. She'kle'malt lived and died in his longhouse there and his widow gave Maggie sixty acres of the homestead. It became known as the "Fitzhugh place" to locals, though its real name *xwl'e'lqt* designated it as the ancestral home of the Lummi. Mason continued his tribal fishing and farmed the rest of the She'kle'malt land after Maggie inherited it, too. They had one daughter, Pearl, two years after they married.[166]

When Mason Fitzhugh died of heart failure at seventy-three in the fall of 1927, he and his children were registered on S'Klallam tribal rolls as well as Lummi, despite his pattern of calling them "white" on census forms. The family buried him at the Eastsound cemetery beside Mary and their sons.[167]

Pearl Fitzhugh grew into a young woman of beauty and humor, and like her aunt Julianne Fitzhugh Reid, had Edmund Fitzhugh's characteristic feistiness. She married Harlan Little from a local part-HBC-Cowlitz tribe family. She became an accomplished commercial fisherwoman like Mason, and partnered with her uncle Tom Phillips. She continued to honor her S'Klallam ancestry, and for many years potlatches were still held in Tom She'kle'malt's old longhouse.[168]

After Pearl's death in 1983, the She'kle'malt homestead (by then called the "Pearl Little Place") became the subject of years of litigation between possible heirs to the last large undeveloped waterfront on San Juan Island. The land, worth millions, was eventually sold with the proviso that its cemetery remain untouched and accessible to the family forever. It still is a peaceful and quiet place.[169]

Thomas Phillips—Mary Fitzhugh Lear Phillips' youngest child, born while she was awaiting trial in Port Townsend. He fished commercially in the tradition of his mother's S'Klallam family. *Courtesy of Laurie and Larry Cepa.*

BILLY LEAR

Billy and Rosalie became a solid Lummi family on their allotment. When Lummi fishermen defied state rules that favored whites and deprived most native fishermen of any salmon, the state charged him with illegal fishing in 1918, as they had Nellie Lane's boys (*see* chapter 5). Their seven adult children founded a large extended family at Lummi Reservation.[170]

In 1947, a family member found his body in the home where the aged widower lived alone.[171]

Mary's Lear descendants at Lummi are numerous and influential. Many are still Catholic and many have led lives of service and activism, including at least one traditional chief.

Though Maggie died at Tulalip School, when Tommy attended he met his wife Leah, daughter of another intermarriage. Her Maine-born father Perrin Preston ran the first trading post on the Snohomish River (near today's Everett) and married Peggy, a Snohomish woman. Tom and Leah had three children whose descendants remain active at Tulalip Reservation and elsewhere. When the couple separated, Tom often lived at his niece Pearl Little's place, where he fished. The quiet, polite man with the ready smile was loved by family and friends who knew him as a logger, fisher, and baseball pitcher. For the rest of his life, Mary's third son told his family of the deep respect he held for his mother, Mary the survivor.[172]

Clara Tennant Selhameten, daughter of
Tsi'lixw, a leader of the Lummi. Her portrait
was probably taken when she and Rev. John
Tennant became Methodist missionaries. *Per-
cival Jeffcott Collection #706, Center for Pacific
Northwest Studies, Western Libraries Heritage
Resources. Western Washington University,
Bellingham, Washington.*

Reverend John Alexander Tennant. Portrait
probably taken when he became a Methodist
missionary. *Percival Jeffcott Collection #704,
Center for Pacific Northwest Studies, Western
Libraries Heritage Resources. Western Washington University, Bellingham, Washington.*

CHAPTER 4

Clara, A Life in Four Acts

C LARA AND REVEREND JOHN TENNANT climbed into a large cedar canoe at The Crossing, site of the Nooksack Methodist mission at today's Everson, Washington. Nooksack headman "Lynden Jim" Selhameten Yelewqaynem captained the eight-man crew who would take them, two other ministers, and his own family downriver after the Methodist camp meeting. The canoe ran low and heavy.

Though melting Mount Baker snow filled the Nooksack River almost to the top of its banks, the Tennants' journey was pleasant. The river's currents, logs, root balls, and boulders always lurked in new spots, but the Nooksack people had canoed the river for centuries. Near Jim's village and the young town of Lynden, they fought through the narrow channel at century-old Devil's Bend logjam. They fiercely pulled through the large whirlpool beyond, but on that day an enormous snag, lodged across the current, could not be seen beneath the swift water's surface just past the maelstrom.

The canoe's prow ran up on the submerged log and lurched high out of the water. The men struggled to control the craft whose stern caught in the whirlpool, but it swung over the middle of the roiling water. Caught, the canoe turned until its full length struck the log. It split in two. The passengers screamed as the wounded canoe tilted up, turned back, and capsized. Everyone went into the glacial water. The whirlpool sucked passengers in the stern underwater, and carried them choking, downstream.

Clara and John clung to one half of the drifting canoe. When he spotted a snag floating in an eddy, he shoved Clara toward it. She clung to the log, but her heavy clothes dragged her deeper into the frigid water. The Nooksack crew had reached the bank, but several

123

jumped back in to rescue her. John fought the current until he grabbed another snag far downstream.

Lynden Jim and his granddaughter surfaced, flung together across the submerged log. He held tightly to the little girl, but the relentless river tore her away and left him holding only a piece of her dress. Her mother, Mariah, struggled ashore with the baby but went back into the river for hours, searching for her lost daughter. Hypothermic, exhausted, and frantic with grief when they found the girl's body under a drift of logs, Mariah did not long survive.

The Nooksacks, Tennants, and others mourned the victims in the Selhameten longhouse.[1]

CLARA

When seen from the distance of time, Clara and John Tennant seem destined to marry despite their disparate cultures and early years spent thousands of miles apart. Certainly, Clara's achievements would have been different without John in her life, and John's would have been equally different and probably less important without her as his partner.

Clara was born into a large extended family that produced many of the most influential *Lhaq'temish* (Lummi) leaders of the nineteenth century and beyond. Her grandfather Saw'rem'ken's seven sons controlled most of the resource territories that extended back into the San Juan Islands where the Lummi originated, and their influence spread ever wider with marriage alliances. Clara's neighborhood as a child was a vast, multilingual one. Saw'rem'ken welcomed a British trader to Lummi Island in 1825 with beaver meat and pelts to trade. If it continued, the trade may have been a major source of the family's nineteenth century material and personal wealth.[2]

Clara's family history has been subject to contradictions even in very early members' accounts, and is still subject to new interpretations. Older witnesses agreed that her father Tsi'lixw, one of the two eldest half-brothers of seven born to Saw'rem'ken and his wives, was a tall, handsome and imposing man whose wisdom earned great respect and admiration. If it had been Tsi'lixw instead of his half-brother Chow'it'sut that Henry Roeder and Russell Peabody met when they arrived at the main Lummi village, *Tam'whiq'sen*, in December 1852, chances are there would have been no Whatcom Falls Mill. While Chow'it'sut gave permission for the men to settle at the falls, tribal oral historians agreed that Tsi'lixw would have seen danger in the permanent invasion of a salmon stream. The results of white enterprises could already be seen at Port Townsend where the previous year, men founded a commercial hub next to the S'Klallam village at the entrance to Puget Sound. The Lummi were fighting a winter epidemic and Tsi'lixw was not available for counsel, believed to have been among the sick.[3]

Two years later, the eloquent Chow'it'sut spoke for the Lummi at the treaty grounds where the limited vocabulary of Chinook was used in a three-way translation that left complex implications unknown to any but the government representatives. Within sight of army guns and based on governmental promises, the brothers signed the Point Elliott Treaty that relinquished forever most of the homeland the Lummi had occupied and managed for several thousand years. The business contract (not surrender) granted important rights, but most land resource territories disappeared into white hands.[4]

Probably in the early 1830s, Tsi'lixw went to his mother's homeland where he married three sisters (or half-sisters) of a noble family from the White River Duwamish, among them Clara's mother. The upriver Duwamish lived between today's Renton and Auburn, mostly at stream confluences and on the benches above the river in a valley occupied for at least 5,700 years. The sisters may have been from one of the longhouses at *Stuq*, located about where the city of Kent is today. It provided top Duwamish leaders for years, and was known for its resource-rich families. They traded at the Hudson's Bay Company's Fort Nisqually and some of the women intermarried, particularly after the company started a farm in their territory.[5]

From Clara's mother (later known to whites as "Mrs. Annie") came family connections to the Duwamish leaders Kitsap, Tsalkub (Curly) at the site of Seattle, and Sealth on Bainbridge Island. She gave Clara and her siblings the Lushootseed language, as well as other female knowledge that was different from Lummi. She outlived her husband by many years and stayed close to Clara after she married John Tennant.[6]

Tsi'lixw's winter longhouse was at *Tam'whiq'sen* on Gooseberry Point, probably one of two that faced each other on today's Lummi Peninsula. It fronted Hale Passage and Lummi Island beyond. There are several versions of the birth order of Tsi'lixw's children by the three sisters. Clara, probably born in the early 1840s, and her closest confidant Sarah, were full sisters. Henry Kwina, the youngest child, was (or was not) their full brother, depending on the informant. They also had two half-sisters, Agnes Seawelton and Mary Yellocanim and three half-brothers: Whi'lano, George Tsi'lano, and Tea'lish George. The exact relationship was not of great importance to the siblings.[7]

While Clara's childhood was that of high-born Lummi girls, she long remembered and related particular events. She found that white people's food was an acquired taste and the first time she tasted "Boston" bread, she got very sick. Clara was unaccustomed to wheat flour and sugar, and they may have overwhelmed her digestive system. She said the first time she drank their tea instead of the ones made from familiar plants, she vomited so her family threw all their foreign tea into the bay.[8]

Clara told a friend about times when she sought protection from *Laich'wil'tach* raiding parties in a series of underground defenses connected by tunnels. If people had to stay hidden for long, someone would sneak out to bring back food. Balancing those memories, she recalled with pleasure the great potlatches when friends and family would join them for days and sometimes weeks. Her beloved uncle, the childless and larger-than-life Chow'it'sut, owned a large potlatch house on Portage Island just across the *swulesen*, the salt marsh path that emerged at low tide. She loved celebrating important life events, visiting, feasting and playing games there with the guests.[9]

Post-treaty, when the government appointed "chiefs" for each group of Coast Salish villages they designated a "tribe," appointees were not always the senior traditional leaders or even the most influential and wise men. The Territorial Superintendent of Indian Affairs, supported by Fr. Casimir Chirouse who knew most of the leading men, skipped over the senior generation and appointed Clara's brother Whi'lano "chief" because, as a devout Catholic, he had only one wife. Although the man who whites called "Davy Crockett" held the position as liaison with the government, people looked to Tsi'lixw for great wisdom. They considered Whi'lano the religious leader and he held prayer services each morning and evening.[10]

In 1874, Clara's brother Henry Kwina, once Captain George Pickett's courier, was appointed chief after the death of Whi'lano. Henry is said to have had several wives and his appointment would not be approved unless he was married to only one. He gave up the others for Mary, former wife of Lt. James W. Forsyth. Henry served as chief until his death at 92 in 1926. By then Clara's much honored brother was the oldest Catholic in Washington State, and Northwest Indian College sits on Mary and Henry's land today.[11]

John Tennant

To understand the man Clara married in 1859 and the life they built together, one must understand the influences of John Tennant's Methodist minister father, Reverend Thomas Tennant, and his mixed-blood mother Christeen Hacker. Their teachings hovered over his adulthood.

The Second Great Awakening that took place during the first half of the eighteenth century changed the face of American Protestantism and led thousands of people to re-think the state of their souls and look for hope. Methodists rejected predestination and taught that people could change their future. The church gave women a public role and welcomed African Americans and indigenous people. An advanced education was not as important for a missionary as was his individual piety and willingness to study as he served. Not yet twenty, Thomas Hardister Tennant of Appalachian Virginia chose the life of a circuit rider to bring the new religion to isolated frontier communities.[12]

Historian Everett Dick wrote of the circuit rider's skills: "Strong lungs, vigorous gestures, copious tears, a ready flow of language, and an ability to describe in picturesque language the horrors of a literal, eternal, burning hell and the joys and bliss of a home in the Heavenly Canaan." Thomas Tennant spent months on the trail with his library, blanket roll, and preaching suit. Teaching people to read was part of his job. He literally had no home and depended on the generosity of people he met for shelter and food to supplement his meager salary. Neither terrible weather nor men in the back row drinking and making jokes prevented his sermonizing. As a young boy, John Tennant absorbed his father's passionate way of changing lives that he would use years later to do the same. He experienced and witnessed first-hand the value of education to rural children.[13]

In 1819 Tennant was one of the first half-dozen missionaries into Arkansas Territory. He spent time on two vast circuits, both of which introduced him to many intermarried couples. The first circuit was mainly farming communities where he did well. However, the Pecan Point's rougher population included southeastern Indians avoiding government control, runaway slaves, Indian-White families from the Carolinas and Georgia, and "Red Bones" (white Louisianans). The determination Thomas developed there would be passed along to his son.[14]

In later life, John Tennant spoke proudly about his mother's indigenous history. That also made up part of his personality and conduct in adulthood as much as his father's religiosity did.

John's ancestry traced to the union of Jean-Baptiste Duchassin, a French settler at Arkansas Post on the southern Mississippi River in the 1700s. Frenchmen at "The Post" married Quapaw women from the nearby village and developed a community French in culture and appearance. Marriage in the isolated Catholic settlement was nor-mally by tribal custom, called a "country marriage" by the French, unless a traveling Jesuit priest stopped in.[15]

Duchassin married Marie-Anne of the Quapaw. Their son Antoine's wife was also either full-Quapaw or of mixed blood. Duchassin men became traders, including some who worked for the St. Louis Choteau clan. When the Quapaw treaty was signed six years before John Tennant was born, some of his relatives were translators who received their pay in land granted to "persons being Indians by descent."[16]

John's mixed-blood grandmother Peggy Guimbelet contracted a "country marriage" with Fred Hacker, who evidence suggests may have also been mixed-blood. When John's mother Christeen was about nine, Fred died. Peggy moved her four girls and one son far upriver to isolated Cadron.[17]

It was there in 1821 that Christeen Hacker converted to Method-ism and married the tall, lanky, handsome missionary with the fire of faith in his eyes and a resonant voice that people even two centuries later claim could carry "seven miles." Methodist rules regarding marriage forced Thomas off the circuit to "locate" and minister to a local congregation.[18]

At that time a hilly area in far northwest Arkansas on the border of Indian Territory (today's Oklahoma) was devoid of white settlement. Unsurveyed, it might still end up as part of the Indian Territory reservation lands. The Tennants, with Christeen's family including several missionary spouses, moved there with others from Cadron in 1827. The missionary-heavy group brought a focus on religiosity and education other Arkansas settlements never had.

Tennant chose his new land within a disputed five-mile-wide strip. He and others believed that the government would eventually draw boundary lines that would not uproot the "old settlers" to give the land to the Cherokee and other tribes moving to "The Nation." And they were right. It was a pattern that young John observed and repeated in Washington Territory.[19]

Christeen gave birth to John on August 6, 1829, her fourth child. The country boy's experiences ran through his entire life like Barren Fork Creek ran behind the family's house in the fertile, water-rich, tumbled limestone hills. They forged him into the frontier "Renaissance Man" to whom Tsi'lixw's daughter tied her future in 1859.[20]

Thomas and Christeen Tennant's farm was scarcely three miles from the Indian Territory border and Cherokee Nation. Their formal address was nearby Evansville, a violent border town where liquor and prostitution were the major products. The Tennant farm's proximity to the Cherokee was good for the family since they became a ready market for their corn, fruit, and grains. Washington County's settlers experimented with fruit tree grafting and turned their small Arkansas corner into the nation's center for new apple varieties. John learned that skill, too.[21]

Behind the farm rose seven-hundred-foot-high Hale Mountain with its springs and a long cave that was a low-ceilinged shortcut to Cane Hill village. Hunting and fishing among the hardwoods, on the tall grass prairies, and in the creek were part of John's contribution to the family food supply. His skills were ever more in demand as the Tennant family grew until there were seven children inside the oak board cabin. Women and men worked tirelessly on the farms where self-sufficiency was the main goal, and where the small slave population worked side-by-side with their owners. Nearly everything John learned from his hardscrabble life on Barren Fork would one day be useful in Washington Territory.[22]

Above all, small Bethlehem Methodist Episcopal Church influenced life within the crowded Tennant cabin. As a "located" minister, John's father was expected to uphold "rigorous standards of personal conduct." The conference expected his family to avoid swearing, profaning the Sabbath, alcohol, quarreling, wearing gold and expensive clothing, and slavery. They were to do good diligently, frugally, and patiently. Most of all, the family was to live their religion's tenets: public worship, family and private prayer, scripture study, and fasting. John learned to fiddle, even if the music at home was mostly hymns. Methodist families like the Tennants soon earned a puritanical reputation among backwoodsmen. If John was ever to rebel, he had a lot to rebel against.[23]

Thomas Tennant still rode out to console, sell books, teach Sunday school, and preach a three-hour sermon with his legendary voice. To avoid mountain lions, he occasionally slept in a tree with his mule tied below. Sometimes he was gone from home for weeks and Christeen managed the farm with the eldest children's help.

The highlight of John's year was the annual camp meeting a few miles away at Salem Springs on the border. For a week Cherokee and settler families camped in a "town," worshipped together, went through emotional conversions, ate and cooked communally. Whatever a family's religion, no one missed the camp meeting organized by the Methodist and Cumberland Presbyterian ministers. John never forgot what those camp meeting "vacations" meant to the isolated, lonely, hardworking people.

When he was six, the nation's slavery issue engulfed the Tennants in a way that he would face again three decades later. Like all Methodist ministers, Thomas was an abolitionist, though he had a slave Christeen brought to their marriage as an inheritance. Voters elected him to the legislature in 1835 during Arkansas' path to statehood when they might legalize slavery. During his campaign he wrote a public letter to old friend and congressional delegate Ambrose Sevier, publisher of the territory-wide newspaper. He objected to Sevier's pairing of the word "fanaticism" with all abolitionists, triggering a hot debate between the two.[24]

John's father had become the biggest name in Arkansas aboli-tionism outside of his presiding elder, Rev. Jesse Haile, who attacked Tennant at the 1838 church conference for still owning a slave. Under church rules Tennant's only option was emancipation. Arkansas law required a bond for good behavior and Tennant believed the man might not comply. When Tennant decided he could not in good conscience free him, the Arkansas Conference expelled him from the church.[25]

At nine, John witnessed his close-knit extended family's religious crisis as some followed his father into the locally-controlled Method-ist Protestant Church and some did not. After two similar cases came before church leadership, the American Methodist Church split into North and South denominations over slavery. John's father remains in Methodist Church history books as a major cause of the cataclys-mic split, and evidence suggests that fifty years later the Northwest missionaries quickly recognized John's family name.[26]

Thomas and family eventually joined the Southern Methodists, but they never ceased to feel the injustice of the pioneering mission-ary's expulsion. The Southern church believed that his expulsion was unlawful, but he never asked for reinstatement as a minister. Instead, he preached when invited and at the camp meetings. He ministered to people whenever he could, but he never again was in charge of a congregation or an official missionary. From then on, John's father entered any public record as a farmer. Thomas and Christeen sent the slave to her sister in another county.[27]

The year of the expulsion, the Cherokee Trail of Tears passed close to the Tennant farm during a bitter winter when at least four thousand Indians died. One-fourth of the Cherokee by that time were mixed-blood like Christeen's family and her Quapaw people (perhaps relatives) were also sent to Indian Territory. It would have been difficult for the Tennants, including a young boy who knew his mother was also part-Indian, to have been unaware of the suffering of thousands passing so close.[28]

Only a year later, the Wright family murders a few miles from the Tennant farm, with the subsequent accusation against Cherokees, then the lynching of three white suspects by a vigilante committee, brought young John another lesson in the damage of injustice. The lynching was watched by a thousand settlers, slaves, and Indians. Only Thomas Tennant, two other ministers, and a judge refused to participate and made a futile attempt to convince the committee that at least some of the men might be innocent. The murders and the possible injustice that followed remain locally controversial.[29]

The injustice of his father's expulsion, of the Trail of Tears, and of the lynchings without trial—all became part of John Tennant.

When he was eleven, his mother and her infant died during her tenth childbirth. Christeen left behind seven children between two and eighteen. She had already trained her oldest girl, Harriet, in traditional native medicine that after marriage enabled her to become a "doctor woman" and midwife in the Missouri hills. The three teenaged girls were capable of cooking, caring for the garden, and sewing, and female family members lived nearby. Four years later, Thomas married Clarissa White Slover, widow of another Methodist minister who gave birth to four more little Tennants and more than earned the title of "Mother" that Christeen's children also gave her.[30]

Washington County's religious founders never lost their focus on education. While most of rural Arkansas paid little attention to schooling, the far northwest corner stood as an island of education. John walked half a mile cross-country to Bethesda Academy, a nonsectarian school for boys started by his father and other trustees of Bethesda Methodist Protestant Church committed to universal education. John next entered Cane Hill Collegiate Institute (CHCI) started by the county's Cumberland Presbyterians.[31]

Students at CHCI included children from prosperous Cherokee families and at least two others studied law in Fayetteville offices. John could not help but learn that Native American children were smart and deserved educational opportunities.

CHCI's first goal was to educate ministers, and Thomas apparently told himself that would be John's path. In 1850 the college received legislative permission to grant college degrees. If John's educational aspirations had ever been religious, they turned to more academic goals. Though he wrote a Bible proverb in Latin in his astronomy textbook, in late 1852 or early 1853 he graduated with a degree in engineering.[32]

No Tennant family stories tell why John did not want to be a minister. Nor do any explain why he wanted to leave home. His older brother James had gone to Texas some years before and if John left, there would be only teenaged girls and young children left to help at home. The fact that both of the eldest sons left implies some difficulty with their intimidating father, by then about sixty-two.[33]

Four years before John's graduation, the Tennants' Evansville neighbor Lewis Evans and a crew (including Tennant in-laws and men from Cherokee Nation) opened the Cherokee Trail, linking Washington County to the Santa Fe Trail route west through Kansas and Colorado. The successful expedition showed the isolated county's young men a route to another life. Arkansas cattle commanded premium prices in far-off California. A $5 cow in Arkansas would sell for $50 if it survived the trip west.[34]

One of the party, John W. Carter, returned from northern California the same year John graduated. He purchased cattle and recruited the newly-graduated engineer with five other young men to drive the stock west to his ranch with him. For John, who had never been far from home, the drive promised high adventure and $8.00 per month. Plus, it got him to the land where fortunes beckoned. John was strong, resilient, and he had a marketable skill.[35]

He left home in the spring of 1853 with seven hundred head of cattle plus fifty horses and mules. On the way to California, John crossed Oklahoma, Kansas, Colorado, Wyoming, Utah, and Nevada. Several of the boys left the cattle drive after an argument, but John kept his word to Carter. They arrived at Carter's ranch near Weaverville in Trinity County on November 10, 1853. John's friend C.C. Seay summed up the journey in his diary: "such a trip as that is enough to try any man."[36]

John's arduous trip west turned him into a seasoned drover who could ride, care for a herd, cook for himself, and thrive under harsh conditions. Having eaten dinner with a buffalo hunting party of Plains Indians, he had learned more about indigenous people. Though the boys had sung hymns around their campfire, he grew less and less religious in California's male-dominated society.

Later activities indicate that John tried at least some prospecting. He stayed in California less than eighteen months before he left for Bellingham Bay, possibly in the company of his new friend, blacksmith Thomas Wynn. Both men seem to have been in San Francisco when Sehome Mine manager Edmund Fitzhugh offered John a job. At the mine, John performed a variety of tasks in its earliest years: surveyor, engineer, and clerk, plus he started to read Fitzhugh's law books. By April 1855 first county auditor Fitzhugh had appointed John his deputy.[37]

⊂℥⊃

In early 1858 now-Deputy Sheriff and legislative Representative John Tennant left the mine and boldly registered the county's first agricultural preemption claim. Over many years, Tennant and Fitzhugh's relationship had its ups and downs and John may have partially been motivated by disgust with his employer, who was the defendant against a murder charge at the time. Other skilled workers soon followed him. The claim lay inside the unratified Lummi Reservation's boundary on the northeast end of *Chah-choo-sen*, a large wedge-shaped "island" between the meandering two main channels of the lower Nooksack River. His action, during a time of uncertainty about where the final boundaries would be, echoed his father's land gamble in Arkansas in the 1820s.[38]

John established the first permanent farm in Whatcom County on the fertile prairie *Si'lat'sis*. Unlike most men who had moved to the bay, Tennant carried a wealth of knowledge about farming. He could assess the quality of soil on a prairie and see the value of marshland where hogs and cattle could happily graze and fatten. He knew the value of a small lake that stayed ice-free all winter and was filled with fish and flocks of waterfowl. The slough protected access to the river and bay. He understood what endless back-breaking work in the field and orchard was and he brought the livestock skills and endurance he learned on his trek west.

John ordered fruit seedlings, berry vines, and green pea seeds, and took official possession of his claim on April 1, 1858. There was no occupancy requirement yet on the unsurveyed land, but he seems to have stayed there occasionally after September 1, probably once he had a crude shelter ready. When he applied for a patent years later, he named his 160 acres *Si'lat'sis,* a tacit admission that he was on Lummi territory. Never again did a settler use the real name of his land in writing.[39]

While working his new land, John's civic involvement continued and over the coming years he committed to dozens of organizations and positions. Soon after taking his claim, he served in the legislature (like his father) and on the Indian Affairs Committee, among others. No quiet newcomer, he introduced several bills that benefited his county and the territorial memorial forwarded to Congress that requested confirmation of the Point Elliott Treaty. He was a vigorous leader in the defeat of House Bill 33 that would have outlawed relationships of any kind with Native women, something that would have been a personal repudiation of the many intermarriages in his own family.[40]

As soon as he entered the legislature, John found himself at the podium defending his political and legal mentor Fitzhugh, who was still under indictment for murder. He met Paul Hubbs Sr. of Port Townsend that session. Two years later, John joined Hubbs' law practice after passing the bar exam when fellow Democrat and then-Judge Fitzhugh led the questioning. Voters elected John (already appointed Deputy U.S. Surveyor) to the county commission in 1862, and he was promptly made chairman.[41]

John obtained appointment as Assistant Indian Agent, which brought in more cash income. He frequently stayed at the Lummi Agency shack on Gooseberry Point at *Tam'whiq'sen* and probably ate many salmon dinners with Tsi'lixw's family. Most likely, that is where he crossed paths with Clara. At the same time, he was the deputy sheriff, which put him in both law enforcement and mediator positions. His equitable actions during the "Battle of the Blockhouse" in 1859 (the bay's only deadly armed conflict), resulted in friendships with Nooksack headmen Humptalem, "Lynden" Jim Selhameten, and others.[42]

Relations between the few post-gold rush residents and the Nooksack villages far upriver were normally cordial. Nooksack leaders made it clear that they wanted to be left alone, other than for their river canoe business, and would be hostile to anyone trying to settle in their territory. The issue that triggered the "Battle of the Blockhouse" was the intended apprehension of a Nooksack suspect wanted in the murder of a Samish man. John's Indian agency superior ordered him to resolve the issue between the two tribes. He talked to Nooksack headman Tallis Kanim (known as "Job" to most whites) in town, but the Native leader refused to either give up the suspect or make restitution to the Samish family, or to even send a runner to the other leaders upriver. Angry, John locked him in the blockhouse as a hostage, a tactic others had already used against the Coast Salish. John then left town for his agency cabin at Gooseberry Point.[43]

Tallis Kanim sent word to John the next day that he would cooperate if released. However, before John's release order reached town, about twenty angry armed Nooksack arrived to free their man, and a general argument with armed settlers started. When "Buckskin" Roessell grabbed a Nooksack musket, he was shot and stabbed, though some witnesses said the whites fired first. Tennant later wrote in his report: "The firing now became pretty general." Five Nooksack men and Roessell died. After the other Nooksack fled with Tallis Kanim, a Lummi runner took word to John at his cabin to come at once. Word also went to the army on San Juan Island at Camp Pickett. Lummi friends refused to allow John to leave for town in the dark and six men guarded his agency cabin in case the Nooksack came for him overnight.

At dawn John found the situation in town chaotic, with some extremists advocating a massacre of all the Nooksack people. Tallis Kanim sent word that he would come back to help get things settled down if his safety was guaranteed, which John could not do. That night the army arrived at the Sehome dock.

John headed upriver ahead of Major George Haller and his escort. Tallis Kanim took him to The Crossing (today's Everson) where John talked to the other headmen at the major Nooksack village. He persuaded all the suspects to give themselves up, and the next morning everyone appeared in town where the five men were taken aboard the *Massachusetts*. The Nooksacks apologized for the melee, based on the Tennant and Tallis Kanim negotiations with the other leaders. Wrote the twenty-eight-year-old deputy sheriff and assistant Indian agent in his report: "The peace now secured is permanent." Major Haller took credit for what John had accomplished.[44]

CLARA AND JOHN

When John Tennant died in 1893, the local newspaper included the following in his obituary: "While in the legislature he became engaged to a prominent and wealthy lady of the territory but, the match being displeasing to her parents, it was broken off. He returned home and was married to the daughter of the chief or tyee of the Lummi tribe."[45]

This unsubstantiated story circulated locally, and it was published with apparent total disdain for Clara's feelings. Had the editor known the histories of the two, he might not have clearly implied that John "settled" for her. In addition to dismissing Clara, the obituary also insulted the memory of John's own part-Quapaw mother and sisters.[46]

There may have been only five or six hundred Lummi who survived the 1852-53 winter epidemic, and more were lost to the local mystery epidemic of 1857-58. John probably saw Clara frequently about *Tam'whiq'sen*. Phoebe Judson called her friend "the pride of her people" and said she was bright, lively, strong, and intelligent. She was also tall like John, unusual for a Coast Salish girl.[47]

The formidable young woman surely reminded John of the women and girls in his own family who were assertive, capable, used to running things, plus knowledgeable about folk medicine and agriculture. Lummi women could live and work alone when the men were gone, as could the women in John's family. Lummi women bore responsibility for the family's health maintenance and nursing those seriously ill, as did the Tennant women. Clara was also physically strong, key for every woman who lived on a homestead, whether in Arkansas in the 1830s or Whatcom County in the 1850s.[48]

The couple shared other traits. They both understood leadership, family obligations, and were the children of community leaders. Her community was built around cooperative activities, as was his. She was religious, something he could understand from a childhood immersed in Methodism.

In sum, Clara was exactly who John Tennant's personal history would lead him toward. Their relationship may or may not have been romantic in the beginning. In rural Arkansas society, as among the Coast Salish, romantic love was not a requirement for marriage. People expected love to grow with time and children.

John met with Clara's family, who had their own agenda for her marriage. If Henry Roeder's report was accurate, Clara's father died in the year of the Fraser gold rush, before her marriage to John Tennant was considered. Along with her mother and sisters, she had older brothers and many aunts and uncles who would judge whether the settler with the odd accent would be a suitable choice for "the pride of her people." From the perspective of Clara's relatives, John first needed to be able to fulfill the obligations of any other husband added to their family. They would absorb the man who had moved onto family-administered agricultural territory that the treaty had placed within the unsurveyed reservation boundaries. The marriage would enable their continued control over *Si'lat'sis* resources.[49]

John Tennant was generally a good prospect. He was strong and handsome, and perhaps the family even liked his height that matched the unusually tall young woman. They had observed his daily behavior as the Indian agent, and his actions during the "Battle of the Blockhouse." John was in a position to mediate with the white authorities who increasingly controlled their lives. He was ambitious and a hard worker. They may have observed his hunting, fishing, and logging skills, and noted that the country boy knew what to do with a carving knife and a block of wood. They may have noticed that he even understood how to smoke meat and fish unlike the city men, and how to use the healing power of plants.

The two men who married into the Lummi family of Saw'rem'ken's sons (Tennant and Philadelphia Quaker Tom Wynn) had something else in their backgrounds that no other settler did, and it may not be coincidental that they were the two the family approved. They grew up in the two Christian faiths most involved in abolitionism and disposed to treat Indians and other non-whites fairly. Thomas Tennant was the well-known abolitionist and Wynn's grandmother operated a stop on the Underground Railroad. Their families had taught them to stand up for what was right. Based on faith and personal history,

John's very demeanor may have communicated an unusual respect that Clara's family did not always experience.

John was undeniably land-hungry and had his own practical motives for the marriage. He may have thought that marrying Clara and keeping the prairie's rightful name was the "just" way to take over Lummi ground. He may have comprehended and been willing to enter Clara's family web of obligations similar to his own extended family's cooperation. Nevertheless, he probably did not understand all the implications of Clara's traditional rights to the land he claimed, or that her family's perception was that his marriage allowed him on that ground only as a "grant" from the family.

John was likely also hedging his bets in case the government failed to follow its long pattern of leaving squatters in place when they finalized a reservation boundary. Clara might be able to claim an allotment if *Si'lat'sis* ended up wholly within the final reservation borders, giving John possession by virtue of his marriage. Since many whites in the area expected the reservation to be temporary, no matter what happened, he still stood to own the land. A few months after the April 1859 treaty ratification, the Steilacoom paper reassured encroachers they were safe because the army force was too small to push them off their claims. Late in the year, the Territorial Superintendent of Indian Affairs officially announced that anyone squatting on a reservation would not be disturbed in "their possessory rights."[50]

In late 1859 or early 1860 Clara became the wife of a white settler, but her intermarriage did not mean she abandoned Coast Salish attitudes toward marriage. Historian Jean Barman found that the culture's women often let their white husbands know that they would return home if they were treated badly. If they were justifiably unhappy, they simply left. An unsubstantiated published tale about the Tennants said that Clara and John broke up at an early date and John sent her home. Her family told her to return because the land was actually hers and she should order him to leave. Given the unstable state of the treaty boundaries before and after ratification, it would not be surprising if Clara and her family thought that they had not only a right of prior occupancy, but a *legal* equity in *Si'lat'sis*. Clara returned to John, and no one ever questioned the marriage's strength again.[51]

John was unlikely to have disdained the legitimacy of tribal custom marriage. After all, his grandparents and other ancestors in Arkansas had followed the French "country marriage" custom. The age difference of perhaps a decade was the familiar pattern in both his family and childhood environment. To disrespect the common Northwest custom would also disrespect his mixed-blood mother, sisters, as well as his grandmother and other maternal female ancestors.

Clara and John were poised to become one of the most influential couples in the county's history. She married a man equal in character, intelligence, and skills. The mature Arkansas farm boy chose his match who would be a partner on the land and in the ambitious life of service and accomplishment he envisioned. Clara's family could not have foreseen some of the new directions her life with John Tennant would take.

When John married, he assumed a dilemma faced by his father two decades earlier. Clara brought two *stseanaq* (Julia and Whis) into her marriage, just as John's mother had brought an enslaved man into hers. The indigenous bondage found among all Northwest coast groups was inherently different from the slavery of John's youth. It was based on loss of social status and personal history after capture and sale away from one's home territory. The *stseanaq* were important members of elite families' workforce who, by doing most menial chores, freed up specialists to carve, weave, make baskets, etc. Without their enslaved labor, large potlatches would not have been possible. Though many lived alongside the family, the intimidating power over life and death underlay the custom. Language difficulties and lack of information prevented them from understanding that the 1855 treaty freed them, and they did not know how to get home even if they could leave. The pre-war federal government seems to have thought the ancient custom would fade away by itself and did nothing to enforce the treaty provision.[52]

Though Clara's family meant to ease a young wife's work burden, John's internal discomfort would have been the same. Her servants were not free. John was a very unlikely *stseanaq* owner. He seems never to have told his father about Julia and Whis. Evidence indicates that John told only his sister Ada, and bound her to secrecy.

However, she told another sister about the situation and his fear the news would kill their father.[53]

Whis was a young Alaskan boy, perhaps ten or so when the Tennants married. Teenaged Julia said later that she was born in British Columbia. Captured as children, neither actually knew where their faraway northern homes were and if John freed them, the youngsters would be homeless and unprotected.[54]

Whatever John's internal dialogue, he made no move to free Clara's *stseanaq* after they joined the household at the farm.

෨

Clara could not have anticipated the farmer her new husband would become. Though Lummi women had long practiced agriculture, she had never seen a plot of tobacco or Jerusalem artichokes. She had not seen five varieties of carrots or a farmyard with cattle, hogs, turkeys, and chickens. On the other hand, John was new to the different salmon species he would help her family harvest every year. He didn't know salmon habits and seasons, their life cycles or the best way to catch them. He did not know the soil of his prairie like Clara and her family did, and the efficient digging stick was new to him. Each partner had farming, food preservation, and preparation skills to share.

John started a journal to prepare for his patent application four years after he settled *Si'lat'sis*. No land office had opened and he was under no real obligation to be on a schedule of residency and cultivation until all the treaty legalities were settled. John built their sturdy 16 x 20-foot cabin near the ice-free lake where the *Ske'laken* village had once welcomed all people to get food in times of winter hunger. The early work comprised mostly land clearing, starting a garden, and planting an orchard—the initial tasks for any homesteader. With trees that could reach 250 feet tall and thick underbrush, "land clearing" was an understatement. John and James Carr (*see* chapter 5) cooperated to widen the waterways and remove obstructions from the slough for a better river and bay access. The *Noos'kwiem* that surrounded their prairie claims was a mystical place of mist and fog, water and marsh, trees and grassland. Soft breezes ruffled the cottonwoods along the riverbank, and sometimes the aurora borealis lit the sky above Clara's home. With John's other jobs that called him away, Clara may have stayed alone to work with her helpers, or gone downriver to her family's home when he was gone.[55]

Over the next twelve years, John's journal chronicled an astonishing drive to develop Whatcom County's first farm. Clara's sister Sarah, her Nooksack husband Albert Descanum, and Clara's brothers regularly worked for the Tennants (while John helped in the fishery). The garden was her responsibility while John did heavier tasks. They planted every kind of vegetable and crop available to find the most profitable. They sold pheasants and venison harvested from the farm's woodlands and prairie. Such zeal would not have been rewarded as abundantly if John had not met John Bennett. The Scot had traveled the world collecting seeds and studying soils and climates before he started a nursery down the trail to town and the two men started to experiment. With Bennett's guidance, and knowledge from his Arkansas youth, John developed the dark red-purple "Tennant Plum" that won prizes and sold widely on the west coast for decades. He planted thirty-eight varieties of apples while he and Bennett worked out which were best suited to Bellingham Bay's growing conditions. John also developed the "Tennant Dwarf Pea" which sold well. Each year, John entered into his journal the weather of the last 6 days of December and paired them with a new year's month to predict the weather during growing season. It was a northwest Arkansas farming custom.[56]

The couple found Coast Salish and Arkansas medicinal plants in common that both families used, though with different names. For example, the same plant was used for "marsh tea" in Arkansas and "swamp tea" by the Coast Salish. Sometimes, John's Arkansan word for a plant could be different from not only Clara's, but also anyone else in town, e.g. "whortleberries" instead of "blueberries."[57]

A few other families trickled out to the river in the early years, mostly other skilled mine employees. Shortly after John's friend James Carr died, Tom Wynn moved to nearby *Ske'laken* prairie with Clara's cousin Jenny and their own *stseanaq*. Blacksmith Wynn had the tools and Carr's grindstone that John needed, and John helped city boy Wynn learn to plow behind an ox team. John frequently collaborated with James Patterson, the Tennessee dairy and beef cattleman who moved upriver, and sometimes herded cattle for him. Patterson, his

Snoqualmie wife Elizabeth (daughter of Chief Patkanim), and their little girls often stopped for an overnight visit with Clara and John on the way home from town or to celebrate Christmas.

The mostly intermarried couples started neighborhood butchering days. Fresh meat turned bad quickly, so a fattened steer killed in the evening was hung overnight, cut up, and canoed to town in the early morning for sale to eager customers. Clara and the other women fed the men working overnight and cooked some of the meat to make it last a little longer at home. When hogs were butchered, everyone worked together to make hams and sausages each family would then smoke or salt.[58]

Clara was an essential partner in the enterprise, especially providing clear communication with workers until John learned the language. He held many public positions and smaller part-time jobs during their first twelve years of marriage, so she often managed the farm with the ever-more-capable Albert and Whis. She produced eggs and feathers whose value to the family income increased after McDonough's store opened downriver to wholesale the neighborhood's commodities to Seattle. In one five-month period in 1877, she sold the trader 117 dozen eggs. Clara often used her "egg money" for clothing and fabric. She quilted blankets for the family and never stopped making baskets. While most farm women were charged with churning butter, John either took it over or they worked together to produce saleable units formed in the molds he made. From youthful experience, John knew how to make almost anything his family needed and with Clara's partnership, they were well-suited to husband the county's best land.[59]

John's Family

Back in Arkansas, the Tennants' situation deteriorated and the Civil War changed forever John's role in the family dynamic, and with him Clara's role. The family farm was caught in the middle of guerilla warfare and the movements of both armies while the U.S. nominally controlled the county for most of the conflict.

John worked like a man possessed, earning money from multiple sources while also serving on the county commission. He may have been trying to raise extra funds to send home. After the government cut mail delivery to the South, it would have been difficult for John to do so, even through intermediaries. In 1862, Washington's Southern settlers learned that new homestead rules denied land to anyone giving aid to the Confederacy. Those with any six-month absence forfeited their claim. If he ever considered it, John could not go home to help his family if he wanted to keep his land.[60]

John almost certainly did not know that his father was a Union spy or that several of Clarissa's family had been killed. Thomas passed information and fed Union officers at his home. The Confederate "bushwhackers" put a price on the elderly minister's head because he continued to loudly support Unionism and abolition. Apparently unaware that he was also spying, they told Thomas they would kill him if he didn't "leave the country or keep [his] mouth shet." He narrowly escaped arrest several times at home and while meeting other Unionists at Dutch Mills under the guise of taking in their grain. When the guerillas tried to get locals to kill the stubborn old man, his friends convinced him they meant it. Tennant and several others spent most of the war years hiding in the damp limestone caves behind his farm, only coming out occasionally at night.[61]

Clarissa and the children brought in the crops only to see them stolen by one side or the other from the barn or hiding place. The Union forces took their horses, including a thoroughbred. Rebels who rode up the lane took clothing and bedding when they couldn't find anything else to steal. Now seventy-two, Rev. Tennant signed a loyalty oath in 1863 in hopes the protection order would end Union appropriation of their food and keep Clarissa and the girls safe from rape when they went to the mill. The order did not keep the family either safe or fed.[62]

In the spring of 1865 with the war nearly over, the Tennant family was starving. Several county women and children had already died of hunger. Neighbors who once would have helped, now were enemies. They had no choice but to enter a loyalist colony, a confiscated rebel farm that offered sanctuary and food to fifty families of men who signed loyalty oaths and raised fodder for Union army livestock.[63]

The war impoverished John's family and Washington County. Six years after Appomattox, the Southern Claims Commission, charged with reparations to the loyalists, awarded them only 40 percent of the value of some goods and livestock requisitioned by Union troops. Led by Thomas, at eighty that year and physically weakened, the Tennants never regained any prosperity. While John had gone to college and his sisters were well-educated, the youngest Tennants never got beyond basic literacy. From thousands of miles away, John and Clara became his financially ruined family's primary advisor and with his older brother dead and married sisters in equally poor straits, almost certainly their major source of cash.[64]

CLARA AND JOHN

When emancipation was enforced after the Civil War, Julia and Whis stayed with the Tennants in some middle ground between family and hired help. Julia married Tom T'ing (former Wynn *stseanaq*) and founded a Whatcom County family. Whis, only a teenager in 1865, never left the Tennants or married. Clara and John had become his family. The tiny man with bowl-cut black hair either lived in the Tennant home or had his own place. He worked alongside Clara and John and took loads of commodities to town, appearing many times in the farm journal and sometimes called "Joseph," his baptismal name. He was a particularly skilled rifle shot and John enjoyed reporting that Whis usually bested anyone else with him on a deer or elk hunt. As the years passed, the public knew him as a well-liked and well-known part of the Tennant household.[65]

The farm crew centered around Clara's brother-in-law Albert Descanum and her sister Sarah, who may have lived on the property most of the time. They worked side-by-side with the Tennants for cash wages, and whenever John was gone Albert managed the operation. Experienced farmers by the 1880s, Albert and Sarah acquired a Lummi Reservation allotment and turned it into a showplace like the Tennant farm. Most of Clara's siblings took allotments clustered on the east side of the reservation close to the Tennants where mutual help was convenient.[66]

Clara and John both came from large families who lived in intimate spaces surrounded by cousins and siblings. It is an easy conclusion that they wanted many children to fill their home, and John sometimes referred to Clara as his "old woman," just as fathers did in Arkansas.

Clara gave birth to John Jr. on May 13, 1863, just after dark, attended by Dr. Boyd who came out from Whatcom at John's request. John's memory of his mother's death in childbirth may have spurred him to find the only medical help available and not to trust the unfamiliar ways of a Lummi midwife.[67]

When the baby was two months old, John returned from town with a Newfoundland puppy. The lake and all its attractions were very near the house. A Newfoundland's sweet disposition around small children, webbed feet for long-distance swimming, and natural instinct to rescue made it a perfect guardian for Clara and John's first-born while he explored his world.[68]

When John Jr. was four months old, the Tennants went to the new government-built Lummi village at the river's mouth for Fr. Chirouse's monthly visit. They slept at the agency cabin for several days until he baptized the children, among them John Jr. In Fr. Chirouse's record, he called Clara by her French baptismal name "Marie" (probably "Marie Claire" in full). Some months later, she suffered a miscarriage.[69]

Sometimes John, Clara, and the baby got sick, but no journal entry forewarned of their little boy's death on January 22, 1866. The weather that month had been foul with constant wind and snow, sometimes blowing "like blazes." John did not say that their son was ill or that there had been an accident, although Jim Carr was summoned to help in some way. John set his journal entry apart with his grief-filled wavering ink border. "And about midnight my little darling boy departed this life—peace be with thee my son—green be the trees that grow over thee my darling, bright the sunshine and sweet the flowers above thee my Love. Soft and sweet thy slumbers my child while thy bright spirit basks in eternal joy."

Carr helped John make a little coffin, while teenaged Nellie Carr or Sarah sat with Clara. Other river families arrived to comfort the couple. They buried the boy in the wind and rain after a day of "laying out" while they tried to accept the terrible loss. John cleared the brush around the grave of his "sweet lovely boy" during the days to come. Filled with grief, Clara and John went to be with her family at *Tam'whiq'sen*.[70]

Baby Bayard arrived on March 29, 1867, fourteen months after John Jr.'s death. When John got home for dinner after a day with neighbors doing pre-season chores, he found Clara in labor and that night "a little boy was born." Bayard's birth was probably attended by Clara's sister, perhaps her cousin Jenny Wynn, and a midwife because John never mentioned Dr. Boyd again. Bayard survived, but the trauma of their previous losses weighed upon his parents. John became an overprotective and indulgent father. Clara and John pinned all their dreams for *Si'lat'sis* on their only child.[71]

◯◯◯

In 1868, John underwent a life-changing experience that slowly resulted in a sharp turn in the family's life. No one had ever stood on the top of Mount Baker. The Nooksack people who lived below believed that man should not go beyond the timberline. Edmund Coleman, charter member of the London Alpine Club and a team that included Tennant (who became ill) had failed to summit the peak two years earlier. Coleman still wanted to look down into the steaming, smoking maw of the volcano that sent fire into the night sky periodically. It erupted again in the spring of 1868, its fiery lava visible in Victoria and it sometimes made sounds like heavy cannon fire.[72]

That summer, Clara and John worked in smoke-filled air while a great Canadian forest fire raged toward them on its way to the Columbia River. Then, in mid-July John severely cut his leg while building a slaughterhouse. Clara nursed him for several weeks before Coleman arrived at their house. John agreed to become interpreter and geographer for a second summit attempt for the team of four. Despite his still-healing wound, John left armed with a month's worth of Clara's bread, bacon, and tea. Knowing her husband was going again to a forbidden mountain, Clara and Bayard said their goodbyes. According to oral history, Clara's family resented the long periods that Clara was left alone, like this one. Her brother Whi'lano and other Lummi men canoed the team upstream to the Patterson ranch at *Sqweha:lich* where they switched to shovel-nose river canoes and Nooksack men who knew the upper river better than anyone. When they camped at ever higher elevations, Tennant did a bit of prospecting and told stories from some gold-hunting forays into the Baker foothills.[73]

The team used homemade crampons for the final ascent of the peak on August 17. A 12-foot-square ice chunk started to slide down a near-vertical wall onto them but stopped before crushing the terrified climbers. Soon after, John fell into a crevasse, but managed to extricate himself. Roped together and using their axes to climb, the four men reached the top at four P.M. Surveyor Tennant was likely the first person to measure the summit hovering above the pall of reddish smoke at 10,618 feet. John and the others felt "at heaven's gate and in the immediate presence of the Almighty." They held hands, prayed, and sang "Praise God from whom all blessings flow." John Tennant stared down into the steaming crater raw with sulphur yellow, reds, and greens against hardened black lava. It reminded him and the others of Hell. They could "sense the fire slumbering under them." The team planted flags on both summits and toasted their feat with brandy. [74]

John's party didn't start down until 5 p.m., roped together and sliding some of the time, crossing snow bridges and ice walls, "as if pursued by a fiend...helter-skelter madbrained [sic]." Coleman was so exhausted he had to be helped down. Lost in the dark, they hiked down the mountain until the Nooksack men heard their shouts.[75]

John had wandered far from his religion since he left Arkansas. But it was perhaps fortuitous that the day after his return home from the mountain two priests visited the Tennants, enabling a discussion of John's deep spiritual experience on the summit. Just two weeks later, he joined the Good Templars, a national temperance lodge, and pledged never to drink again. There were stirrings of change.[76]

∞

Two years later, the territory's agricultural census showed that profitability of the scattered farms along the Nooksack had begun to separate out by soil quality, commodity choice, effort, and knowledge. The Tennant farm was valued at $2,000, twice that of John's friend Tom Wynn's farm, but others lagged far behind the two. The Tennant and Wynn barns were comparatively very large, and John had built a smokehouse, root cellar, and milk house. Though the land office had still not opened, Clara and John's farm was well-established and he could ease up a bit and try a new adventure. Clara would be left behind once again.[77]

Daniel Linsley of the Northern Pacific Railroad approached John to help with an exploration trip over the Cascades. John had been recommended as the perfect man for Linsley's partner and so he was. He had unmatched experience in rough terrain for a non-native. His language and negotiating skills were crucial to obtain canoes, labor, and supplies. The two were a good personal match also, both engineer-surveyors from ministerial families.

Albert Descanum joined the team to bring additional upriver experience and language ability. The brothers-in-law brought a further advantage (probably not realized by Linsley): they were the husbands of two important women. Clara and Sarah's connections, whether family or trade, would help their husbands (and friends) obtain hospitality from the Upper Skagits and Sauk-Suiattles whose assistance they would need. If Saw'rem'ken and Tsi'lixw's names were also known to tribal leaders east of the Cascades, the party would not be strangers in the Coast Salish sense, i.e. intruders to be cautiously viewed with suspicion of their intentions.

Once again, Clara waited and worked.

The party traversed the Cascades and descended rivers as far as present-day Wenatchee on the Columbia River, though sickness sent Albert home. John met not only the leaders of the upriver tribes, but also powerful Chief Moses on the eastern side. He was part of the first exploration of Lake Chelan by whites. He traversed the upper Stehekin Valley alone. He and Linsley were the first non-Natives over Indian and Linsley passes, the first to climb Indian Head Peak, and they made the first known non-Native examination of Lake Wenatchee and its river through Tumwater Canyon and down to the Columbia.[78]

ଓଡ଼୦

One position John took on again that used his college education and supplied additional income was Deputy U.S. Surveyor. Without proper surveys, the U.S. Land Office that opened in Olympia in 1872 could not accept applications for patents or the counties ultimately issue deeds. Thereafter, he surveyed Whatcom County roads, the plats of Ferndale and Marietta, and townships suitable for agriculture. One summer he surveyed the Tacoma railroad terminus, a job courtesy of Daniel Linsley. Leaving for three months after his other dangerous trips probably did not endear him to Clara's family. Neither did his participation in the resurvey of Lummi Reservation's northern border, ostensibly to straighten lines. What it really meant was the loss of a long and wide strip of land that was given over to homesteaders.[79]

John and a partner opened a surveying and real estate office at nearby East Ferndale after the land office opened. He bought 240 additional acres and helped other settlers do the same, as well as fill out their homestead applications properly. The Nooksack tribe had no reservation because they did not sign the treaty, but they were eligible for "Indian homesteads." By then, John was actively opposing the new upriver settlers who had no history with the Nooksack families and wanted them driven away to the Lummi Reservation. He assisted his friends with the applications and, with other Nooksack-connected supporters Holden Judson and James Bertrand, witnessed their "fitness" to own and farm a piece of their traditional homeland.[80]

John did not survey alone. Over the years, Albert and Whis assisted him, and probably other brothers-in-law. While he surveyed the eastern townships for Indian and regular homesteads he took an apprentice, the young Nooksack man Jim Uchochanon (Jim Kelly). Uchochanon knew all the village and resource locations that Nooksack families, if they applied for a patent, could continue to hold. He also patented his own before he became a surveyor across the Canadian border where he had family.[81]

Unlike some others, Clara and John lived in their snug two-room log house for over a decade, most likely with one or more additions tacked on. In 1872, when the patent application went in, Bayard was a growing boy, and there was enough money to build a proper farmhouse. John sited the two-story home in a meadow at the north end of what is now called Tennant Lake. The steamer brought lumber from the Utsalady mill on Camano Island, and expert builder Harry Post walked down the trail every day from his home with the Wynns

The Clara and John Tennant house. Built in 1872 under the supervision of master carpenter Harry Post, the home was still occupied 140 years later. The back sections may have been the earlier dwelling. *Percival Jeffcott Collection #1263, Center for Pacific Northwest Studies, Western Libraries Heritage Resources. Western Washington University, Bellingham, Washington.*

to do the carpentry work. As usual, Post used fitted joints and mortises instead of just nails, which enabled the home to last well into the twenty-first century. John did a lot of the work and gained experience which he would put to good use a decade later. Clara and John surrounded their home with flowers. Photos hint that they may have integrated the cabin into the back of the house.[82]

On John's birthday following completion of the new home, the Tennants received a singular "honor," which friends carefully planned in advance. All the neighborhood families met at the Wynn house with food and drink. Two scouts went down the trail about 9 P.M. to prepare for the surprise event and were confronted by two big watchdogs bounding toward them, barking loudly. John came out on the front porch in his night clothes, shotgun in hand. The startled men told John his neighbors would soon arrive for the "shivaree." He and Clara dressed quickly. Said the local newspaper editor: "Dancing kept up till morning, except that at midnight a recess was taken for refreshments...[it] was the first organized sociable held in the Nooksack Valley, and we congratulate Mr. Tennant on being the recipient of such mark of esteem."[83]

The roomy new Tennant home became the neighborhood's favorite spot for parties. Children slept upstairs while their parents ate and danced reels, waltzes, and square dances all night. If John still remembered how to fiddle, he probably took his turn. Clara and the other women especially enjoyed the occasions that brought them out of homestead isolation and the boring tedium of their chore-filled lives.

John had largely abandoned legal work when he began to seriously work on his upcoming homestead patent application and all it required. After Judge Fitzhugh left, for some time he was the only trained lawyer in town, even if he had no further interest in regularly appearing in district court. Voters elected him probate judge twice, starting in 1876. He oversaw estates, married couples, and appointed guardians for children whose father had died since mothers didn't legally qualify. After his re-election, the *Mail* editor said Tennant had performed to everyone's "eminent satisfaction." Even his opponent, a former judge, agreed there was no one better qualified.[84]

John turned his attention to education once seven-year-old Bayard started school in the small log building on Mary and Solomon Allen's land. Three years later in 1877, voters elected John County Superintendent of Schools. He was already the probate judge in addition to his farming and surveying duties, but that did not seem to deter him from the extra time commitment. Both Clara and John were committed to their communities.[85]

John immediately began to professionalize the district teachers by establishing certification in line with the legislated territorial standards. When he encouraged the teachers to take competency exams in reading, writing, spelling, geography, arithmetic, physiology, history, and the theory of teaching, not many appeared. When he made exams mandatory, he also inaugurated teachers' institutes to meet at the same time. They immediately became popular gatherings for teachers, usually isolated in one-room schools, to share information and encourage each other. He organized six new school districts as rural homesteads proliferated. At the same time, he successfully fought off a movement by a long-time teacher and his allies to stop the cost-saving consolidation of Whatcom and Sehome districts earlier split apart with equal controversy (*see* chapter 5).[86]

Superintendent Tennant traveled by horse and canoe to make unannounced visits to the little schools scattered across today's Whatcom and Skagit Counties. He checked on the teachers' competency and what problems they might be encountering. One day he walked into Bayard's school just as his son was being punished. Clara and John's pampered boy and his cousin Harry Wynn had a reputation for finding myriad ways to get into mischief and give their teacher problems. There Bayard stood in front of the class with his head covered by the teacher's black scarf. Furious at his son's humiliation and forgetting professionalism altogether, John lost his temper and berated the teacher in front of the class. News of his unfortunate outburst spread rapidly among shocked parents.[87]

It is clear that John Tennant could never be just one thing. Perhaps today he would be labeled someone who could not say "no." In the twenty-first century, it would be unimaginable for a person to be superintendent of schools, county commissioner, and run for probate judge at the same time. There were days when John moved between three different meetings at the courthouse. His farm demanded time and he was beginning a new spiritual life. No one seems to have ever publicly questioned his competency or energy for any of the jobs.

୦୫୬୦

Clara's life took a different turn because another life was calling John. She would soon leave her Catholic faith behind and cast her spiritual lot with her husband, despite her brother Chief Kwina's leadership of the Lummi Catholics. And with that change came an entirely new focus for the rest of her marriage.

It's hard to say when or why John Tennant felt the religion of his youth call to him so strongly. His Arkansas family credited their decades of prayer. Perhaps it was his experience on Mount Baker's summit, or the conversations with the priests immediately following. Perhaps it was the happy gatherings at Lummi for a week of sacraments, worship, celebrating, and feasting so reminiscent of the camp meetings in Arkansas, or the visits of Rev. Charles Tate, a Methodist missionary who traveled south from the Fraser River villages to convert the Nooksacks at their invitation. Something prompted John to think deeply about how he wanted to live the rest of his own life.[88]

During the years of pressure on tribal-custom couples to legalize their unions, Clara and John had a civil ceremony on February 13, 1876. That summer he taught Sunday school at the old Wynn schoolhouse to twenty-five children gathered from the river neighborhood. Perhaps Superintendent of Schools Tennant approached a reunion with his church from the education angle, since Methodists promoted literacy and the public schools met only three months a year. No one recorded how Chief Kwina felt about his sister's civil rather than Catholic wedding and her husband's Methodist Sunday school.[89]

Events in the next two years slowly drew John into dramatic changes. He was already marrying couples as the probate judge. Missionary Rev. A. J. McNemee arrived in Blaine to start proselytizing after the Methodists had abandoned the bay settlements to the more established Catholics some years before. Rev. Tate and Captain John (a Nooksack lay preacher) held regular services at Jim Selhameten's longhouse for Lynden settlers and the Nooksack. Methodism had already re-entered John's life on a regular basis at the Sunday school.

Three Methodist missionaries decided to hold a Ferndale camp meeting in June 1877 in Billy Clark's meadow by his ferry landing, easily accessible to the river neighborhood and to people they hoped would come out from Whatcom. John helped organize the grounds in the traditional pattern and attendees followed the old cycle: prayers before a common breakfast, divine service, lunch and informal meetings, preaching and fellowship meetings, a rest period before dinner, the exhortations to conversion and an evening-long revival. The settlers sat on one side and the Indians (Nooksack and perhaps some Lummi) sat on the other. The camp meeting plunged John back into the hymns, sermons, emotions, and exhortations to live a better life that he remembered from his youth. Years later, one of the missionaries fondly remembered Clara teasing him because he had not yet found a wife. A second camp meeting followed at Semiahmoo after Tate stayed over with Clara and John and perhaps encouraged him to look at his life more deeply. Introspection leading to conversion had always been the goal of circuit riders. John embarked on a year of self-examination.[90]

The next spring, John wrote to his sister that he might soon die, but he was trying to live a more religious life by attending Methodist services. In a maudlin exaggeration of how bad his behavior had been so far, John wrote that he grieved over his wasted life and said "it was all leaves." He asked for all of his sisters' prayers that his talent might not be "wrapped in a napkin."[91]

That summer, when John worked on the second camp meeting site, he cut his thigh long and deep with a large knife. He bled so badly and for so long before bandages could staunch the flow he fainted. Clara expertly cared for her seriously wounded husband. She gained even more respect from her adopted community.[92]

The wound didn't stop the family from attending the camp meeting. The three converted after listening to the missionaries' emotional exhortations to turn their lives toward God. Apparently Clara responded first, because John credited her with his conversion. When John volunteered to start preaching, the presiding elder licensed him the same day to serve the people of his own area. It was a singular jump over the usual study requirements. The superiors probably recognized his talent and spirit, and also the surname of one of American Methodists' first missionaries. Within weeks, John conducted the funeral for a hunting accident fatality, and that winter said the final words over the fresh grave of a murderer finally cornered and shot by a posse.[93]

Clara continued to run things at the farm with Albert and Whis when John was away riding, walking, and canoeing an informal circuit, preaching wherever friends and acquaintances gathered to hear him. When he wasn't preaching, farming, holding probate court, or inspecting schools, he read theological books that would someday lead to full-fledged ordination. Clara was not left out of the church duties, because Methodist clergy wives had their own requirements to help with charitable activities. She was supposed to welcome everyone and provide for their comfort at John's services as well as organize and cook for the communal meals the Methodists called "love feasts." When she attended church conferences with John, attendees treated her the same as the other "cultured" women, according to her friend Phoebe Judson. Clara and John gained a reputation for keeping an open door to preachers and church members.[94]

John's missionary activity was very different from his father's. The Northwest was a diverse place in which Methodists would never be the majority religion. There were Catholics, Mormons, Asian religions, and the unchurched who prayed at home. Missionaries in the West found that for most settlers, religion was a Sunday-only faith, but the Coast Salish did not separate spiritual and secular activities. The Nooksacks and Lummi lived their religion like the missionaries did, in a daily demonstration of spirituality. Clara's people had been solidly Catholic since the 1840s, but few totally abandoned their traditional spirituality. The Nooksacks had largely abandoned their cursory affiliation with the Catholics and were open to the Methodists who had welcomed their own Captain John (settler James Bertrand's Nooksack brother-in-law) as a lay preacher.

John's conference expected him to address social issues. Northwestern Methodists campaigned against the abandonment of Indian families by white husbands. In addition to their long-standing belief in personal temperance, they saw alcohol as a major cause of the abandonments and supported local prohibition. Clara and John, by their example and encouragement, were also to demonstrate their commitment to keeping the Sabbath holy in a place where most people forgot Sunday observance. The church forbade gambling and raffles for any reason, even if John wanted to raise money to build a church at Ferndale, which he did.[95]

Like everything in which John Tennant became involved, his participation and responsibilities for the church conference quickly grew. They could count on him to preach far afield, including occasional visits to Orcas Island's few interested people. In 1884 he got the Ferndale church built, contributing his own labor and the couple's savings. By then John had been instrumental in the two major institutions that signaled the permanence of a western frontier community: schools and churches. People of many denominations usually helped build a church for that reason. The first one built symbolized the community's ability to gather diverse families, to eat together, to rest together from the hard life they led. It provided someplace "in town" to hold other types of meetings.[96]

At the same time, John became chairman of "Indian Work," a post he held intermittently until his death. To the conference, he was an obvious choice with his own heritage and his Lummi wife. That brought him into closer contact with his longtime Nooksack friends while he supervised the running of the new mission school, church, and dormitory they built at The Crossing's major village. By then, the Nooksacks were the largest Methodist congregation in the county, soon reaching 125.[97]

An anecdote in John Tennant's obituary reads: "At one time he and his wife were stationed among the Modocs at the Lava Beds, and endured great hardships, subsisting principally from bread made from the seeds of the water lily." This vivid anecdote must have come from the Tennants, though any records of their (perhaps very brief) service at the Oregon reservation have not been found. It may have been in the early 1880s when Bayard was away at school, the farm was successful, and John did not have a permanent assignment.[98]

ADA

John had not seen his Arkansas family for more than twenty years, but would soon be more involved than simply sending money. His long absence from church and home had distanced him both emotionally and geographically. His widowed sister Ada Pyeatt's new marriage to a son of influential Presbyterian minister John Buchanan deeply angered him when he heard about it. The Tennants and Buchanans had been estranged since the 1839 vigilante lynchings which Rev. Buchanan had led and Rev. Tennant opposed.[99]

The family warned Ada not to marry George Buchanan, but she was "so willful and such a fool." John quit writing to her. When she told her family she wanted out of the "hell on earth" marriage after twelve years but omitted details, they were unsympathetic. In his "miserable jealousy" the man moved Ada and her children to Kansas where he abused all of them, including sexual abuse of her daughter Eva.[100]

Ada finally revealed all after Eva died a young wife and mother herself. Ada had no money of her own and Buchanan threatened to harm the Tennants if they came to get her. When the family informed him, John's heart softened, perhaps urged by Clara's kindness. They invited Ada and her son Henry to come to them and John explained how different life was in Whatcom County, and about his intermarriage. He told her that Clara was the reason for his return to the Methodist Church, that she had saved his life when he thought he would die from the knife wound, and that she was "respected in the best of society." The letter Ada received implies that John wanted to make sure that she brought no airs of superiority with her.[101]

With time and planning, Ada and teenaged Henry Pyeatt escaped to her sister Harriet's Missouri home and left for Washington in April 1883. They took little other than family mementoes and Ada's new teeth. She left the Buchanan name behind on the two-week journey.[102]

Clara opened her home and heart to Ada and Henry for over seven months. John helped them file on land six miles away and he built them what Ada called a "real nice little boxhouse." The Tennants provided provisions for the first winter and work began on the homestead to support Ada's dream of "a good life for two people who came with nothing."[103]

Ada and Henry were lonely on the isolated homestead unless John and Clara came down the trail for a visit. Clara never got over her fear of horses and resolutely walked if John rode his horse. At Christmas, when Bayard was home from school, the Pyeatts spent the holiday with the family. John gifted both women with a pattern and wool for a new dress. Clara gave her impoverished sister-in-law slippers, an apron, and calico for quilting. John refused to let them go home through a winter storm and impassable trails for three weeks, during which the boys became best friends. Wrote Ada to her sister Miranda in Texas: "They have been just so good to us...Clara has been a sister indeed to me." She soon wrote that she possessed a peace she had never known.[104]

John hired Henry occasionally and Ada went to work in his real estate office before she became a certified teacher and found a teaching job. John's younger sister Nettie, her husband Peter Pyeatt, and his brother Finley migrated to Whatcom County within a few years of Ada's arrival, but left few tracks. There is no record of help from Clara and John, though they probably did. Nettie and Peter left after Finley died in 1889.[105]

BAYARD

Clara and John's son grew up handsome and intelligent, even innocent in his protected world, according to those who knew him. The Tennants spoiled him, from his pet canaries to his education. Probably at John's insistence, they sent him away to the Methodist Church's Olympia Collegiate Institute.[106]

Bayard was sick when he came home for that first Christmas with Ada and Henry. All his advantages and the love of his parents could not protect him from tuberculosis. The "white plague" caused one in seven American deaths at that time. In February, John asked Ada to help after the school sent Bayard home because he was worse. Perhaps she tried some of their mother's Indian healing ways and Clara may have tried hers, but they did not help. John sent the teenager to southern California for treatment in September 1884, though Clara apparently vehemently disagreed. Sanitariums clustered around Los Angeles where victims hoped the dry warm climate and sea winds would alleviate or cure the disease. Such a choice was available only to the well-to-do, and the Tennants had hard-won savings.[107]

The climate and treatment seemed to help for a few months, but then stopped six months after Bayard arrived in California. The sanitarium telegraphed John to come get his boy immediately. He left the next morning. When the doctors told John there was no hope, he and the dying eighteen-year-old started for home. They both wanted to get back to Clara so Bayard could say goodbye. When she heard they were close to arrival, she sent a horse for Ada so she would not have to wait alone. Albert, Henry, and Whis took the canoe to Whatcom to meet the steamer. When they arrived back at the Tennant dock, Ada was shocked. Bayard "looked like a corpse." Clara told her that she didn't know how she could have managed if Ada had not been at her side that awful moment.[108]

Clara, John, and Ada did everything they could for the beloved boy who was reduced to whispers. He complained very little, but when a sharp pain struck him in the side while his parents slept, he told Ada he was dying. He talked calmly about his death and they prayed together. When his parents woke up, he told them not to grieve too much. That was an impossible request. Bayard died on March 8, 1885, just a week after he got home.

Two days after Bayard's death, the funeral brought together two hundred family and friends to console his grieving parents. They buried him in a silver-trimmed casket beside John Jr., and Clara tended his flower-bedecked grave every day.[109]

Clara's grief was difficult for others to watch. One report said that her long black hair began to turn white. She had "spells" in which she seemed to stop breathing and her companions thought she had died. What they did not understand was that Clara's reactions were consistent with the Coast Salish grief process. Her sister Sarah and other family members stayed with her much of the time. A few years later, Clara told her friend Phoebe Judson that she believed if John had let her keep Bayard at home and used an Indian doctor that he would have recovered. This may have consumed her thoughts after the funeral.[110]

Ada wondered if Clara would ever recover. John told her that he didn't know what to do next, and would love to go "clear away" for five years, but nothing could change until Clara's grieving eased. She declared that she didn't care about her home or farm anymore without Bayard and gave his pet canary to the Pyeatts and other things to people who knew him.[111]

While Clara was sunk in grief, John made plans to leave. They would go to Orcas where no established congregation existed, but they knew many of the island's intermarried families. John wanted the Pyeatts to take the farm so he would feel "safe" about it, but Henry was young and already responsible for two homesteads. He knew he could not handle those and also manage the extensive Tennant place, particularly since Albert and Sarah had moved to their new allotment. John and Clara understood. They gave Henry some livestock, then rented out their farm to a young couple John knew.

When she recovered enough, they moved very quickly. Clara and John walked away from *Si'lat'sis* and never returned.

John had taken on the father role for young Henry who had protected his mother and started his own farm. The Tennants stayed at Ada's for three days before they left. John praised what the teenager had accomplished, encouraged him to stick with his hard work, and assured him that he would soon have a good farm on one of the best pieces of ground in the county. And then Clara and John were gone, less than two months after Bayard's death.

In a tribute to the love Clara and John had given to his family, Ada wrote to her sister Miranda about her loneliness. "How we do miss Brother John's folks. We could always go there any time and it was like home. Now we feel like we have no place to go. We have lots of friends but no connection to visit."[112]

CLARA AND JOHN

Clara and John, mourning their son and their dreams, arrived at Charles Shattuck's Eastsound dock. For $100 a year and any donations from cash-strapped homesteaders, the Tennants would work to increase the Methodist congregation. It had grown from the original three after he converted twenty-six more people at a revival. His

The village of Eastsound on Orcas Island, 1906. The town had grown around the Episcopal Church (left) and the Methodist Church whose steeple can be seen on the right. The Episcopal Church had more money and outside help when it was built, compared with the Methodist Church built by a small, cash-poor congregation under the supervision of Rev. John Tennant. *Unknown photographer. Courtesy of Orcas Island Historical Museum, all rights reserved.*

ability to reach hearts had been clearly demonstrated. John rowed his canoe as much as fifteen miles through heavy currents and sudden windstorms to half a dozen preaching points on three islands. Sometimes he walked miles inland to reach families he pastored. And then he waited and hoped that people would come to listen to his preaching and sing the old Methodist hymns that comforted him.[113]

John wrote to Ada that they were "as well satisfied as they would be anywhere," and Clara was feeling much better. She had much to do to help John, to build a small home and to start her garden, so much to occupy her mind. The couple had once lived in a small cabin. They had survived the near-fatal canoe accident on the Nooksack, and now the loss of their last child. They had the strength to live the simple life of missionaries.[114]

They began holding services in the primitive log school, which contrasted with the pretty Episcopalian Church whose members protested John's use of a public building. His congregants were not the islanders with money to spare and East Coast financial support to build their church. Soon the Tennants built and nicely furnished a tidy three-room house facing the beach.[115]

Christmas continued to be the island's biggest event. Settlers came out of the woods to canoe the two fjords that split Orcas into three peninsulas, and they didn't make the effort for just one day. The island's two ministers added a new dimension to the usual raucous overnight party at the Shattucks' store. Facing Christmas services for the islanders, Clara and John would have to pretend that the first holiday without Bayard was still a celebration. John wrote to Ada and "begged so hard" that the Pyeatts made the winter journey to the islands to be with them. Ada found John's appearance alarming after eight months, and blamed it on his "large work" rather than his grief. She found that islanders liked and admired her brother for his "kindness, and fidelity and energy." One islander concluded that Episcopalian Rev. Sidney Gray was also well-liked, but he lacked John's magnetism, intelligence, and money-sense.[116]

Christmas was an interfaith holiday on Orcas for those who were religious, despite the rising competition between the two churches. The crowd just wanted to wring every bit of celebration they could out of it, so they started at the Episcopal Church with a tree lighting on Christmas Eve. Then everyone tramped across the muddy road to the log school, where John led a prayer meeting. Shattuck's was probably the next stop for most people. The next day, everyone gathered again at the school where John preached a "heart-searching sermon on the birth of Christ, equal to a bishop's," observed his sister. A "basket dinner" at long tables built for the occasion followed, starting with nuts and candy for the children. It all kept Clara busy.[117]

Ada and Henry accompanied the Tennants to another place on the island that weekend for preaching and a Sunday school session. Enoch May and his indigenous wife took the four home with them. When the Pyeatts left for the mainland, they carried their gift of silver dinner spoons from Clara and John. Ada concluded her holiday letter to her sister with "I am ever so proud of them."[118]

The old missionary, abolitionist, and spy Rev. Thomas Tennant died six months after Bayard. Weakened by extreme old age, he was lovingly cared for by John's stepmother and the local siblings, but after his death his two families began to argue and fight over who should inherit the farm. Because John was a lawyer, the large blended family expected him to mediate from across the country. He would surely alienate someone and that turned out to be his sister Miranda. Christeen's children believed the farm had been purchased with her money and Miranda insisted from Texas that the second family should not inherit. John had to inform her that the first family had no more inheritance rights than any of Thomas Tennant's second family.[119]

A year after Bayard's death, John started to plan a real church for Orcas and its congregation, grown to forty poor and scattered people who had donated only $36 the entire year. He wrote to his presiding elder to leave him there since a family would starve, but he and Clara knew how to live on clams. Just as he had in Ferndale, he threw everything into the building project, including his and Clara's savings. The church trustees borrowed money, got started, and applied for a grant. With the guidance of a trained carpenter in the congregation, John and the men worked for many months until they could worship in the unfinished space. By then over budget and in debt, they hoped the Extension Board in Philadelphia would soon send money.[120]

John's congregation had grown to over one hundred members, converted by his preaching and care for them. The congregation was exhausted financially and physically from working on their church. Some farmers had even taken second jobs just for money to contribute, which broke John's heart. He wrote to his presiding elder that they might lose the church because they'd put it up as collateral for a loan. When Methodist headquarters finally sent a grant, the men quickly finished. John had been ordained after eight years of study and tests, so he and Clara proudly donated the preacher's chair and stand he would use. At the dedication, he made a final appeal for help to pay the remaining $110 debt. In eight minutes, the community and visiting ministers donated every penny.[121]

To Orcas Islanders, John was "indispensable" and Clara, the "good Christian woman" fit in with everyone else. They wanted to keep them on the island, but that was not to be. John had become a congregation and church builder, and Lynden, a growing town of sixty-five people north of Whatcom, was ready for a real church.[122]

CRBD

For two and a half years after the deaths of Bayard and John's father, Clara and her husband focused all their energy on missionary activities. For the first time, the farm and all its chores were gone. Building a future around their son was over. Instead, John built congregations and churches. He rode the circuit through all kinds of weather to preach, as his father had done. He married people. He buried people. He was the secretary of his Methodist conference. He kept an eye on the Nooksack Mission's development.

It was a lot for a man in his late 50s.

In early November 1887, ten years after John rejoined his church and devoted his life (and Clara's) to its growth, he suffered a stroke that paralyzed his entire right side. The Lynden church project was already underway, funded in large part by the Tennants. Once again, he had put his muscle as well as his money into the project. Perhaps with a premonition, he had signed a new will just a week before. Clara nursed John round-the-clock at the little house they had built in Lynden until he resumed preaching only two months later. Though he may not have been able to get up on the roof anymore, construction went forward. By July the church was ready to occupy, boosted by the women's strawberry festival fundraiser to buy chandeliers.[123]

As he often had, John added work instead of cutting back. When he and Clara attended the annual conference meeting, once again he became chairman of the Indian Affairs Committee. He started the conference on the path to a better boarding school for the Nooksack people. The Tennants hosted the quarterly Methodist meeting after the dedication of the Lynden church, which required them to head up a large hospitality effort. The rest of the time, he preached twice on Sundays, held Sunday School between the two services, and hosted a prayer meeting on Wednesday evenings.

On November 27, 1888, one year after the first stroke, another one struck.

The Lynden *Pioneer Press* expressed the community's hopes for his recovery. On New Year's Day, it announced that he would be back in the pulpit the next Sunday for two services, assisted by another minister. Optimistically, the editor wrote "It is quite probable that services will be held regularly from this time, as Rev. Tennant is steadily improving in health and strength." The congregation missed the stirring sermons given in his thrilling voice so like his father's, but now his voice surely was weakening or impaired even if his message of salvation was not. The people didn't seem to care.[124]

CRBO

John didn't stop. He formally retired, then returned to pastor the Nooksack Mission where services often lasted three hours. He supervised the building of a new church for the Nooksack at The Crossing (today's Everson), but he could not write the membership's formal records as he once had. His health failed again.[125]

John had a third stroke in early April 1892. The Bellingham paper noted that he was not expected to survive. No more optimism about his future. It was front page news and the editor reminded people of his important role in the early county's history. A few days later, the paper repeated the lack of hope. Nursed by Clara (and probably Ada), John was in "comparative comfort...but occasionally suffers intense pain. He does not expect to survive long and calmly awaits the last summons." Contrary to expectations, John did not die, but he remained nearly helpless and unable to walk. His final accomplishment, the Stickney Island School for Nooksack children, opened that year.[126]

For another ten months Clara took devoted care of her paralyzed husband of thirty-four years. The ice was a foot deep on the river when John Tennant died at age sixty-three on February 12, 1893. At his funeral, the appropriate message for the large crowd was that he had fought the good fight, finished the course, and kept the faith. Clara buried him next to their sons at the new Lynden cemetery where they had been moved after the Tennants and Judsons donated the land. The *Bellingham Bay Express* noted that Clara was "faithful to him unto death" and repeated the farm's reputation as the finest in the county. Erroneously, it and the *Daily Reveille* called him half-Cherokee and the son of a long-time Cherokee missionary, which started an enduring myth.[127]

CLARA

When John died, Clara was undoubtedly emotionally and physically spent after caring for him during his ten months of paralysis. The court affirmed her competency to administer the complex estate, as John wished. Calling Clara his "beloved wife" in the 1887 will that gave her everything, John trusted her intelligence and wisdom. Her inheritance included 74 theology books, an organ, and a buggy. Not only was there property in Ferndale, Marietta, and Lynden as well as the farm to manage, but the couple had substantial savings in the bank.[128]

For the next ten years, Clara husbanded the property and money she and John had built up together. Sarah and Albert's son-in-law Peter James, a Duwamish lawyer, collected rents for Clara and advised her on legal matters. She turned extra cash from rents and the sale of property into bonds. She lived up to the faith her husband had placed in her.[129]

No evidence makes clear what Clara's other activities were during those ten years, but she continued to live in her small house near the Lynden Methodist Church that John had given the last of his energy to build. She remained devoted to her adopted religion and her many friends in the church. Clara knitted and sold socks which led friends to think she had little money, but she may have been doing it to raise money for church projects. She probably continued to show interest in Stickney School across the river that the Tennants and "Lynden Jim" Selhameten had worked together to establish. Clara remained Ada's closest friend and probably enjoyed being Great Aunt Clara to Henry's children. Four of Clara's siblings still lived at Lummi with their families, and it is unlikely that she failed to renew and strengthen her relationships with them. Whis had gone to live on one of the Nooksack homesteads, and stayed active in the Methodist Mission.

James Selhameten Yelewqaynem, Nooksack leader of Sqweha:lich village across from the young town of Lynden. He was the second husband of Clara Tennant and donor of the land for the Stickney School. *Percival Jeffcott Collection #1347, Center for Pacific Northwest Studies, Western Libraries Heritage Resources. Western Washington University, Bellingham, Washington.*

CLARA AND JIM SELHAMETEN YELEWQAYNEM

Clara, daughter of Tsi'lixw and "Mrs. Annie," was a resilient woman who had thrived despite major changes in her life.

After ten years, Clara's life entered its fourth act when two old friends married at the Lynden Methodist Church. Clara was about sixty, and "Lynden Jim" Selhameten was somewhere between seventy-five and ninety-two, depending on the census or who was estimating. Their marriage record said he was seventy-five. Clara, tall and imposing, must have towered over Jim's four feet, five inches.[130]

Both of them were well-known, important, and respected elders among both white and indigenous communities. They had their own shared history over half a century and probably longer, including the canoe disaster that nearly killed them. Newcomers may have failed to recognize the couple's place in county history and decades of concern with the spiritual and temporal futures of everyone who lived there. Bellingham's *Evening Herald* wished happiness to two deserving community-builders.[131]

In addition to friendship, both people had impeccable genealogies, each closely related to all the influential head men in their respective groups. Both knew multiple languages. Methodist records noted that Jim was the first convert "on the Nooksack River," and his *Sqweha:lich* longhouse had sheltered river travelers and worshippers alike in the old days. He had worked tirelessly with the Tennants to build the Nooksack congregation and its schools. It was Jim who donated a piece of his homestead for Stickney Indian School.[132]

Jim Selhameten Yelewqaynem had a very long history with settlers. Travelers exchanged salt water canoes and Nooksack shovel nose river canoes at his village. A major trail to the Fraser River began across the river from *Sqweha:lich*. Jim and his men had worked as packers for Russell Peabody, moving supplies to the Boundary Survey crew up that trail. Jim and one of his earlier wives had helped move Lynden founders, the Judsons, and their belongings upstream to the Patterson ranch across from his village, which started their long friendship. He was not the paramount leader of the Nooksacks, but he was the best known to whites, and a man who recognized that his people could not keep the intruders out permanently.[133]

Jim Selhameten filed the first Nooksack Indian homestead in 1874, supported by John Tennant's affidavit. He selected 160 acres around his village which kept his family's home intact. He had to swear that he had severed his tribal ties and would live as a white man. It was, of course, malarkey. When no one prevented him from obtaining the papers, the way was open for others to do the same without fear of losing their identity.[134]

Clara's new husband had also fulfilled the headman's obligation to take care of orphans and the poor over many decades. According to friend Phoebe Judson, "many of the sick and unfortunate, the lame, the halt and the blind found a home in his camp to end their days in peace." After his intermarried sister Nina McClanahan and her husband Dan died, Jim stayed involved in their four children's lives while they lived across the river with the Judsons. He raised the half-Nooksack children of Whatcom merchant Charles Richards after he deserted them and their despairing mother committed suicide. John Tennant, Jim, and the missionary society almost certainly worked together to send the brilliant little boy Johnny Richards, raised in Jim's longhouse with his mother's Nooksack values, on to an eastern college and a degree in engineering. Other settlers' children remembered his kindness and friendship, and one dedicated his memoir to Jim.[135]

At Jim's advanced age, he had a long marital history. Some said he had been married a dozen times but the settlers knew only of two or three wives he had outlived. John Tennant had officiated at Jim's last marriage in 1890, but he had long been alone when Clara married him. They were two lonely, accomplished people who found comfort in each other during their last years.[136]

Clara moved into Jim's cabin that had replaced his longhouse for a residence, and the impeccable housekeeper probably got things tidied in a hurry. A Lynden pioneer son who knew them both wrote that Clara "accepted all her original way of life. And was content."[137]

Clara and Jim's time together was brief, only about three months. She contracted pneumonia in the rainy, windy, cold autumn months. Phoebe Judson visited her the day she died, and was surprised that her old friend was able to give specific instructions for her funeral. Clara wanted to wear her black silk dress, be in a "handsome" casket carried to the church where John had officiated. She wanted to be laid to rest next to John and their two boys. Clara died on November 28, 1903, and her wishes were fulfilled by all those who loved her. Her headstone also bears her father's name. As both a Nooksack and a Methodist, Jim would have seen that the guests were well fed and taken care of with the help of her friends and family, but it wasn't what the newspaper wanted to talk about.[138]

A Lynden paper printed news of Clara's funeral with the (apparently) surprising news that $2,000 had been found in her trunk and she owned considerable property. Two months later, when the probate case started, the *Bellingham Herald* printed an article that said "Odd as it may seem this old Indian woman left wealth in real estate and money to the extent of about $12,000." It mentioned her gold and silver coins, bank notes, plus mortgages and notes payable to herself. The comparable sum in 2016 would be about $320,000. The paper surmised that she had guarded her holdings with a "miserly instinct which seemed bent on amassing a fortune with no apparent object in view save to have plenty of money." It then called her a "simple old child of nature." Bellingham's other major paper ignored her death.[139]

Clara had acted upon the teachings of both of her worlds. She had followed her traditional teaching to conserve and accumulate for when times grew bad and there were necessities she could not produce herself. She honored John with the way she lived up to his faith in her abilities. Money gave her entrance to the advantages of the white world and power for those who had it. If she chose to help someone, she could.

Clara's probate case went on for two years after her siblings challenged the will that left everything to her new husband. Many legal maneuvers culminated in a civil court trial. When a compromise was reached, Jim still got most of the estate (including the buggy and organ), and following her example, he built it even larger before he died in 1911.[140]

CHAPTER 5

Nellie, An American Family

J IM CARR WAS DYING. With every labored breath he knew the pneumonia would not be defeated. The fever would not break. The chills would not cease. The coughing would not stop. He was going to die and his too-young Sto:lo (stah-lo) wife Nellie and their baby would be alone in the cabin.

What happened next became family legend.

The dying man told Nellie to get his horse and hurry to Sheriff Fred Lane. "Go get my friend. I want to see him before I die. I want to tell him something."

Lane's land claim adjoined Carr's, but the sheriff was often miles away in town, sometimes in the islands. She thought Lane had taken the canoe to his place in town, but she ran down to where she saw his horse tethered. Lane was still there and saw Nellie's distressed face. When he asked what was wrong she gave him Carr's message.

Back at the cabin, Carr told Lane that he was dying and said "I want you to take good care of my wife and baby."[1]

Helene "Nellie" Carr had no local family. To return to her mother near the Fraser River demanded that she find someone to canoe her upriver to *Sqweha:lich,* then find a Nooksack escort to take her up the trail into Sto:lo country. The trip would take days and it was early 1867. The weather veered from clear and cold to snow and rain. The Arctic winds that funneled down the river to the prairies might come at any time. It was too early in the year for such an arduous journey with a baby.[2]

The too-young wife became a too-young widow. F. F. Lane did not take her home to her family. No one did.

Lane married her instead.

NELLIE (HELENE)

Nellie came from the village of *Math'qui* (Mat'kwee) in the Interior
Salish world of Halkomelem-speakers, now called the *Sto:lo*. They
have lived along the lower Fraser River for 10,000 years, where the
physical environment differs from that of the coastal villages. After
the turbulent river's turn west not far north of the international
boundary, it flows almost placidly to its delta where the world's largest salmon runs still start for home.

During Nellie's time, the Sto:lo lived in a multitude of villages
between "the evil one" (Lady Franklin Rock) at the mouth of the
Fraser Canyon and the delta. They commanded 105 miles of abrupt
jagged mountains, long Ice Age lakes, prairies, and numerous tributaries. The river was the primary food source and highway for the
people of each watershed. The Sto:lo knew "its floods and shallows,
its winter ice, its deep pools, rapids, beaches, snags, and rocks as inti-
mately as a child in a large city knows his own block." The highway
brought coastal visitors, some friendly and some not.[3]

The two-day paddle from the delta forty miles to *Math'qui* took
less time going downriver, but there were always friends and family
to visit along the way and any trip could take more time than anticipated. The name *Math'qui* ("easy portage") referred to the short distance to drag a canoe south to the Nooksack River tributaries.

Nellie's world of the broad alluvial plain was broken here and
there by a solitary low mountain associated with a lake and river. The
size of the shallow lake beneath Sumas Mountain varied seasonally
and was home to millions of birds and other wildlife. On Nellie's
southern horizon, Mount Baker and the Cascade peaks soared. If
a warm winter Chinook wind blew from the south, the mountain
snows melted quickly and severe flooding endangered the villages.
Nellie and her family had to be prepared to move to higher ground
momentarily. Like the saltwater Coast Salish villages, Sto:lo ones
didn't always last forever.

The Sto:lo people were bound loosely together by shared territories, language, and their common immortal ancestors who long ago
transformed into geographic features. Marriages strengthened ties,
including those with the Nooksack families down trail and tributary
with whom they shared some resource sites.

When British explorer Simon Fraser stopped at *Math'qui* in 1808, he noted the elaborate carvings in the village's 640-foot-long cedar house. During Nellie's childhood, the longhouse was still the primary dwelling for about fifty people. The village's most important asset, the salmon smokehouse, ensured winter survival and provided a commodity to trade or sell to the Hudson's Bay Company (HBC). *Math'qui* prairie hosted the most important deer-hunting area for all the Sto:lo, and the village women and girls grew large numbers of vegetables there.[4]

Because the Fraser linked thousands of people whose habits and dialects changed minutely but continuously from delta to canyon, it brought sickness along with travelers. Epidemics entered the watershed through the indigenous trading routes two generations before the HBC built Fort Langley in 1827. The first killed perhaps two-thirds of the thousands of Sto:lo people, and those that came in the 1790s via the coast added enough deaths to finish the destruction of 90% of the dense population. Nellie's people remembered the epidemics with oral history and place names. They called one spot "a lot of people died at once" and another was "people container" for a mass grave.[5]

Laich'wil'tach raids intensified with the arrival of the HBC forts because they offered seasonal jobs, after which they plundered. Up to seventy invaders in each of as many as sixty ocean-going canoes paddled and sailed upriver from the coast as far as they could navigate. Despite epidemics, in the nineteenth century the valley was still so densely populated that raiders could find thousands of people at twenty-four watersheds in a matter of a few days. It was far easier for the raiders to kidnap and plunder along the river than among the scattered salt water villages. The Sto:lo increased their village defenses of reed-covered pits, caves, tunnels, and rock walls facing the river. The defensive sites at Nellie's village and others inside sloughs and side channels gave the Stol:lo more time to organize against an attack because the war canoes could not enter shallow water.[6]

Family memory and documents put Nellie's probable birth date in 1851. A catastrophic failure of the Fraser salmon runs made it easy to remember. It was also about three years after a killer measles epidemic, and a time of village abandonment and the building of new ones. During Nellie's childhood, the places of traditional cultural interchange along the river had to contend with constant foreign influence and the host of pressures and opportunities it brought: sickness, jobs, trade, new technology, a gold rush, and missionary activity that competed with indigenous spirituality. At the same time, once the British forts were built, some newcomers entered the Sto:lo matrix of friendship and marriage.[7]

The 1858 Fraser River gold rush brought unprecedented numbers of Americans to Nellie's village via the river and the Whatcom Trail. Little Nellie witnessed the invasion of about thirty thousand men whose largest campground was at nearby Chilliwack River's prairie. *Math'qui* families found new opportunities to sell salmon and other goods to miners desperate for fresh food and supplies as they trekked north into the canyon. Miners also brought abuse and crime but some men appreciated the Sto:lo's traditional hospitality, and occasionally that resulted in intermarriage rather than rape and disrespect.[8]

The smallpox epidemic of 1862-63 may have killed twenty thousand First Nations people in today's British Columbia, about two-thirds of the population rebuilt after the previous scourges. Only one group there was spared its genocidal force—Nellie's people, the Sto:lo of lower British Columbia. Why?[9]

The answer lies with the arrival of Oblate Father Leon Fouquet in November 1860. By the end of December, the physically fragile priest had visited dozens of villages and baptized some five hundred persons. Given her French baptismal name, "Helene," that may have included Nellie. He established St. Mary's Mission (today's Mission, B.C.) across the river from *Math'qui*. As smallpox loomed two years later, the few mission priests obtained vaccine from Victoria and started to inoculate the Sto:lo. They vaccinated over eight thousand First Nations people, settlers, and Nooksacks to the south. Other places experienced major village abandonment, consolidation, and cultural disruption. The Sto:lo survived nearly intact numerically and culturally, among them Nellie and her family.[10]

The large stone across the river from *Math'qui* kept the century's challenges in mind anytime Nellie's family saw it. The Sto:lo told that in a long-ago time, their leaders were turned into the stone because they did not adopt new ways to preserve and protect traditional culture. Nellie's people saw lessons in the stone to guide them in their own time of change and uncertainty.[11]

Efforts to find tangible facts about Nellie's early history within this context have stymied researchers. Custom did not include a surname in the way required by American documents so women gave their father's name, their village name, or something else. Those on Nellie's adult documents include Healwas, Holmes, Howen, Halls, Holms, even George. Her own clearest statement was when she gave "Halms (an Indian name)" for her father on a marriage certificate. Some of the confusion may stem from the problems of nineteenth century script coupled with county clerks lacking familiarity with Halkomelem sounds. No one seems to have called Nellie by her baptismal name "Helene" until it appeared on probate records after her death. She told a great-granddaughter that she had three brothers and she went home to her *Math'qui* family throughout her adult life. Family has discovered little else of her early history.[12]

The picture of Nellie's early life must be drawn from that of typical *Math'qui* girls of her time. Fort Langley had become a major factor in the lives of the Sto:lo after the HBC switched from the fur trade to salmon. Sto:lo historians believe that when it was built in 1827, the families saw it as just another resource location. They made it a trading partner for their salmon, cranberries, nuts, meat, shellfish, and other excess products. Employees and traders from First Nations families controlled the fort's incoming products more and more as the years passed. They wanted the store's useful and decorative merchandise, including some clothing, but families drove hard bargains for their equally attractive commodities. The fort also offered Sto:lo men cash work logging, stevedoring, and at other jobs. Women profited from their baskets and other handmade goods.[13]

Even with the presence of the HBC and the mission across the river, Sto:lo life continued much as it had with the additions of the new trading partner and new religious activities to add to the traditional ones. Winter continued to be a time of inside activities, but sturgeon fishing made the season different at *Math'qui* from that upriver and on the coast. Fishermen used flexible poles as long as 60 feet to probe river bottoms for the white prehistoric-looking fish that could weigh a ton and provide an important winter diet addition.

When the spring eulachon run began, everyone gathered in camps at the mouth of the Sumas River to harvest thousands of the small oily fish to boil and smoke. Summer salmon harvests were nearly identical to the coastal villages, though the migration of coastal people with family ties to the Fraser fishery was heavier than to other locations. *Math'qui* families moved to upland camps in the fall for the men to hunt bear and mountain goats, and women to gather late plants and berries for food and medicines.

The Halkomelem word for "relative" is the same as "friend." The greeting of "Hello, how are you?" was really a spirit-to-spirit inquiry about the well-being of body and soul, a much deeper greeting than that of English-speakers. These concepts were so deeply ingrained that during late fall trips to the delta, one of a family's numerous stops to visit along the way could turn into a winter's stay, or even a permanent move.[14]

Few (or no) women ever remained spinsters, according to anthropologist Wilson Duff's informants. Nellie's people liked large families and the bountiful environment supported them. Sto:lo girls generally married young, very soon after their puberty seclusion and skill-learning time. Unlike the Coast Salish whose young women usually married someone from a distant village, a husband most often chosen by Sto:lo parents came from a geographically adjacent group regardless of the language or customs. For a girl like Nellie, marrying an American who spoke a foreign language would not seem too much different. The Sto:lo were less tolerant of divorce than the coastal families. It may have been almost nonexistent among elite families who often took the deserting wife back home to her husband, especially if there were children.[15]

James Carr

Ship's carpenter James Carr was a New Yorker born in 1826. Perhaps he learned the craft from his father or as an apprentice at the docks of New York harbor, but he left no other clues about his early life other than his profession. He was Frederick F. Lane's friend in California and Lane's own shipbuilding background in Massachusetts may have led to crossed paths.[16]

Carr arrived at Whatcom in mid-1853 likely with Henry Roeder's first mill employees. Carr and Enoch Compton didn't like the work or their bosses because they tried a squatter's claim on *Shais'quihl* (March Point) where they encroached on Caroline Davis Kavanaugh's Samish territory (*see* chapter 2). The men built a cabin and took individual claims to the north and south of her family's now-seasonal village. They raised one crop on the fern prairie, but retreated to Whatcom in the face of Samish hostility and their exposed position when the *Laich'wil'tach* raiders were showing no mercy to isolated settlers on land or water.[17]

Back in Whatcom, Carr worked on the construction of Roeder's *H.C. Page,* a seventy-foot schooner-rigged scow, the third commercial vessel built on Puget Sound. The slow flat-bottomed vessel was a reliable carrier of livestock and large shipments, and was the only local vessel other than Coast Salish canoes. When settlers organized a militia company for the Treaty War a hundred miles south, he was one of the few men who didn't enlist. He was probably more valuable to the local community repairing boats and equipment.[18]

By spring 1857 now-"Captain" James Carr was living with the Roeders and piloting the *Page* around the Sound. His duties included obtaining goods for local wives who lived far from stores. It was not business-as-usual in April when Northern canoes followed him up the Sound for days from Port Townsend water. The Olympia newspaper told readers that the troubled *Page's* previous captain had been shot by a crewmember just a month before, and that apparently was how Carr got his new position.[19]

The sparse all-male electorate made Joseph Jewett the second county sheriff, after the first drowned during a drunken nighttime canoe ride with some friends. Jewett did not stay long and the county commissioners appointed Carr the new sheriff in January 1858, a few months before the chaos of the gold rush began, and a month after former Lieutenant Robert Hugh Davis was appointed deputy sheriff. Carr conveniently resigned on May 19 just as the population exploded into the summer's social chaos. It freed him to concentrate on his job with Russell Peabody's pack train to the U.S. Boundary Survey Commission depot on Chilliwack prairie in Sto:lo territory.[20]

Two years after the survey crew moved east, Carr and his California friend Lane had moved in with another New Yorker, shipwright
James Taylor. All of them boarded at the home of William Woods
and his Samish wife. Taylor, Carr, and Lane began their longtime
work association on the construction of Roeder's much larger vessel,
the *General Harney*, an eighty-eight-foot-long schooner-rigged scow
capable of carrying much larger cargoes for settlers, the army, and the
Boundary Commission headquarters at Semiahmoo Bay.[21]

Carr began the transition to a piece of ground on the *Noos'kwiem*
a few miles downstream from John and Clara Tennant. Taylor and
Carr took adjoining (even overlapping) claims on a slough with
access to the meandering river. The two men did more boat repair
and freighting from that base. Their sheltered location within reservation boundaries (like Tennant's agricultural claim) gave them
direct access to the best water route inland on the Nooksack River to
the old HBC trails north to the Fraser River.[22]

Tennant and Carr began to help each other. Tennant helped Carr
build a "house" over two days in December 1862 so he could establish
residency. Carr owned his own scow (perhaps in partnership with
Taylor and Lane) that, along with Tennant's Salish canoe, could
move farm or logging commodities to town. The men went back and
forth to help each other cut timber, hunt, and bring in hogs and cattle
from the marshes. Carr owned a grindstone and some blacksmithing
equipment which helped when there were barrels and tools to fab-
ricate, as well as axes and saws to sharpen. It was Carr who built the
little coffin when the Tennant's toddler died.[23]

In the early 1860s gold miners had moved hundreds of miles up
the Fraser River to the "Cariboo." Carr went to work as a drover on
Roeder's new venture driving cattle to the distant gold fields. When
Roeder made his first trip north in July 1862, the crew camped at
the former camp of the Boundary Survey. The trail led through the
Math'qui prairie. Carr and Nellie probably met during that first cattle
drive north or as he returned. She remembered 1862 as the year she
married him, though it may have been early 1863 after he and Tennant finished the cabin.[24]

The flood of miners who passed through the *Math'qui* neighborhood after 1858 seemed endless to Sto:lo families. These men were

unlike the many Fort Langley employees married to Sto:lo women. Unruly, defiant, and ungoverned, most of them presented immediate dangers of assault and rape to the women and girls. They were equally dangerous to fathers who tried to intervene. Nellie's family may have considered integrating Carr into their family and village network to be a good solution to serious problems, in the same way many Fraser River Canyon families had already done.

Nellie's marriage at age eleven or twelve (as she repeatedly confirmed) to thirty-six-year-old American James Carr was not necessarily unique. In fact, colonial settler marriages in British Columbia at the same time had similar age patterns. Nearly half the brides were teenagers as young as twelve, and grooms averaged eight years older. In the nineteenth century American West, there were many pre-teen brides, enabling the men to legally file for more land. The 1850 Oregon Donation Claim Act gave couples double the acreage and made marriage to very young girls more acceptable to Pacific Northwest settlers. The first Washington Territorial Indian Agent married a fifteen-year-old before he headed to his new post, and defended large age differences as a response to harsh frontier life that made girls grow up fast. Most U.S. states set the age of consent for girls at ten to twelve for most of the nineteenth century, which was a time of general marriage inequality and paternalism.[25]

From Carr's perspective, Nellie would provide a home life and domestic labor at his American land claim. Without a documented legal marriage, Nellie would be entitled to nothing in Washington Territory if he deserted her. In British Columbia there was continual pressure on white husbands to regularize their marriages, but to do so required a long journey to Victoria for the license. That became another excuse for men who wanted an "out" so they could eventually abandon their wives, and many missionaries actively discouraged legal marriage to a First Nations woman. Nellie's "custom of the country" marriage with its exchange of goods and obligations followed the general pattern of the time in Canada's HBC country.

Nellie remembered her wedding. She said she was "taken from her home by Jim Carr," a description that implies a wrenching experience for the too-young wife. Family members have believed that he did not give a big enough gift to her parents, said to be a hundred sacks of flour, which descendants did not think enough to make up for the loss of a daughter. Carr may have given other goods or labor, but people remembered only the flour. With the miners and drovers passing through *Math'qui,* the flour could have been turned into a larger value commodity by selling it in smaller quantities at inflated prices, but this was not part of the memory passed down.[26]

The basic facts remain: pre-teen Nellie had no customary right to choose her own husband and Carr was about twenty-five years older. Indigenous and a minor, she would have no legal rights in the United States. These add an element to the relationship that by any standard today would be considered sexually abusive and criminal, as her family sees them.

Carr brought Nellie home to his cabin on the *Noos'kwiem.* He continued to transport goods in his canoe and scow, as well as bartered tasks with Tennant. Like many before him across the frontiers of America, Nellie provided required evidence that he was living at the land claim, and he could roam at will. He added hogs and cattle, and with Tennant cut and sold wild hay from the sloughs and wetlands along the river, much of which they had no right to take. Like on nearly every American farm, the chickens and garden would have been Nellie's responsibility.[27]

As young as she was, Nellie still presented advantages as a farm wife. In addition to her labor, she could find and prepare local foodstuffs since her family would not have let her go into a marriage without those skills. Nevertheless, her routine in the isolated cabin was alien to the longhouse life of her childhood. Carr expected his very young wife to cook and clean alone. The learning process may have been long and challenging, but she became a memorably excellent cook and talented artisan.

If she was lonely and homesick, Nellie had the occasional company of women who spoke her Halkomelem language because two wives from *Su'math* lived in town. Nearby, Lummi wife Clara Tennant probably spoke Halkomelem as one of her secondary languages, as would many others who came down the river from the Nooksack villages.

Nellie and James lived on the *Noos'kwiem* between four and five years. Some of her descendants maintained that he took their first baby away from her, but the evidence is sketchy. A "James Carr Jr."

lived on Orcas Island in 1885, and if he was their son, a recorded birthdate of 1853, not 1863, was a clerical or transcription error. Carr Jr. was baptized and confirmed at the Lummi Reservation church in 1893, which would put him near Nellie and her family. She gave birth to Lucy Carr in 1866 or early 1867.[28]

Nellie's husband died of pneumonia in early 1867. A Nooksack River winter included slogging through icy flooded sloughs and wetlands after livestock, and working outside in the ever-changing weather. Settlers suffered from few diseases common to their former homes, but exposure could lead to pneumonia, deadly without modern drugs. And so, despite any remedies available from his culture, or Nellie's or Clara Tennant's, Jim Carr died in the little cabin. He left behind a widow of perhaps sixteen, far from home and alone with little Lucy. The only thing he could do for her at the end was to extract Fred Lane's promise to care for her and the baby. She had no right to the land or custody of her American child. He left no will that would give her even his personal effects and tools.

FREDERICK F. LANE

Frederick Fomme Lane would one day teach his children to sail the family schooner, and a navigational light would be part of his family's life as one was in his youth. He carried west his expertise and family's maritime history from the village of Annisquam, Massachusetts, near Gloucester. He was much more than a mere California gold rush prospector come north for the Fraser rush, as some have described him.

Fifty-five years after Wampanoag leader Massasoit welcomed the Pilgrims, his son Metacomet and allies revolted against the colonists' insatiable hunger for land. One of their victims was James Lane, an English carpenter on Lane's Island, Maine. His son John decided that a move down the coast to Cape Ann, Massachusetts, made sense. One of Fred Lane's other ancestors had been the first to colonize the place thirty miles northeast of Boston that faced Newfoundland's cod-rich Grand Banks.[29]

By the end of the 1600s, Annisquam residents built boats as well as fished, and when a local man invented the schooner in 1713, their future as shipbuilders was cemented. The Lanes lived and did business on Lobster Cove off the small tidal Annisquam River. It was perfect for ship construction and trading vessels because neither its entrance nor tall masts could be seen by passing pirates. If they found their way in, Lanes and other defenders lining the narrow channel found them easy targets.

Fred Lane's ancestors built their fortune upon each maritime advance by Annisquam residents. They built and commanded ships to sail the world, while cousins became major players in the Grand Banks fishery, working out of Lane's Cove and Lanesville on the cape's ocean side. Fred's male ancestors intermarried with the Griffins and Phippins, the other major maritime families. On Lobster Cove, his great-grandfather Gideon took command of one of the era's largest trading vessels, and each generation made their mark in peace and in war.[30]

Fred's grandfather (Gideon II) and his wife bought an imposing five-bedroom Greek Revival home high on the wedge of land between river and cove. The mansion (sporting thirteen columns for the thirteen colonies) in which Fred Lane would grow up stayed in his family for over 120 years. Gardens and lawns sprawled above the moorage for Lane family ships.[31]

Fred's grandparents married the same year Captain Robert Gray and the *Columbia* returned to Boston from a voyage to the Pacific Northwest and around the world. Once the "Boston men" found that sea otter pelts attracted Chinese buyers, and goods like tea, silk, and porcelain yielded huge profits at home, new ships for the China trade were in demand. Fred's grandfather commanded the largest China-trade ships of his time, calling at ports around the world and turning over their cargo several times. In his spare time, Gideon II sired eleven children, including Oliver Griffin Lane, Fred's father.

Oliver qualified for full ship command at age twenty-two, notably young for the size of ships under his hand. He married Charlotte Phippen, daughter of a shipping family as his own mother had been. When his father died the same year, they moved into the big house that overlooked the family wharf and warehouse, home to Oliver's journeys to New Orleans, France, and South America in the cotton trade.[32]

Charlotte and Oliver had two boys before Frederick Fomme arrived on September 25, 1829. The family's life revolved around the comings and goings of the ships. His mother devoted herself to the (Universalist) Village Church's charities and Sunday School to occupy her lonely months. When Captain Lane had been gone from home too long, she would tell Fred and the other children "Take the glass and go to the attic. See if your father's ship is coming in." Sometimes Charlotte with some or all of the children accompanied him on globe-circling voyages that lasted as much as a year. Few other commanders sought such family togetherness, but the Lane children received an unparalleled international education. When at home, the Lanes were known for their open-door hospitality.[33]

Fred and his brothers explored a boy's paradise around their home. Lobster Cove was Annisquam's main "street." Seafarers, fishermen, merchants, and Penobscot Indians all contributed to the clamor and bustle around the Lane wharf, store, and shipyard. Boulder-strewn "Dogtown" behind the village was five square miles of swamp, moor, overgrown pasture, and huge "Squam Rock." The black and white tower of Annisquam Light perched high on a rocky bluff just over the hill from Fred's home. The keeper welcomed children to use his spyglass to spot ships carrying fathers and brothers, or to look for the sea monster the Penobscots and others had seen since 1600. Every year some men and boys did not return from the Grand Banks or from the trading voyages, as it had always been. Some of the lost were Lane cousins. For seafaring families, there was inherent danger in their lives beside and upon the ocean. When Fred was ten, a series of December storms hit the unprepared Cape Ann mariners and left beaches littered with bodies of two hundred area residents and other debris.[34]

Whatcom County histories and family legend portrayed Fred as a Yale University graduate, but there is no evidence that he ever attended Yale or any other college. The truth is that Annisquam Lanes did not go to college. They studied at the clapboard Leonard School, where navigation was an important part of the curriculum in the upper grades. Boys usually went onto the fishing boats by age twelve or they went to sea. School was held in the winter and they could attend until they were 21.[35]

Extended family surrounded Fred, like Nellie's world at *Math'qui*. His uncle Captain Gustavus Lane owned a store on the cove to sell cargo he acquired around the world. Aunt Hannah married a distant Lane cousin who was the other local commander equal in stature to Fred's father. Uncle Gideon III built and commanded ships as did Uncle Davis Lane. Griffin and Phippen relatives added to the family tradition that Fred absorbed from birth.[36]

It was Fred's father Oliver, however, who earned singular fame for never making an insurance claim in his thirty-four-year career of command on the high seas. Oliver combined safety and speed, unlike most other masters who chose one or the other.[37]

Fred Lane did not go prospecting in California from 1849 until he headed north about 1857, as generally believed. He stayed with his family business most of those years. His father may have left for San Francisco with a full hold as soon as they could after the gold strike news arrived. The Lanes seized the opportunity to make money by supplying miners' needs, not prospecting. The 1850 census listed Captain Lane as a Sacramento lumber merchant, both older brothers ship masters, and twenty-one-year-old Fred as his father's clerk in port. If they arrived in San Francisco with a lumber cargo for the city's construction boom, the brothers may have been taking it upriver on smaller vessels and selling directly off their decks as most others did. The next year, Fred signed on to the *Georgia* as a "mechanic" (probably the ship's carpenter) and returned to the East Coast, perhaps to coordinate the next Lane cargo for California.[38]

That same year, 1851, Oliver took command of the new 670-ton *Victory*, the kind of full-rigged tall ship immortalized in paintings, which Fred's father was said to give a clipper's speed. Fred returned with him to San Francisco in June 1852, with a cargo that included anything useful, from tobacco to cement and bricks, even beds and dishes, plus seventy paying passengers, guaranteeing healthy profits for Fred's family.[39]

It seems likely that Fred continued to sail under his father or brothers. Oliver next took over the new, spectacular 195-foot-long ship *Neptune's Favorite*, called the best that ever called Boston home by the newspaper. On its second voyage to Shanghai, Oliver shaved the time from Philadelphia to San Francisco down to a phenomenal 116 days, despite losing much of the rigging rounding Cape Horn. After a final adventure racing eight others to San Francisco in 1856, he was ready to retire, saying that he had reached his youthful goal to command both ship and cargo on one of the finest ships out of Boston. The Lanes continued to entertain men who had repeatedly signed on with him and did what he could to help needy former crewmen.[40]

Captain Lane's retirement may have prompted Fred to stay in California, particularly because the maritime industry was in transition. The "Boston men" had resisted the turn toward steamships out of fear of explosion, but the speed getting miners to California could not be denied. Fred's first cousin George Lane had left the family's great sailing vessels to command a steamship for the Pacific Mail Company. Ship crews had changed from hometown boys to immigrants with little loyalty to ship or captain. Expansion of American industries opened new opportunities for ambitious young men who had an adaptable skill like ship carpentry. Fred's older brothers joined the family business as their father phased out, but he sought adventure on land in the West instead.[41]

Fred did some prospecting in California, but when, where, or for how long is unclear. He later showed considerable knowledge of gold-bearing rock formations and called Nellie's first husband James Carr and John Fravel his mining "pardners."[42]

"The Great Panic" of 1857 prompted many men to migrate and Fred Lane arrived in Oregon in the fall, ready to find a construction or boat repair job. The following April, Fravel wrote to him from Whatcom, where he and others were excited about the Fraser River gold rush and the young settlement's prospects. Fred read the letter to men gathered on a Portland street corner, and made his plans to sail north.[43]

Fred already had a family informant about Puget Sound's promise. His cousin John Griffin served as first mate during the *Victory's* voyage to San Francisco in 1852 and was supposed to take the ship over from Fred's father. However, he met pretty passenger Almina Richards and jumped ship to marry her. He incurred the permanent wrath of the entire Lane family except Fred (who could have had a hand in the romance). Subsequently, Griffin captained cargo vessels from California to Puget Sound and back with lumber.[44]

Fred Lane, at twenty-nine a blue-eyed lanky six-footer, disembarked at Sehome in June 1858, joining thousands of men on the beaches. It was sixty-six years after Robert Gray's return to Boston with news about the Pacific Northwest that transformed the Lane family's business. If Fred continued on to the gold mines, he didn't stay long. As the Fraser rush dissolved, he saw men disassemble the boom town of Whatcom, but in his words, he was one who did not head north to the Cariboo rush. "Being more susceptible to the allurements of a life on Puget Sound, I remained," as did many others tired of chasing gold.[45]

Lane worked at several, probably overlapping, jobs. Like James Kavanaugh, he did the back-breaking work of felling trees for the Boundary Survey for a season. He worked with the only other men qualified to repair and build boats, his friends ship carpenter James Carr and shipwright James Taylor. The trio is believed to have shared the profits from a scow they ran to Survey headquarters at Semiahmoo with supplies. Scows landed on beaches and carried a large cargo, but they were not very seaworthy in rough waters and bad weather, which Lane knew how to handle.[46]

During the county's first years, sheriffs didn't last long, as Carr exemplified. The county commission accepted Sheriff Enoch May's resignation on January 17, 1860. The erstwhile miner turned saloon keeper-hotelier had a penchant for card games of dubious integrity. He tended to be around when something bad was happening, but not as a peace officer. Being sheriff was not good for him or for the community, and the commission appointed Fred a few minutes after the town's other Massachusetts native resigned.[47]

Sheriff Lane was no administrator. Property taxes, as well as liquor and peddlers' licenses, were the county's only source of cash revenue. Four months into his term, the commissioners ordered Fred to turn over all funds and account for his efforts to collect delinquent taxes. He submitted his resignation the next day, but the commission refused it until they got their money. After he complied, they accepted his resignation due to "retaining money in his hands belonging to the county" and the local Quaker, Thomas Wynn, took over.[48]

Lane went prospecting that summer into the upper Nooksack River watershed with John Tennant and three others in canoes piloted by Tennant's Nooksack friends. The expedition found only adventure, but Fred's diary revealed his new respect for the Native men who had knowledge and skills equal to his own, but in much different waters and vessels. It was Fred's last fortune-hunting trip.[49]

Lane decided to go home when the Civil War began in 1861. The timing was right. He had neither married nor found his fortune, but had some money. The army and boundary survey, who were the two major boat repair customers, were gone. Many of the Lane men at home were on ships that could be commandeered by the government or attacked, his parents were aging, and the youngest sister Ann Eliza had married a U.S. Army officer. It was time for the bedrock Yankee seafaring family to consider their place in the conflict with the South where they had done business and knew many people.

Lane caught a lumber ship bound for San Francisco and his personal log of the trip hints at his joy being back in his most familiar environment. They raced the *Leonora* down the Strait of Juan de Fuca, "hammering away," then stopped outside Neah Bay to take on fresh halibut from Makah traders. Once on the open waters, he stood on deck alone under starry Pacific skies calculating the length of a comet's tail.[50]

When he left the steamship in New York after only twenty-two days instead of four months under sail, he found a city buzzing with war news. He headed home, and the visit turned into residence for the duration of the war. The family managed to continue to sail to the Far East and he said he worked in China for several years, perhaps again as the family's port clerk who would oversee purchase and sale of goods. When the war ended, he left the sea in San Francisco with his cousin John Griffin, who had a job offer from Henry Roeder to take command of the Whatcom-built scow *General Harney*.[51]

At Port Townsend, the cousins caught a ride to Whatcom with the mail carrier, Clara Tennant's uncle Whi'lano ("David Crockett"). The heavily laden canoe battled rough water in a squall. Not used to canoes with Coast Salish commanders, the storm intimidated Captain Griffin. Lane said "Why John, these Indians are the best boatmen in the world." Despite Whi'lano's skill, the three men spent a cold wet night on a Whidbey Island beach after the craft capsized. They recovered the mail, but Griffin's navigational tools went to the bottom.[52]

Fred Lane called February 1, 1866, his official claim settlement date at the unsurveyed edge of Lummi Reservation. He expected to be left alone like Tennant and the others. The three maritime friends are believed to have operated a cooperative boat building, repair, and freight business at the protected spot on the river's sloughs. His claim seems to have overlapped with Carr's in the absence of a township survey, and it only took final shape after his friend died and Lane took over the claim Carr never registered with the county.[53]

Lane split his attention with law enforcement duties in 1866-67 after voters elected him to the post of sheriff despite his previous questionable actions. Exasperated Sheriff James Kavanaugh was happy to turn all the travel, poor pay, politics, and trouble with settlers and army alike over to him. The conflicts he inherited with the army over who was in charge of American civilians in the San Juan Islands grew so lengthy and heated that he declined to run for re-election.[54]

NELLIE AND FRED LANE

Fred Lane pledged to care for Nellie and Lucy when James Carr lay dying. Years later, he officially documented that his tribal custom marriage to Nellie Carr occurred on March 30, 1867, not long after his friend's death. The couple, with baby Lucy Carr, established their required "exclusive" residence at his (or Carr's) small cabin on April 7, if Fred hadn't already finished his new four-room, 20 x 26-foot cedar cabin. The thirty-eight-year-old man of the sea and his sixteen-year-old bride had five years to develop their claim enough to submit a patent application when the General Land Office opened. There were forest giants to fell, orchard and garden to plant, outbuildings and livestock pens to build. And Fred Lane was a seafaring man, not a farmer.[55]

By the time of her second marriage, Nellie must have looked more like the woman seen later with her children in a formal portrait. She had high cheekbones and thick dark hair that framed an expression both capable and strong. F. F. Lane looked more like her father than her husband by then, and the visual contrast grew ever stronger with the passing years.[56]

Voters next elected Fred superintendent of schools, to begin when his sheriff term ended in fall 1867. The new office came with a salary of $25 a month in scrip worth 20 cents on the dollar, usable only at the coal mine store. Any kind of money in the depressed two-industry community was still an incentive to run for a salaried office. Since the only school was at the Sehome mine where his cousin's wife Almina Griffin taught a few children, it was not a difficult job. Though Fred had exaggerated his formal education, he claimed to have done some teaching in Massachusetts. He was demonstrably well-educated and interested in the needs of children, and he was now a stepfather.[57]

Like other indigenous wives whose husbands held a second job to supplement their income when farms were not yet fully productive, Nellie probably spent a lot of time alone. When Fred was home, he worked on the buildings or helped their neighbors before he left again, and evidence suggests that he continued to do some freighting and boat repair with Taylor. The intermarried Solomon Allens and Reuben Bizers moved to the lower Nooksack in 1868, which brought women familiar with Nellie's Sto:lo culture close to her. Mary Allen, an Nkla'pamux from the wild upper Fraser Canyon and Nooksack Sally Bizer both spoke Halkomelem.

Nellie gave birth to August in 1869, the same year Fred's brother Charles Augustus died of yellow fever in Rio de Janeiro while serving on Oliver Jr.'s ship. The choice of names to keep Lane family members alive in Fred's memory became a pattern as babies came along regularly after that.[58]

The 1870 Territorial Census showed that Nellie and Fred's farm income lagged behind the productivity of Tennant, Wynn, and others. The largest commodity came from the market garden which probably required the labor of both people without the presence of in-laws to help, unlike the Tennants and Wynns. Fred's parents had large gardens and an orchard on their Annisquam acreage, so the seafarer had some familiarity. He also took a "free" crop of fifteen tons of wild hay from the river bottoms, a resource that should have been the exclusive property of Lummi families. Maritime work may still have supplemented the Lane income.[59]

Despite his frequent absences, Fred made enough progress in the next two years to apply for his patent. With the help of neighbors, he had erected a 30 x 30 barn and planted 175 fruit trees. In November 1872 Fred received Patent #291 from the new land office in Olympia and three years later recorded his deed. Nellie's labor in the home-stead's development was assigned no value or recognition in either document.⁶⁰

The year 1872 heralded the birth of Nellie's third child (or fourth if James Carr Jr. was her son). The second baby with Fred Lane, Annie Phippen Lane was given the name of his youngest sister and his mother's maiden name. For the next twenty-one years, Nellie was never without at least one child under four. Nine of her children lived or died in that little cabin before the family moved in 1884. Common in her culture, babies came every two years except once, when Nellie went four years between births: Oscar E. (1874), Nathaniel Phippen (1876), Charlotte (1878), Constance (1880), Frederick F. Jr. (1882/83), a baby who died at birth in 1884, Oliver Griffin (1885), Helen Francis (1889), Charles Francis (1891), and Lucy Medora (1893). Midwife Mary Allen helped with at least one of the births, perhaps most of them at the *Noos'kwiem* and Nellie became a midwife herself. When Fred was in his sixties, the local newspaper made a point of comment-ing on how large and young his family of eleven (living) children was, emphasizing the word "young." There might have been thirteen chil-dren in the home instead of twelve, but little Lucy Carr died at nine, the same year Nathaniel was born. They named the last baby Lucy for her deceased half-sister, and the younger namesake said her mother told her stories about the first one when she was curious and wanted to "know" her in a sense.⁶¹

After Oscar's birth in 1874, Nellie and Fred took their first step toward legal marriage during the same period other tribal custom intermarried couples felt they had to do the same, pressured by "new" informal moral codes and territorial laws. They took out a marriage license January 15, 1875, from a county auditor who ignored Nellie's previous tribal custom marriage to James Carr and recorded the event as her first one. On May 2, their precinct's justice of the peace (and fellow intermarried husband) Seriah Stevens married them. Such ceremonies were usually the excuse for a general neighborhood "basket dinner" and all-night dance. The favor done for a dying friend had turned into a solid marriage.⁶²

Though Nellie was Catholic, there is no record that the pair ever had Fr. Chirouse bless their marriage, as the church often did for tribal custom marriages. Perhaps her husband, raised in the Universalist Church, declined, though he never stood in the way of the children's baptisms and Catholic faith. There is anecdotal evidence that the Lanes and several other intermarried couples, including the Tennants, married—again—in one large ceremony at the second Methodist camp meeting in 1878.[63]

It was difficult to keep a competent school superintendent in place in the early 1870s with only one person to handle every problem out in the county. After well-liked Superintendent John Griffin and Almina moved to March Point, the commissioners appointed his cousin Fred to step in again, followed by his election. He immediately created a local district for the Allen School at the Nooksack River's mouth so responsible parents were on the scene to handle problems. He continued to create local districts with parental boards until there were sixteen scattered across what later became Skagit and Whatcom counties. The expanding position was an independent and authoritative one, and complainants had no right to appeal Fred's decisions. This made him unpopular with townspeople when he split their district into Whatcom and Sehome, resulting in a disparity of funding. He ran for another term and won a rancorous election but did not finish his term.[64]

When F. F. Lane died many years later, residents remembered the former superintendent's devotion to the schools. The *Reveille* called him "brilliant of mind and a schoolteacher of natural bent." He worked for a per diem "so small it did not pay for the shoe leather he wore out during his visits to the posts," usually traveling by canoe between schools. He once told the editor: "I only did my duty. I knew there must be a beginning and as I had experience in school affairs in Massachusetts, I simply pulled off my coat and went to work. The salary was no object and as I had considerable money I paid my own bills and in some instances paid for the filing of papers in the territorial capitol in Olympia."[65]

What Lane's "school affairs" experience was in Annisquam, other than as a student and at sea reading on his own, is not clear. Perhaps he really did teach there for a time when he periodically returned, though records do not show it. It is questionable how truthful he was about money being "no object," given his obvious awareness that he was discussing his place in local history with the local newspaper. With a farm that was not among the best and a growing family, Nellie might have disagreed.

Fred was not done with public service yet, though it made more work for Nellie with so many young children. After he resigned from the school position, county Democrats urged him to run for the legislature. His previous run-ins with angry residents over school issues were not forgotten and at least one opponent "was violent in his denunciation." After his defeat by a LaConner banker, he never ran for office again until he became Justice of the Peace late in life.[66]

The farm was doing better by the end of the 1870s, but never so well as his neighbors. Nellie churned and sold butter and many dozens of excess eggs. It was a valuable contribution that constituted most of their increase in farm income. When once they had owned no cows, their need for milk grew to a four-cow herd. Their hogs supplied ham, sausage, bacon, and fresh meat for the ever-expanding family. Nellie and Fred bought staples and other items downriver at McDonough's store where she delivered her eggs and butter. On the same day they shopped, they usually traded potatoes and apples for credit. Despite his later claims that money didn't matter during the years all the children were home, expensive items were only a treat. Most extra money went to denim and calico for Nellie to sew into children's clothes, plus shoes, socks, hats, and jeans. However, Fred once bought Nellie an expensive bar of rose soap, and one Christmas he brought home the luxury of a keg of maple syrup. It is not hard to envision extra-special flapjacks on Christmas morning for the children.[67]

Farm chores and household tasks did not entirely consume Nellie and her family. Independence Day was always a big event for the Nooksack River settlers and their Lummi neighbors. After the McDonoughs lost their government contract for a trading post at Lummi, their open ground at the new site in a corner of the Allen land became the community gathering place. One year, five hundred people from reservation, town, and farms arrived for softball, a picnic, horse and foot races, plus contests for everyone. After the crowd stuffed themselves with the midday dinner, Fred rose to give the holiday's main speech. The newspaper enthused that it featured "beau-tiful and well-chosen remarks and apt quotations of poetry." Perhaps Fred didn't have a degree, but he never quit acting as though he did in a community of people with average education or none at all.[68]

෮෨෯

A problem in the 1880s sent Nellie's life in a new direction. Fred took out a loan in both names from the mother of his political enemy from the school election. It is unlikely that Nellie understood the dangers of putting up half of their land as collateral. Any default would make the full amount immediately due. Electa Fouts could sell the land and take the loan amount plus any profit. The first year, Fred paid only the interest. Then he paid nothing. Fouts immediately foreclosed and set about to sell the parcel. Her son, the defeated election opponent, was by then deputy sheriff. He served the summons, but had to find Fred in town because Nellie wouldn't open her door to him. They lost the land, but Fred had already purchased a new piece with the loan.[69]

The new land on Lummi Island faced the reservation across ¾ mile-wide Hale Passage. Nellie and Fred continued to live on their homestead until they sold the rest of it (by then under both names) at the end of 1883 for $1000, giving them a healthy sum with which to start over. Soon after they moved, Nellie had a baby who died at birth or shortly thereafter. Probably buried in a little casket fashioned by its carpenter father, the infant was Nellie's eighth Lane child. By Christmas the next year, she had given birth to baby nine, Oliver.[70]

Nine-mile-long Lummi Island lies across the circle of Bell-ingham Bay, its dark humps on the roadless southern end silhou-etted against the western sky. It is never more than three miles wide and its sunny farmland on the north end faces the other San Juan Islands. Today it is little more than a five-minute ferry ride across Hale Passage from Gooseberry Point, but in 1884 that was a substan-tial water barrier. It was a major part of the Lummi homeland with traditional villages and reef fishing operations, but the government had failed to keep its treaty agreement and removed the island from the reservation.

Before the Lanes arrived, only Christian Tuttle, an Indian hunter from the California wars, had permanently imposed upon Lummi activity on the island. Hostile to the Lummi from the beginning, Tuttle took a homestead in the middle of the fertile north end. He expected the government to dissolve the reservation soon and the Lummi would be forced to leave the area entirely. To his frustration, no one forced the Lummi to leave the island and the reservation did not expire. The Lummi found Tuttle's fences annoying and "harassed" his sheep and cattle when they passed through his fields. Tuttle's poorly hidden contempt made compromise and better relations impossible. When Wade Hampton Beach and his First Nations wife from Vancouver Island started a logging operation and distributed mail from a little post office, it gave the Lanes and a few others a sense of permanent community.[71]

Nellie and her fifty-five-year-old husband's new farm included timbered uplands and a triangular spit jutting into Hale Passage. It provided some protection for boats moored behind it when November gales and their high waves rolled in, although nothing as secure as the *Noos'kwiem* sloughs had been. The setting almost duplicated Lobster Cove, the protective watery "street" of Fred's youth. The family built a new, larger home next to the base of what became known as "Lane Spit." True to form, Fred immediately petitioned for a school since five of the junior Lanes were of school age. Although the school was organized, it failed from lack of attendance and wasn't revived for three years, which resulted in the oldest children's spotty education and gaps in the younger ones' years in school.[72]

The first year had to have been very difficult for Nellie with seven children under sixteen to feed, clothe, and care for, while starting over. Children did chores, but that helped their mother only so much. Even Nellie's new garden wrestled out of the virgin soil and underbrush would not be immediately productive and deer eagerly ate tender plants they could reach. She was cut off from her friends on the river, and Nancy Beach may not have spoken a common language other than Chinook jargon or elementary English. Clara Tuttle was half-Chetco tribe from California, but though she and Nellie had similar personal histories of marriage to men decades older and large families, no one has suggested that the two were friends. Tuttle seems to have kept his wife isolated, possibly because she had been raised

Lane Spit. The photograph of the spit on Lummi Island and Hale Passage was taken about two decades after F.F. Lane sold most of the family land, but shows the configuration that led to vessels ramming Lane Spit. The electric navigational light that replaced the Lane kerosene one is slightly visible above the trees on the spit (indicated by the arrow). *Image 1999.0114.000094. Gift to the museum of Bill Richardson. Whatcom Museum, Bellingham, Washington*

with a white family and he (sunk in his bigotry) wanted her to avoid Native people. The census always listed her as "white."[73]

Fortunately for Nellie, someone new moved to the island the year after she arrived. Caroline Bowden followed her son Albion there to build the first store and wharf. The Bostonian widow was about 15 years older than Nellie, and she took her own homestead very close by. It helped that Nellie had lived among whites so long that her English was fairly fluent.

In the isolation of their first island years, Nellie and Caroline were both in a raw place without their old friends. They became both teacher and student for each other. Nellie was an expert cook of regional seafood. She steamed clams, and made nectar from them. She rolled other clams in flour and fried them up tender and golden. She smoked salmon and knew the island's edible and medicinal native plants. New Englander Caroline probably brought her own clam recipes that would be familiar to Fred. She taught Nellie to cook the Lane children's favorite plum pudding made from the fruit of their own trees.[74]

The friends also shared an expertise in fiber arts. Nellie spun wool against her thigh on her Salish spindle whorl and wove. Caroline taught her to use a spinning wheel and perhaps to knit, if Nellie didn't already know how. Shared interests nurtured the women and helped them provide for their families. In Nellie's future, knitting would become her springboard to an independent business.

Four years after Caroline arrived, the women watched as Episcopalian Albion Bowden and Catholic Annie Lane were married by a Congregationalist minister on New Year's Day, 1889, at the Lane house. Nellie was seven months pregnant at the wedding with Lane baby number ten. In the years to come, the close friends welcomed two more Lane children, six shared Bowden grandchildren, and together mourned a baby lost and two accidental deaths of grandchildren they both loved.[75]

With the maturing Lane workforce and Fred's carpentry skills, the family quickly developed the farm. The house faced the water, backed by four outbuildings, a pasture, and Nellie's garden. Where the land rose behind, two big orchards fronted a large crop field and Fred had many of their fruit saplings shipped from the East Coast. (In the twenty-first century, a walnut tree still towered beside the county road.) The family sold apples and pears, but Nellie canned most of the cherries and plums. Fred and the boys built a root cellar to shelve her canned fruit, along with bins of apples, potatoes, onions, cabbages, and squash that would keep over the winter.[76]

In Lane family tradition, Fred owned a two-sail, single-masted sloop. It was especially good in a headwind, and with a five-ton capacity it was big enough to carry the Lanes' products to market in Seattle. There, Nellie and Fred sold their fruit and nuts, often trading some for supplies the family needed. Nellie sold her extra butter and eggs, and sometimes canned fruit. When they sailed the sloop to the city, the Lanes usually left the smallest children crying on the beach in despair and fury at being left behind with older siblings to care for them.[77]

Fred turned his uplands into a logging operation. The older boys worked with their aging father, moving logs down a primitive road to the beach and towing the filled boom across the bay to town.[78]

As the boys grew older and stronger, they accompanied Nellie to *Math'qui* and the Fraser River fishery. She took all her children to visit their grandmother and they long remembered the fun of wading into the river shallows and grabbing salmon, though Nellie scolded them for taking ones meant to spawn. Sometimes she bought wind-dried salmon that did not have to be boiled before eating from the upriver people, but at home she kept her large smokehouse busy with local salmon. Occasionally, unscrupulous men who knew the contents of her front yard smokehouse landed on the moonlit beach to rob it.[79]

The waters around Lummi Island abounded in shellfish and other edibles that hadn't been so easily available up the Fraser River. Nellie relished sea cucumbers and raw sea urchins, though they weren't part of her youth, but her children did not share in her delight. In addition to clams, she grew increasingly skilled with oysters and mussels, favorites of her Bostonian son-in-law and probably her New England-born husband as well.[80]

Days for the younger Lanes combined hard work with play. The level spit was a safe playground without the Nooksack River's dangers. Fred gave his children sailing lessons on breezy days in the blue sloop, tacking back and forth or running before the bay's winds. They sailed across the nine miles of open green water to town, to Gooseberry Point, or to nearby Portage Island. Those days took Fred back to his own childhood lessons in Cape Ann waters. When age robbed him of the physical ability to sail his sloop, his sons took over.[81]

Starting with August's marriage in 1890, Lane sons' Lummi wives inevitably drew the family into the reservation families' orbit. Now in-laws, the Lummi continued their summer encampment across the island at Village Point where twenty canoe reef fishing teams competed against the deadly efficient technology of white-owned fish company traps.[82]

Nellie's home on the spit put her in a more exposed position than she had been on the *Noos'kwiem.* Her fear of Northern raiders persisted decades after they no longer came south to raid the Coast Salish and Sto:lo. She still taught her children to watch for war canoes and run back to the house if they saw them entering Hale Passage. Despite the spit being the Lane family's paradise, there actually were people to fear, but they weren't Northerners.[83]

Criminals used Lummi Island to smuggle Chinese immigrants, liquor, and opium from Victoria, as well as for other illegal activity. They were so ruthless they dumped the work-seeking Chinese overboard if they were pursued by authorities. Even piracy was a danger to boats in the area. In addition to the occasional raids on Nellie's smokehouse, outlaws stole a large amount of meat, salmon, and other foods from her storehouse during 1893's severe winter. Fred believed they had fled to nearby Eliza Island where criminals often hid out, but three months later police found two thousand pounds of his potatoes stored at a Whatcom restaurant. The newspaper did not reveal how police could tell they were Lane potatoes.[84]

Outlaws were not the only culprits Nellie had to put up with. New Whatcom High School students and their teacher once "borrowed" the Lane skiff and canoe while on an outing. They arrogantly told authorities they "forgot" to return them. They thought the small craft were "not valued very highly," though they had left the Lanes with no way to reach their sloop moored offshore.[85]

The island's population continued to rise as did its community life. It was left without mail service when Wade Beach moved to Bowen Island, British Columbia. Post office officials rejected one of Solomon and Mary Allen's mixed-blood sons for lack of education and asked Fred to re-open the post office in a small cabin near the spit. Islanders came to Nellie's home every week after mail was fetched from town or was dropped off. A year later, Fred turned the cabin into a small trading post until their daughter Annie's husband took over postmaster duties and moved the office to the couple's store at Beach.[86]

Fred and other islanders petitioned the county school superintendent to give the island another try at a school that would hold classes the required three months in a two-year period. Any education island children got was in their own homes or off-island if they had someone to board with. Now on the local board, Fred and other fathers built a log school during the cold wet gray of February 1888. They included sliding wood panels to keep leaves and rain out of the glassless windows and started classes without desks. Four years after the islanders so eagerly built their school, the state superintendent condemned it. The men built a new one farther away from Lane Spit but more centrally located for the island's twenty-three families. The Lanes' trudge to school was much longer, especially in winter's darkness after the term expanded to seven months.[87]

Because Nellie spoke good English, she could enter the island's community life. As an island pioneer and member of the Ladies Aid Society, she worked to establish a non-denominational Sunday school eleven years before the community welcomed a resident minister. She took her regular turn hosting the group in her home.[88]

Island birth records also show Nellie's work as a midwife, perhaps from her earliest days there, and she presided over the births of her island grandchildren. Expectant farm wives still often sought out Native midwives because they had a more confident attitude than fearful Victorian women with little knowledge of their own bodies and the birth process. Having lost her own infant, Nellie well understood the fears of women giving birth isolated from their mothers and familiar surroundings.

Living a difficult journey from town, island parents feared serious injury or illness of a child. On March 23, 1895, Nellie lost ten-year-old Oliver to meningitis. Once afflicted, there was little anyone could do other than to comfort the boy and try to cool the raging fever. Nellie and Fred buried their son in the family cemetery where he joined Nellie's granddaughter (and namesake) "Nellie" Bowden who burned to death only a month earlier. The island mourned with them and no one had a stomach for social meetings that week.[89]

Five years after the family moved to the island, Nellie and Fred took on a major service role for the wider community and Salish Sea mariners. Weather and darkness presented serious problems in Hale Passage where strong tides ran around Lane Spit. Many large vessels had plowed into it in the dark or fog. When the territory became a state in 1889, two fast steel boats were brought around Cape Horn to improve the Seattle-Victoria commercial route with regular stops at Whatcom. One of them steamed down Hale Passage in the fog and ran into the spit with enough force to nearly cut the boat in two. It took two weeks to refloat the steamer and halt the disruption of the Lanes' quiet life. This was the last straw for Fred and Nellie, whose family was the first assistance for grounded boats and their passengers. Having grown up just over the hill from Annisquam Light, Fred knew that a navigational light would inevitably save lives and money over time, given the perennial fogs and storms. He petitioned for a lighthouse on the spit.[90]

Federal officials approved a light similar to others being erected in the San Juan Islands. The wooden "stake light" located on the spit a mile inside Hale Passage's entrance from the main shipping channel had a small fixed light twenty-seven feet above the water. Though not as high as a lighthouse, it was visible for six miles. It brought a new rigorous daily schedule to Nellie's family life. Someone had to climb the post and light the kerosene lantern every evening, year around. Younger Lane generations memorized the lightkeeper's credo: "The light shall not fail." It was a treat for grandchildren to walk with Grandfather Lane out to the end of the spit and light the beacon at night and return in the morning to extinguish it.[91]

୯୫୨୦

Unwanted notoriety came to Nellie's husband in 1899. Fred found himself the defendant in two criminal actions. At seventy he may have been under financial pressure because he sold off 126 acres of the farm to outsiders, then advertised nearly 58 acres that included Lane Spit, and mortgaged more land.[92]

Fred stood before a Seattle federal grand jury accused of two charges of selling illegal liquor to Lummi residents. Tribal police accused the former sheriff first of illegally selling his "raspberry juice" to a teenager. The second charge was an alleged sale to an adult. The teenager had been sent to the island to see if Lane was selling wine after others bought some, and returned with a full lard can of evidence for Judge Hillaire Crockett's crusade against white liquor-sellers. Despite family connections, if Fred continued his wine sales, the Lummi people would no longer consider him a friend.[93]

Prosecution witnesses testified to seeing relatives and friends intoxicated after going to Lane's trading post and buying wine. Fred's witnesses countered that a person would be sick before they would be drunk. Fred attributed the strength of his "wine" (his own term by then) to the lateness of the raspberries, but claimed it was never intoxicating before. The defense never called Nellie to back up her husband's assertions that it was just for dinner, but the all-white grand jury did not indict him. When they considered the second charge of sale to an adult three days later, the victim's wife said her husband was so intoxicated from Lane's wine that she and their children would not go home in his canoe after they ate dinner with Nellie and her children.[94]

For a man who had served his county as sheriff, superintendent of schools, and recently local justice of the peace, the arrests were embarrassing. In hindsight, they also forewarned of future actions that were less than honorable.

Two intriguing statements may shed light on the Lane marriage in its later years. The second victim's wife said that Lane was in the post office cabin when the family arrived and he went to see if anyone was coming "to help." According to the wife, Nellie sold the wine to people when Fred was not there, but in this instance, she came in crying. Another witness under defense questioning said "the Indians have not talked about making it so unpleasant for Lane that he would leave the island." The same veiled threat had been raised in the first proceedings. Again, Nellie was not called to the stand, and again the jury did not indict Fred. The illegal liquor sales may have become an issue in the marriage when Lane children married into the Lummi community he was taking advantage of.

Three years after the unwanted publicity, Fred decided to divorce Nellie, his wife of thirty-five years and mother of his twelve children. The divorce case has always raised questions about exactly what happened, the reasons for the action, and why the case was allowed to proceed at all. It may have had something to do with the liquor cases, as well as a confused tangle of real estate transactions that stretched over many years. By 1902, selling off the remaining land seemed more important to Fred than the logging and fruit business as the boys moved toward different futures. He was seventy-three, but Nellie was only fifty-one and they still had three minor children. The balance of power in the marriage had probably changed, though perhaps Fred resisted losing any of his control. Nellie may have strenuously opposed some of his activities, both the real estate and the wine sales, but it is all speculation.

When Fred filed for divorce, he alleged that tiny Nellie was very strong and had a violent temper. He accused her of repeatedly assault-ing him, including two days before he filed. Fred claimed to be mis-erable and couldn't live with her anymore. He claimed that she was unfit for child custody because of her illiteracy and temperament.[95]

The very next day, Nellie was presented a summons which she could not read. On the same day, she signed away her community property rights in exchange for forty acres, her house, and a lot in the Marietta townsite on Solomon and Mary Allen's land. Not even Nellie's children helped her retain an attorney to interpret the legal papers, to defend against Fred's allegations, to request financial sup-port, to ask for shared custody, or to obtain her rightful share of the property. In contrast, Fred's lawyer was Ed Hardin, Vanderbilt Uni-versity Law School graduate and the mayor of Whatcom.[96]

The judge took Fred's allegations and testimony at face value and entered Nellie's default. It is most likely that no one told her when she was required to appear, or she had no transportation across the bay to town. Oddly enough, Fred finally treated her more fairly in the divorce than he was required to, despite his assertions of domes-tic violence, which makes the divorce more perplexing. Perhaps he realized that Nellie's (alleged) behavior might have been affected by the sheer exhaustion of thirty-five years of small children, the phys-ical labor as their mother and his wife, and the care she was giving to her elderly spouse. He had also exaggerated or lied to get what he wanted. Again, the truth remains unclear.

The judge declared the Lanes' considerable assets to be com-munity property despite the document Nellie had signed. They had come to an agreement on an equal division before the court date. He accepted Fred's ridiculous claims about Nellie's abilities to care for children and gave the elderly man custody to support and edu-cate them. Although Nellie received the forty acres, house, and lot, the judge awarded no alimony or support for her thirty-five years of domestic labor. She was handed half an outstanding mortgage to pay.

What happened afterwards is another puzzle. The couple con-tinued to live on the property together, in one house or two. The youngest three children (Helen, Charles, and Lucy) had both parents available every day. In later life, they had only loving positive things to say about their mother. Nellie's daughters never mentioned a violent temper.

Well-educated older sister Constance, home from Pennsylvania's Carlisle Indian School, lived nearby and could help with the children's lessons. Lane children began to study at Carlisle in 1896, seventeen years after its founding to "civilize" the rebellious Plains chiefs' sons and daughters. The first Lane child arrived six years after the Massacre of Wounded Knee when more Native leaders' children were sent there. The school's intentions might have been benevolent, but the venture is now viewed by many Native Americans and others as committing cultural genocide in many of its students. During 1895, recruiters traveled to regions that had not contributed to the student mix and the following July teenaged Constance left for Pennsylvania, not to return home until she finished school four years later. Fred's reasons for sending her and later siblings, and what Nellie's reactions were, went unrecorded. By that time some island newcomers opposed the attendance of children with any Indian blood at the community school that Fred had fought so hard to establish. Fred may have wanted the children to see more of the world as he had by leaving home. Perhaps he wanted to make it possible for his Massachusetts kin to get to know them before he died. Perhaps he didn't want the remaining children to marry into the reservation, or he secretly thought that Nellie was still "too Indian." Perhaps all were true.[97]

Carlisle's mission was assimilation, particularly using the example of students returning home stripped of their "Indianess" and taught Euro-American ways. The Lane children must have made uniquely attractive recruits. Though of mixed blood, they lived close to a reservation but were not of it. Older siblings had married into the reservation and their father had been a county school official. They were assimilated already and would be excellent role models both in their community and in the school. Five of the youngest Lanes attended for various lengths of time until mid-1915.

There was one problem with this seemingly perfect and unforced recruitment. Nellie was not an "American Indian." She was a Canadian First Nations woman. Enrollment was restricted and her children should have been technically ineligible. They had never lived on a reservation and they attended public schools. Carlisle bypassed these difficulties by registering them as Lummi, perhaps using August's marriage as the rationale. They also registered them as Nooksack, the American group often intermarried with Nellie's *Math'qui* people, and perhaps the origin of her mother.

The long-term results of the Carlisle attendance were a mix of the experiences of many Native American families across the West whose children attended government boarding schools. All three of the girls married non-Indians. Fred Jr. died of tuberculosis he caught at the school. Several worked for a time at a government boarding school or an Indian agency. The ones who attended used the skills they learned there. Unlike most boarding school students, the Lanes did not experience the extreme cultural disruption that was the lot of other students. They told their parents they liked the school and kept positive memories into late life.

NELLIE

Nellie was not completely without financial and emotional support after the divorce. It is not clear if Fred continued to contribute money, but she was not awarded any by the court. She had her land, her house, cows, chickens, the sheep, and Fred was responsible for the youngest children's support. Married daughters Annie and Constance lived almost next door and Charlotte worked in town. August and his growing family lived on nearby Portage Island where Nellie built a loving relationship with her grandchildren. Nathaniel and his wife lived on the Lane farm while he worked with his brothers logging and fishing until they moved to Orcas Island to be near her family. Nellie's friend Caroline Bowden still lived close by, too.

Nellie was strong and resourceful and she built her own flock of one hundred sheep. The island was still largely open range and she was the sole owner of forty acres, though her flock may have also pastured on Portage Island's prairies. She wasn't the first Native wife to have her own flock, but Nellie turned hers into a viable producer of more than wool and meat for the family.[98]

Nellie applied her traditional knowledge about fiber with her new skills to making yarn balls, and knitting socks to sell. Eventually abandoning her spindle whorl for a spinning wheel, she did not allow curious small granddaughters to touch it. Whenever she completed 100 pairs of socks, she filled large baskets with raw wool, yarn balls, and the socks. She took them across the bay and wholesaled her products to The Fair Department Store so she could buy groceries and her children's clothing. She wasn't an unknown at The Fair, since their man Charles Norman had been one of the Lane children's teachers and bought land from Fred. The store had a reputation for paying the highest price for quality farm products and keeping "the confidence of every person, merchant or patron." The Fair was a favorite of locals, and the quality of Nellie's work had to be high for the store to carry it. She had become one of Whatcom's early female entrepreneurs.[99]

Knitting was a traditional Euro-American craft, but it should not be surprising that a Sto:lo woman adopted it with enthusiasm. Northwest indigenous girls learned to spin and weave from female elders and the products of a woman's hands were hers to keep, give away, or sell. The spirit attached to beautiful and intricate handwork still crosses cultural fences between women. Nellie switched from her spindle whorl to Caroline's method that produced yarn faster, more evenly, and with less physical effort. The busy mother's finely executed knitting could make family clothing and marketable goods within hours, rather than the weeks and months traditional weaving might take. Tradition did not close Coast or Interior Salish women's eyes to new technology that would improve their lives. Nellie passed along her new skills to two more generations.[100]

Nellie earned money in other ways. She wasn't very good at milking cows but did so to sell milk, butter, and eggs to campers after the neighboring Granger family started a resort. She sold her canned fruit, and perhaps lucky campers bought her smoked salmon, too.[101]

Most notably, Nellie became the Lane Spit light keeper. She was better fitted to climb up the light than elderly Fred and it wasn't an unusual job for a woman. Oscar kept the required log for her. An unconfirmed source reported that she received $7 a month to maintain the small but important light. With her son's assistance,

Nellie served the public safety for years until the government installed an automatic light.[102]

NELLIE AND FRED

A tangle of questionable real estate maneuvers involving Oscar and Fred clouded the years between the divorce and Fred's death. Fred became a stooped, thin old man, white-haired and balding, though his gaze was still imposing above a mustache and long beard. At 73, he may no longer have been mentally vigorous after a lifetime of hard labor and after his death, a lawsuit accused him of encouraging and plotting fraud. There is no way to tell how the odious idea was born, but Nellie's inability to read and understand legal language became a critical element of what transpired during the years leading up to her lawsuit.[103]

Nellie had more important concerns than land values at the time. Six months after the divorce, Fred Jr., now twenty years old, arrived from Pennsylvania with tuberculosis. Many young victims died at Carlisle, prey to the disease in the common sleeping rooms, and never seen by their families again. Having lost Lucy Carr, Oliver, and a baby at birth, Nellie faced a much slower heartbreak.[104]

As the island changed in ever larger and faster ways, beach property values rose, including that of Nellie's forty acres. Shingle mills and Carlisle Cannery brought in hundreds of American and Chinese men, and large numbers of Lummi canoed over every day to work. One shingle mill was at Lane Spit on the large parcel Fred sold in 1895.

Nellie's need for interpretation of legal documents made her vulnerable to fraud, even by family. First (in very confusing language) she signed off half of her land to Oscar and his wife as a "gift." Three years later, a deed put the twenty acres back in her hands but was recorded only later at the request of a man who bought five years of the timber and road-building rights on the property for a paltry sum. Nellie played no part in the negotiations and was designated "a widow by divorce" in the papers, though Fred was still alive.[105]

Thirteen months later, Nellie leased twenty of her restored forty acres, three cows, fourteen chickens, and her house for an entire year for only $50. The lease included an option for the newcomer to buy it all within a year for $500, a very good deal for the buyer as beachfront land values rose. An unusual provision in the lease option required that, if she requested it, he would build her a "shack or box house" with no more than two thousand feet of her own lumber. In essence, this left Nellie homeless unless she wanted him to build a shack. No friend or family member witnessed the signing to explain the lease's implications. Though Nellie's English was good after four decades among the whites, the question remains of how much she understood about "timber rights," "lease," and "option to buy." Family members indicated that she and Fred shared a house for a time, so she may have moved to his house to care for her ex-husband. She did not sell.[106]

Fred continued logging with his sons despite his advanced age. The island's six mills could use whatever old growth trees the Lanes felled. On February 21, 1909, he left after breakfast to check on some burning stumps one hundred feet from the house and never returned. The family found his body hours later pinned between a trunk and a heavy branch fallen from a burned tree. Under a headline about the death, the *Herald* paid tribute to his early contributions to the law and schools. Like some other intermarried men's obituaries, the paper never mentioned Nellie.[107]

The *Reveille* approached Lane's death differently. It was more interested in his intermarriage and personality than his accomplishments. The editor complimented him on not abandoning his Indian wife when "better" society arrived, and said Fred had once told him that it would have been dishonorable to do so. He had also told the editor the divorce was due to incompatibility, which was probably closer to the truth than his divorce accusations. By declaring the Lane children among the Sound's best citizens, the editor actually paid tribute to Nellie's mothering.[108]

They buried Fred beside his children on the island.

During the estate probate, Judge Hardin (Fred's divorce lawyer) appointed a guardian for the two youngest children. Victor Roeder (son of Henry) wanted the appointment to "guard" their interests. A companion appointment at the time showed his true attitude when Nooksack Tribe teenager Daniel Swanaset saw the banker sell the Indian homestead he inherited from his father. Roeder managed to find ways to claim the entire proceeds as one expense or another until the boy was penniless and landless.[109]

The minister whom Nellie had helped bring to the island supported Roeder's appointment by calling her "not a fit or proper person" because she was an uneducated Indian. It was not an unusual argument in Washington State to keep a Native wife from taking on legal powers. Hardin appointed Roeder and ordered a private sale of all Fred's property.

NELLIE

A year later Nellie realized that her minor children had benefited little when Roeder and a new judge sold Fred's waterfront land to W.L. Showers at a price under the appraisal value, and Roeder's fees took more from their proceeds. Though she probably knew nothing about the Swanaset probate case, Roeder was repeating what he had done before. She discovered that Oscar was in the process of selling Showers more land—her land. She found that he had previously tricked her into signing over the property to him by telling her he would pay the taxes and mortgage to protect her "frugal and limited savings." Nellie did not realize it was a sale deed and had continued living there without paying her taxes and mortgage. She had no warning that things were amiss until she found out he was selling the land that by then was worth considerably more than after the divorce settlement. She started to believe that her ex-husband had a hand in the fraudulent action before his death.

When she went to Oscar and his wife, they said she had no rights or title to any of the land being sold, and they didn't need to account to her for anything. Oscar offered her a "life estate" lease on the house and two acres, if he could sell the rest. Nellie had had enough. She talked to friends and hired a respected law firm who got the county auditor to examine the web of transactions that started with the divorce.

Nellie filed suit accusing her son and his wife of fraud and stopped the sale. She alleged that Fred "aided and abetted" the original fraud out of "hostile feeling and enmity against [her] that continued beyond the divorce." In truth, the county auditor should have examined closely the transactions involving lots and partial lots around the time of Fred's death and beyond.[110]

By using Superior Court, Nellie Carr Lane took charge of her own affairs and sought justice from the same system that the father of their 12 children used to get an unjust settlement nine years earlier. Her lawyers made strategic use of the very incompetence arguments others had used to take her power and financial support away.

A *Bellingham Herald* writer saw a good story and put Nellie's lawsuit on page one of the November 20, 1910, issue. It is clear that Nellie's lawyers, who doubtless knew the value of sympathetic publicity, helped with the story. They even added ten years to her age. One of the story's three major headlines told nearly the whole story: "Mrs. Nellie Lane, Full-Blooded Indian Woman, Bowed by Weight of 70 Years, Starts Legal Action to Recover Property Out of which She Claims She was Defrauded Through the Machinations of Her Half-Breed Son and Her Former Husband F.F. Lane, First Superintendent in Whatcom County." A smaller headline on page two added: "Infirm woman, Who Finds That her Estate is Limited to Two Acres…Tries to Get Back What She Thought She Owned." The article gave an unflattering description of the young people's "machinations," plus Nellie's statement she had had "perfect confidence" in her son, and consulted him on all her business dealings.

The Lane clan found itself in the middle of a public mess while Nellie sought to establish her title and prove she was "induced to deed the land to her son by fraudulent methods." Oscar claimed that he was contributing to her support all along, but when the details came out in court, he just looked worse. Not only had his mother never received any support or compensation for the land, but the young couple had not repaid substantial loans from Nellie. The loans may point to her self-sufficiency or to loans made from money she needed. Since she had not been paying the mortgage and taxes because of the lies, she offered to cancel the other debts if the land were returned to her. Oscar never filed a defense. Negotiations began.[111]

Months later, Nellie and Oscar signed a compromise settlement, witnessed by three other Lane children, indicating family participation as well as lawyers. Nellie sold her twenty acres to Showers while Oscar and his wife signed over the main homesite to her. It was an admission that they had defrauded Nellie. She had her home and two acres back under her control as well as land she owned in Marietta on the Nooksack River.[112]

There is no evidence that the family failed to heal the wounds left by the dispute, although family memories could be different. Nellie had many busy years left with her children and grandchildren. As some married into the reservation, she was drawn along with them into closer ties. She took trips to *Math'qui* for the fishery or for the hop picking season in the Chilliwack Valley when families gathered as they did in the Puyallup Valley. She made trips to town to sell her goods. There was a garden to keep, salmon to smoke, and fruit to can. She had her job tending Lane Spit Light with Oscar's recordkeeping help. In 1915 the last child returned from Carlisle after five years away and Nellie's obligations for the younger children were drawing to a close.

Nellie and Daniel Daley

In her sixties, Nellie married Daniel Daley in early September 1915. The *Herald* reported that the pair married on Lummi Island, but were moving to Chilliwack, "her former home." No county record for this marriage exists, but three years later they got a license and had a Methodist ceremony in Blaine on January 30, 1918. Daley, a never-married illiterate immigrant, was born in England to Irish emigrants. By the time of the 1918 ceremony, the couple was back living on the island where he worked as a laborer, probably at one of the mills or fish canneries. On the 1918 record, Nellie fudged a bit about her age, subtracting nine years from her 67 to put her closer to Daley's 53.[113]

Before Nellie's church ceremony, she wrote her informal will and bequeathed the last of her acreage to her daughter Lucy Medora and the Marietta lots to Charles. The rest of the children, well-established in adulthood, were to receive $1.00 each to prevent protest. Nellie excluded her new husband entirely. Three years later, the Daleys sold Lucy and her husband the two acres around the house that Nellie had fought so hard to keep. The transaction ensured that Lucy actually got the land willed to her and Nellie received fair value while alive. It is not clear if the Daleys stayed there, but the marriage failed before long. It is possible that Nellie's will and sale to Lucy was connected to the split, but there were other serious marital problems. There is no divorce record, but Nellie reverted to her Lane surname.[114]

NELLIE

Nellie's eyesight failed and she needed the assistance of the children and grandchildren who surrounded her in her final years. She lived for a time with Helen and also on Portage Island with August's family.[115]

Nellie Carr Lane died on June 27, 1929. At 78, she had outlived seven of her thirteen children. August, Fred, Annie, and Nathaniel had died since the divorce. Thirty-five grandchildren and thirty-nine great-grandchildren survived her. Calling Nellie a "pioneer of the county," the *Herald* never mentioned Frederick F. Lane, reminiscent of his obituary which never mentioned her. The family buried their matriarch at Lummi Reservation Cemetery, instead of with Fred on the island. Descendants (who number in the hundreds) annually honor her memory in the traditional way and flowers can be found at her headstone. Large reunions of one branch or another confirm the enduring ties between Nellie's descendants.[116]

AN AMERICAN FAMILY

The Lane children's lives illustrate the falsity of enduring stereotypes about the progeny of nineteenth century intermarriages. They were not failures. They did not become misfits who fit into neither culture. They forged the legacy of Nellie and her husband as individuals.

August, the eldest, married Lizzie Adams from Lummi and moved to her father's allotment on Portage Island where he logged, fished, and farmed. His first of eleven children was born before Nellie had her last two. August took an active part in the Lummi fishing rights movement in 1916 when he was a tribal policeman with his brother. He led a group of Lummi fishermen who seized a Croatian purse seiner's net in water above the low tide mark in violation of the treaty. August was arrested. The incident brought more attention to the escalating dispute that ended with the brandishing of Lummi firearms. The Croatians finally realized that the reservation fishermen would never willingly tolerate illegal fishing.[117]

Annie Phippen Lane Bowden had six children with Albion and ran two stores on Lummi Island before they divorced. She ran the Beach store alone until her re-marriage. She lost three children: one at birth, little Nellie to a brush fire, and Peveril in a sledding accident. Her daughter Anne Frances majored in music at prestigious Washington University in St. Louis and taught for over 30 years. Her sister Clara had a long nursing career in Honolulu. Annie died at 47 in the 1918 worldwide Spanish influenza epidemic.[118]

Oscar Ernest, named for one of the Lane sea captains, was also a Lummi Reservation policeman during the fishing confrontations. He most of all the children adopted Fred's love of sailing and raced his own boat. He married Lucy Finkbonner, Tulalip-educated daughter of the first Lummi Reservation farmer-in-charge and his Kwantlen wife Mary from Fort Langley, British Columbia. Though one of Nellie's earliest children, Oscar never spoke his mother and mother-in-law's Halkomelem. This may indicate the speed with which Nellie learned English and used it with her children.

Oscar and his wife lived on the Lane property while he logged with his brothers. After the 1910 lawsuit, he obtained a late allotment by doing as many Washington mixed-blood people did. He enrolled as "Omaha" to enable tribal adoption during a time of national wrangling over tribal rights to do so. He received less desirable land near Old Lummi Village, but he fished and was a carpenter (like his father). In the centuries-old Lane tradition, he built a fishing vessel that he took to Alaska. Among the five children who survived him was the third Frederick Fomme Lane.[119]

Nathaniel Phippen's first name honored Fred's disabled cousin who became the nationally famous painter of Cape Ann known as "Fitz Henry" Lane. Like his older brothers, Nathaniel had a spotty education and logged with them. At nineteen, he was hailed by the wider community for his heroic (though unsuccessful) efforts to save his niece from death in a brush fire. Also the child of an intermarriage, his wife Jessie Moore's parents founded the village of Olga on Orcas Island. Her mother was the daughter of Chief Sealth's niece and a British Columbia Chemainus leader. Their only child died, after which they moved back to Lane Spit. The local hero died three years before Nellie, a few days short of his fiftieth birthday.[120]

Fred chose his beloved sister Charlotte's name for the second daughter. The Annisquam town historian lived in the Lane mansion and hosted Nellie and Fred's children from Carlisle. The spinster was renowned for her hospitality and turned the Lane mansion into a summer boarding house for creative people, including Rudyard Kipling. Nellie's Charlotte was already seventeen when the Carlisle recruiter arrived, and did not go east. She worked as a "domestic" until she married Minnesotan Henry B. Miller, an older machinery operator at one of the mills or canneries. They had at least two daughters on the island before they moved to Seattle.[121]

The year 1895 was the critical junction in the Lane siblings' lives. It separated the younger five in education level and future occupations from their older siblings who had only been intermittently schooled on the island.

Constance, the sixth Lane child, left for Carlisle on the train at age sixteen knowing only that she had family in Massachusetts, which probably felt like a very tenuous connection to home. She could not have known how her world and view of her place in it would change when she exchanged the calico dresses sewn by Nellie for dark Victorian uniforms and high-button shoes. Students at Carlisle came from the Aleutians to Florida, but she alone was registered as "Lummi." Constance walked through the new campus entrance to join a culturally diverse indigenous student body permitted to speak only English. That wasn't a problem for her since she didn't know any native language. The school's director tried to make it as pleasant as any nineteenth century boarding school could be, and many activities were available to soften the loneliness of the alien environment. The year after Constance arrived, the new head of the nation's Indian schools took over and de-emphasized academics because she thought the children were intellectually inferior. Any sense of nurturing that had existed was at least formally gone. Even so, Constance immersed herself in debate and other activities. She also became one appreciative teacher's classroom assistant her third year. The school exposed her to visiting native leadership examples, including Carlisle alumni who led tribal delegations to Washington, D.C. and the medical hero of Wounded Knee, Dr. Charles Eastman who taught at Carlisle for a year with his non-Native wife.[122]

The first Lane child to venture out with her father's confidence behind her, Constance's world grew. She was the first young Lane to spend Christmas holidays in Annisquam with "Aunt Tot" and the big Lane clan. Under the "outing system" she also spent at least two summers in Maryland private homes. Constance married Fred Bumstead, son of the English shipwright who built Oscar's racing sailboat. Her education led to membership in Lummi Island's literary society and the couple appeared frequently in social news before she became a widow with a small child at twenty-eight.[123]

Constance took cooking jobs before she and her child moved back in with Nellie. She took on her late father's role guiding the younger children's education, including correspondence with Carlisle about her siblings, who she wanted to attend there. Though she disdained Tulalip Boarding School's quality, she taught sewing there after Carlisle's director found the position that gave her financial independence. She moved to Cordova, Alaska, after remarriage.[124]

In the early 1940s, people who wanted to enroll in a recognized tribe had to complete and return paperwork within a deadline. Constance still lived out-of-state and though she was sent the forms, she never returned them even though all her siblings enrolled in Lummi Nation. Because of her carelessness, oversight, or lack of foresight, her descendants remain ineligible for enrollment.

Fred Jr. followed Constance to Carlisle when he was sixteen. He chose farming as his field of concentration, which meant long hours at the school farm that fed the staff and students. In 1903, Carlisle sent him home with tuberculosis, contracted in the dormitory or from the cows, which was still common. He improved enough under Nellie's care that he planned to attend Chemawa Boarding School in Oregon, but was too sick to go. After eight years, Fred died in 1911 despite his mother's devoted care. The *Herald* called her son "a most estimable young man."[125]

Helen Francis, given Nellie's baptismal name and that of Fred's brother who died in childhood, had been Nellie's eleventh childbirth in twenty-two years. At seventeen she entered Carlisle as an eighth grader, a more advanced level than previous Lane students because her local education had been longer and of better quality. She studied office administration and worked in the school office, as well as the laundry and sewing room. Her busy activities were not enough to keep her from missing her mother's pies and applesauce, crabs and oysters. She missed the soups: duck, fish, and clam chowder she left behind for bland dining hall fare. She missed the soft summer dresses and the knitted wool sweaters that Nellie made for her. It may have been extreme homesickness that got her sent to the school's Quaker benefactor "Miss Edge's" Philadelphia home for some recuperation.[126]

By the time Helen arrived at the school, the institution was once more organized like a traditional prep academy. She joined the debate society, the Catholic Club, and wrote front page essays for *The Carlisle Arrow*, including one that was reprinted and reviewed by the Milwaukee, Wisconsin, newspaper. Throughout her adulthood, she remained proud of her school activities and other accomplishments at Carlisle while plagued by ill health.[127]

It was exciting to be at Carlisle during the years it fielded the best football team in the nation, including victories over the Ivy League schools. To most of Helen's fellow students, the football field was another battleground, one on which they were the victors. Since Helen's boyfriend was Jim Thorpe's best friend, she also became friends with him before Thorpe went on to win dual Olympic gold medals in the decathlon and pentathlon.[128]

When Helen's father was killed a few months before her graduation, her work, study, and activity-filled third year became more chaotic. Her cousin Helen from Annisquam took her to Aunt Tot for two months after a side trip to Gettysburg battlefield. She wrote to her classmates via the student newspaper, telling them she loved Annisquam's beauty and charm, and that she was healing. She was happily enfolded within the Lane family, but returned to celebrate her graduation. Her fellow graduates represented seventeen tribes from Alaska to the East Coast, but only twenty-six graduated of the fifty who had initially enrolled. The faculty encouraged her to go to an eastern secretarial school, but she wanted to go home and eat her mother's duck soup and go to a square dance where her brothers were the fiddler and caller.[129]

Intermarried like her older sisters, Helen and her son were abandoned during World War I when her husband lied that he had joined the army. She later married John Baptiste Finkbonner, the son of the Wounded Knee army commander's daughter Teresa Forsyth Finkbonner. Helen lived the rest of her ninety-four years on Lummi Reservation where as an honored elder, she was a valuable contributor to the *Lummi Elders Speak* book project.[130]

By the time Charles followed his sister to Carlisle in 1910, Lane children had been enrolled almost continuously for fourteen years. However, Fred Jr. was dying of the tuberculosis contracted at school and Helen was also having health problems there. To continue sending Nellie's children east was a calculated risk, pitting a free academic education and experiential opportunities the average Whatcom County teenager never had, against the possibility of illness and death.[131]

The next eligible child, Charles, had already nearly died in a sailboat accident. Born when Nellie was forty-one and Fred sixty-three, he never knew youthful, excited parents untouched by hard work and tragedy. Though Charlotte had been denied entrance as too old at seventeen in 1896, Charles left for Carlisle at nineteen, where the short but sturdy youth entered the blacksmith program. It was a difficult course that taught manufacture and repair of farm implements and gates, plus horseshoeing. Charles was also a debater, but most of his energy went to blacksmithing.[132]

It is certain that he enjoyed the 1912 football season when Jim Thorpe and his teammates beat West Point, a team that included sons and grandsons of Wounded Knee "battle" soldiers and officers. Victory held great symbolism for the Carlisle "Indians" dressed in blood-red uniforms, among whom were players related to the massacre's victims.[133]

Charles never got the chance to graduate. Nellie wrote to the superintendent in 1913 that she needed his help at home, and the director paid for the train ticket, leaving Lucy, the youngest Lane, at school. Charles was already highly skilled, having gone on three summer apprenticeships, the last with Jason Passmore, the recent inventor of a way to stretch and tighten barbed wire fences, an invaluable advance for western farmers.[134]

After only two months at home, Charles received a good job offer. Someone outside of Carlisle had given his name to the Supervisor of Indian Employment in Washington, D.C. Carlisle officials told the Supervisor that he had a "splendid" record and added many praises that spoke to Nellie and Fred's parenting abilities. Charles left for Montana's Crow Agency near the site of the Battle of Little Bighorn. The government had sent many children and grandchildren of Crow war chiefs to Carlisle, so Charles may have already known some people at the reservation. Allotments had been granted only nine years before and his blacksmith services were greatly needed. The Crow clans' history, their existence among incoming land-hungry settlers who usually hated them, and the tribe's brutal struggle to survive was a different story from what Charles had seen at Lummi. And yet, it was also the same. Many Crow daughters had married settlers there, too.[135]

When Charles returned home after about a year, he married a Lummi widow, Addie Warbus Gardner, like him the child of a British Columbia First Nations mother. He blacksmithed and lived most of the rest of his life at the Lummi fishing village along the Nooksack River. He and Addie had fourteen children, but only three lived to adulthood. The couple were greatly loved by their many other relatives.[136]

Lucy Medora, born in 1893, was Nellie's last child. They named the infant for both her long-deceased half-sister and her father's cousin Medora. In many ways, she was a Lane of a different era from that of her eldest brother August, married and with a large family by the time she was born. Lucy's parents divorced when she was nine and she didn't start school until age twelve. When she finished sixth grade at sixteen, she left for Carlisle with Charles to begin five years of high school. Unlike Charles, she stayed for her entire course. Nellie told the school that her meager income wasn't enough to afford train tickets for Lucy to come home for a visit.[137]

The petite teenager said later she never got homesick and didn't mind being so far from home at a school her sisters had liked so much. Despite what she said, she never adjusted to the institutional atmosphere after life on her Northwest island. After her first six months, she moved back and forth between Carlisle and private homes where she attended public school and helped out in the kitchen to earn her board. The first was Miss Edge's house where Helen had recuperated from one of her illnesses. Lucy spent twenty months in another where she attended the local high school for most of two years. She seems to have thrived on the combination of family living situations and public school, alternating with Carlisle and all its student activities, where she could usually be found with her brother for Christmas and Thanksgiving holidays. Because of her irregular presence at Carlisle, she seems to have fallen into the cooking course by default and during her last summer outing, she took over the home's cooking and baking completely. Lucy reported that whenever she was on campus, Helen's friend Jim Thorpe enjoyed flustering her. "He was famous. I was a waitress and I had to wait on his table. When I'd go past him, why, he'd whistle…I'd turn as red as a beet."[138]

At a time when none of the children from Lummi Reservation went on to high school, the Lanes' youngest studied opera at Carlisle when she was on campus. Her lack of consistent presence at the school made it impossible to devote herself to the rigorous daily lessons needed for serious voice development.[139]

Lucy was on campus much of 1914 when Congress investigated the entire staff for a failure to emphasize academics enough for the students to go on to college, despite the school's stated focus on being a prep school. Reports detailed many other kinds of abuses, which led to criminal prosecutions and the closure of Carlisle within a few years.[140]

When Lucy arrived home after five years, she found nearly everything about her family's lives and the island changed. A cannery sat atop the spit and electricity had arrived. And Nellie re-married just a few months after her daughter returned.

Using the cooking skills she learned from Nellie and at Carlisle, Lucy took a job at Tulalip Boarding School. The confident young woman, not even five feet tall, did not fear the intimidating director, Charles Buchanan. "He would pound his fist on the table and I would pound right back," she said. She later operated a hotel restaurant before she married Charles Patton, a man forty years her senior, and they had two sons. They lived in a "beautiful home" on her Lane land, according to the *Bellingham Herald,* as her mother had planned.

Chief Tsi'lixw (William) James of the Lummi. A renowned weaver of wool and cedar like his mother Frances James, he descended from Nellie Lane, Mary Fitzhugh Lear Phillips, and Sarah Descanum (sister of Clara Tennant). *Photo courtesy of Chief Tsi'lixw.*

Frances Lane James (Chetopia), Nellie and Fred Lane's great-granddaughter, is pictured with her traditional Coast Salish spindle whorl and wool yarn at her reservation home with Lummi Island in the background. Her blankets and baskets grace museums, galleries, and homes of admirers around the world. Inducted into the Northwest Women's Hall of Fame in the years before her death at 88, she was credited, with her son, for keeping the art of weaving in cedar and wool alive with decades of teaching grateful students. *Photograph by Candace Wellman.*

Left a young widow, she married Lawrence Handeyside, a veteran of two world wars. Lucy contributed to *Lummi Elders Speak* before she died an honored Lummi Nation elder who had been a member of St. Joachim's Catholic Church for all her ninety-four years. Family members recalled her dancing a jig at Lane family square dances even in her last years.[141]

In the twenty-first century, Nellie's numerous descendants continued to build a legacy of community action in tribal government, the military, education, sports, arts, and religion, though many probably did not know how far back some traditions went on both sides.

Lanes have included museum-honored basket makers and weavers, elected and traditional office holders, dancers, teachers, a Peace Corps member, tribal and county school board members, state sports champions, college staff, canoe pullers, fishermen, an archaeologist, a doctor, and other medical personnel, as well as spiritual leaders both traditional and Catholic. Lane men and women continue to smoke and barbeque salmon for appreciative consumers as Nellie did 130 years earlier.

೧ૐ౩

In 1981, a Lane descendant and his son noticed a home's roof in flames as they passed by. It was a busy roadway but no one had stopped to help or alert the residents. The pair turned their truck around. They rescued a mother and child alone and unaware in the burning house.[142]

The day could have ended in the loss of two lives, but did not. A different kind of legacy, the rescue was set in motion more than a century before when the too-young widow married the county sheriff.

Conclusion

CROSS-CULTURAL MARRIAGE CLUSTERS are known to have existed in mid-nineteenth century Washington and Oregon Territories. Others are probably yet undiscovered across the American frontier where, as in Whatcom County, tribal custom marriages followed a pattern that began in the earliest days of Spanish settlement of the New World. Historically, the cross-cultural marriages appear to be found where Euro-Americans sought to move onto tribal lands near villages, starting on the East Coast. White settlements where a sizable male workforce existed with few eligible women of their own culture may have generated a large percentage of cross-cultural marriages.

Understanding the contributions of intermarried women adds to the complexity of frontier history. Those wives and mothers can, with new research, be brought forward to the position of community mothers, as were the earliest white women settlers. While most community histories bestowed primacy honors on the "first white woman" and the "first white baby," a new look should be taken at who were the first married couples, and who was the first child born to them. As *Peace Weavers* demonstrates, Native wives made valuable contributions, but they went largely unacknowledged when their community's story was written. Assumptions that their children grew into misfits caught between two cultures also need to be discarded to view their destinies as individuals.

With many Hudson's Bay Company intermarriages in British Columbia, Bellingham Bay's blended community was not unique. However, in Washington Territory, a larger percentage of unions that did not involve the HBC began at that location than at any other yet found. Early legal complications and tribal custom marriages that went unrecorded prevent a final total, but the list of intermarriages in Whatcom County's first two decades continues to grow.

In contrast to the other early towns in Bellingham Bay's "neighborhood," to be intermarried in Whatcom County was entirely appropriate. No blended community grew at Coupeville on Whidbey Island or at Port Townsend, despite the presence of hundreds of eligible Coast Salish girls. Most settlers there were mariners and "money men" developers who brought wives with them, went elsewhere to find a bride, or abandoned their first (indigenous) wife to enhance their "city father" image. Neither community had the overwhelming bachelor workforce coupled with an absence of unmarried white women that Bellingham Bay had.

In the mid-1870s, a heavy influx of married white couples attracted by homestead laws, plus the establishment of Protestant churches, led to social changes that made Bellingham Bay communities more like Port Townsend and Coupeville. Aging intermarried men gradually left government leadership roles or were forced out by men with "legal" marriages to white women who imposed their own social standards. Still, the outcomes of the intermarriages differed as much as do those of twenty-first century couples.

The aging of the "old settlers" of Whatcom County coincided with a national belief that Indians were soon to die away in the face of a superior civilization. Writings portrayed them either as "savages" or as a "dying race," to be pitied and romanticized. Many descendants of intermarried couples who were "living white" gradually left behind close relationships with their reservation cousins. As much of their native heritage was either buried or romanticized the memories of Native grandmothers were gently placed into the proverbial closet. On the reservations, the memory of white grandfathers went into a closet as well, and identification became wholly indigenous.

The young Native American women who married Whatcom County's prominent settlers and army officers came predominantly from their villages' leading families. Though the four women profiled in this book had limited control over who they married within their own family's agendas, they were not simply the drudge and sex object of popular myth. They and others possessed the ability to adapt to their environment as well as bring their own values into marriage and new friendships with women of the invading culture. They influenced their husbands and administered their homes, as well as helped to build a wider community by their own actions or the children they gave birth to. Family and friends knew them as loving mothers and good neighbors who broke through stereotypes brought west by pioneer women and men. They maintained ties and integrated husbands and children into their own family complexes, and several helped build the new blended community. They became mediators and interpreters of both cultures, weaving a peaceful community together.

Caroline Davis Kavanaugh married to fulfill her father's agenda to keep peace among the alien peoples who shared geographical space. Her tenacity allowed her family to keep part of her own Samish family's traditional inherited land.

Mary Fitzhugh Lear Phillips lived her life in accordance with the S'Klallam people's self-identification of "The Strong People." Her resilience and survival skills enabled her descendants to become leaders in a new century.

Clara Tennant Selhametum helped to build new communities through church-building. She exhibited leadership that took her family's values of service and obligation into a blended culture without losing her own identity.

Nellie Carr Lane personified the community mother. Through her own actions and those of hundreds of descendants, she contributed to Lummi Island's community development and Lummi Nation's future.

Culturally biased attitudes of new Whatcom County residents coupled with ignorance of the intermarried women's contributions predominated over the century that followed the deaths of these four women and others. In the twenty-first century, change came as Lummi Nation, Swinomish Tribe, and others emerged as regional leaders in the fight for water, fish, and sacred site protection. Among those emerging leaders were descendants of many intermarried women.

In 2015, Bellingham replaced Columbus Day with Coast Salish Day.

Appendix A

Mary Devoes v Samuel Strange.
3rd District Territorial Court, Jefferson County. Series 2, #173
(1878)

Outgoing Justice Joseph R. Lewis' decision triggered indictments of "old settlers" with long tribal custom marriages to Native women. Neither Devoes nor Strange was a Native American.

Mary Devoes, an Irish immigrant, sued Samuel Strange for back wages for housekeeping and farm labor after their six-year relationship ended. Strange responded that he didn't owe wages for a common law marriage. She countered that they never were married and his defense would be an illegal contract. Justice Lewis ruled they only had a contract for "open and notorious fornication…in open violation of the law." He dismissed the case.

The law cited (Leg 5 Acts 1866, p. 82) declared that "marriages may be solemnized by any regular ordained minister and priest, Justice of the Peace, District or Probate Judge…a license shall be procured…there can be no legal marriage save only in accordance with the provisions of the statute."

Lewis added: "The rule is based on reason and morality. The plaintiff…asks this court to compensate her by compelling the defendant to pay her the wages of her sin and immorality. She and the defendant are equally guilty and the court…will leave these parties…to wallow in the filth it has found them in."

Appendix B

Territory v Charles Beale: Indictment for living in open and notorious fornication.
Territory of Washington, 3rd Judicial District. In the District Court of Whatcom County of the June Term, 1879. Judicial Review by Chief Justice Roger S. Greene.
(*Bellingham Bay Mail* 6/14/1879)

After the Lewis decision, and subsequent criminal indictments of long-married tribal custom husbands for "open and notorious fornication," Chief Justice Greene issued a review of the series of contradictory and confusing territorial marriage laws and amendments. Greene's opinion on the nature of the marriage contract ended the criminal proceedings.

Excerpts follow:
"The marriage contract stands, among all contracts, chief. It exists not by the law of a particular nation, but by the law of all nations. It is before all nations, and it is the legitimate source of them all..."

"...where the relationship of parties apparently living together as husband and wife, is in question, the presumptions of the law are always that they are married."

"The great weight of legislative, judicial and speculative authority is that marriage among English-speaking peoples, and particularly throughout the United States, is a civil contract, and needs for its validity nothing more than the mutual assent of two persons legally capable of making and fulfilling such a contract. Such is our English common law. And a statute, therefore, providing for a license, publication, witnesses, an officiating civil or religious officer, or ceremonies of any kind, is not held to make these formalities necessary to constitute a marriage...for it is not the act of the State, but the act of the couple, that makes the wedding."

Notes

If not cited in full, sources in the notes can be found in the bibliography of this work.

Introduction

1. Irene Jernigan, Finkbonner genealogy. Irene Jernigan Papers. Primary record citation withheld by request.

2. Gretchen M. Bataille and Kathleen Mullen Sands, *American Indian Women*, 130.

Chapter 1

1. Ingersoll, *To Intermix With Our White Brothers: Indian Mixed Bloods from the Earliest Times to the Indian Removals* and Pascoe, *What Comes Naturally: Miscegenation Law and the Making of Race in America* inform much of the introduction.

2. Hyde, *Empires, Nations & Families*, 1, 5; Larry E. Morris, *The Fate of the Corps*, (New Haven: Yale University Press, 2004), 187-202.

3. Harvey J. McKay, *St. Paul, Oregon 1830-1890*, 14.

4. Pascoe, *What Comes Naturally*, xiv.

5. Sam Pambrun, descendant of Frenchtown's earliest settlers, in conversations with the author, 2014.

6. The following focus on intermarriages at some of these locations: Robert Foxcurran, "Les Canadiens: Resettlement of the Metis into the Backcountry of the Pacific Northwest," *Columbia* (Fall 2002): 24; Cecelia Svinth Carpenter, *Fort Nisqually: A Documented History of Indian and British Interaction* (Tacoma: Tahoma Research Service, 1986); John B. Jackson, "Mixed-Bloods on the Cowlitz," *Columbia* 12, no. 1 (1998), 12-16.

7. Sylvia Van Kirk, "Tracing the Fortunes of Five Founding Families of Victoria," *BC Studies* no. 115/116, (1997/1998): 149-79.

8. Jones-Lamb, *Native American Wives of San Juan Settlers*, details the lives of many HBC couples, though at the time it was written, access to some sources that would have enhanced accuracy were not available.

9. The approximate number of intermarriages was estimated starting with a list begun by Howard Buswell, (HBP, CPNWS) and added to by the author over the years through sources that included family knowledge, legal cases of many kinds, unpublished interviews, anthropologists' research notes, church records, family genealogies, published histories, newspaper articles, and county marriage records.

10. Suttles, "Post-Contact Culture Change Among the Lummi Indians," 47.

11. Jeanette Taylor, *The Quadra Story: A History of Quadra Island* (Madeira Park, BC: Harbour Publishing, 2009), 27-39; Mike Vouri, "Raiders from the North," *Columbia* (Fall 1997), 24-35.

12. Teresa Eldridge, "Fifty-five Years on Bellingham Bay," *American Reveille,* 6/14/1908.

13. Entries for Blocks 1 and 8, Whatcom County Auditor, "Abstract of Whatcom Lots 1856-1872," and "Book of Liens H," "Deeds G," 39-40.

Out of fear of the Roeder family's continued local power, Howard Buswell coded Roeder as "Captain Vermillion." He noted in 7/1952 that "The basic fact was widely and well known by old timers generally." His source interviews were Lizzie Adams Lane Malmberg who said she was the wife's cousin, 7/4/1952; teacher and Lummi resident Florence Boone, 12/30/1947; Lummi Angeline Alexander 1/26/1967; and an undated interview with Hallie Lysle Campbell, whose (white) parents arrived in 1854 during the Lummi marriage. HBP, CPNWS.

14. Roth, *History of Whatcom County,* 1 and 2.

15. Jacqueline Peterson, "The Founders of Green Bay: A Marriage of Indian and White," *Voyageur, Historical Review of Brown County and Northeast Wisconsin* (Spring, 1984). Reprinted at www.uwgb.edu.

16. Acts 613 and 614. Abbott, *Real Property Statutes,* 462; Roger Newman, personal research re marriage laws.

17. Acts 615 (1859), 616 (1866), 617 (1866), 618 (1866), 619 (1868), Abbott, *Real Property Statutes;* George Richardson Hall and Fanny (Kumshelitsa), Whatcom County Auditor, Book of Liens "H." January 1855.

Only in 1869 did Whatcom County establish a marriage record book, after the final law was passed. Later laws in 1881 and 1883 did not mention color. Abbott, *Real Property Statutes,* 463-65; Roger Newman, personal research re marriage laws.

18. Jeffrey, *Frontier Women,* 5-7, chapter 4.

19. *Bellingham Bay Mail* 6/21/1879; The following 12/1878 indictments are all from 3rd District Territorial Court: Terr. v Fritz Dibbern (#48), Terr. v Henry Barkhousen (#51), Terr. v Charles Beale (#52); Terr. v Alexander Hemphill (#53), Terr. v Richard Wooten (#54), Terr. v David Whitehill (#55), Terr. v Shadrach Wooten (#56), Terr. v Enoch Compton (#57), Terr. v James Taylor (#59). All in 3rd District Territorial Court Case Files, WSA, NW.

20. "Henry C. Barkhousen," Interstate Publishing, *Illustrated History of Skagit,* 639.

Chapter 2

1. Vaughn Ploeger interview, 4/27/2011; James Kavanaugh III, in Jeffcott, *Nooksack Tales and Trails,* 426; Dick Fallis, "Military Fort Beckoned as Glamorously as Cinderella Ball," *Skagit Valley Herald,* 1982.

2. "Swinomish Princess was Sister-in-Law of Jefferson Davis," *Anacortes American* 2/27/1913; Jeffcott, *Nooksack Tales and Trails,* 421-27.

3. Dick Fallis, "Sweetheart of Padilla Bay," *Skagit Valley Herald,* 2/20/1982; Hilbert, *Siastenu,* 4, 26-7.

4. Caroline and Sarsfield Kavanaugh affidavits 2/15/1917 in Roblin, "Schedule of Unenrolled Indians." Suttles, research notes.

5. Sampson, *Indians of Skagit County*, 27-28; Roberts, "A History of the Swinomish," 54-56; Olive Munks in Loutzenhiser, *Told by the Pioneers vol. 2*, 179; Trebon, *First Views, an Early History*, 4.

6. Sally Snyder testimony and judicial opinion, *Swinomish v U.S.* #233 (1953) before the Indian Claims Commission. Copy in NWEC, CPNWS; Charles Luchman and Carmen Shone, "Lushootseed Village Life in the Skagit Watershed 1855," Skagit County Historical Museum program, 2/11/2001.

7. U.S. Census, Whatcom County 1870-1910; Washington Territorial Census 1885, 1887; Tombstone, Fernhill Cemetery; "Sister-in-law of Jeff Davis, Indian Princess, Dies at 91," *Anacortes American* 2/13/1919; Kavanaugh affidavits, 2/15/1917, Roblin "Schedule of Unenrolled Indians"; Suttles to author 12/2000 re family names from Sarsfield Kavanaugh; Ploeger Interview, 4/27/2011.

8. Sampson, *Indians of Skagit*, 29; Hilbert, *Siastenu*, 4, 26-7.

9. U.S. Dept. of Interior, BIA "Recommendation and Summary of Evidence"; Boyd, *Coming of the Spirit*, 59, 158-69; E.C. Fitzhugh, 6/1857 report quoted in Samish Indian Tribe, "Petition for Federal Acknowledgment."

10. Hall/Kumshelitsa marriage record, Whatcom County Book of Liens H, 348 and Deeds A, 19.

11. Davis genealogy in Jefferson Davis, *Papers*; David Adams, research re Robert and Katherine Auter Davis.

12. Morris, *Becoming Southern*, xvii, 108.

13. Hermann, *Joseph E. Davis*, 41; William Davis, *Jefferson Davis: The Man and His Hour* (New York: Harper Collins, 1991) 23-24; Hudson Strode, *Jefferson Davis: American Patriot 1808-1861* (New York: Harcourt Brace, 1955) 30; Cooper, *Jefferson Davis, American*, 30; Clement Eaton, *Jefferson Davis* (New York: Free Press, 1977), 7.

14. Davis genealogies in Davis, *Papers*; Morris, *Becoming Southern*, 120; Hermann, *Joseph E. Davis*, 93; Jefferson Davis, *Papers* 2:12.

15. Jefferson Davis, *Papers*, 2:12-13.

16. Sam Olden, "Mississippi and the U.S.-Mexican War, 1846-1848," *Mississippi History Now*, www.mshistorynow.k12.ms.us; Tim Harrison, "Mississippians in the Mexican War 1846-1848," *DeSoto Descendants* 24, no. 2 and 4, 2006. Reprinted on USGen-Web.com; Davis, *Papers*, footnote 10/31/1846 re NARA RG 94, 1st Miss. Muster Roll; *Vicksburg Daily Whig*, 11/14/1846.

17. Davis, *Papers*, 2:228-29; 1850 U.S. Census, Wilkinson County, MS.

18. Treaty of Point Elliott, available in many sources.

19. Harmon, *Indians in the Making*, 78, 96.

20. Karen Meador, "An Unlikely Champion: Jefferson Davis and the Pacific Northwest." *Columbia* (Winter 2004-5): 12-21.

21. Capt. Fred R. Brown, *History of the 9th U.S. Infantry, 1799–1909.* (Chicago: R.R Donnelley, 1909) n.p.; Sheila Biles, West Point Archives, to author, 12/5/2000; Coffman, *The Old Army*, 60, 143, 272; Cooper, *Jefferson Davis, American*, 283.

22. Jefferson Davis to Joseph Davis, 8/25/1855 in Cooper, *Jefferson Davis, The Essential Writings*, 112-14.

23. *Pioneer-Democrat*, 2/8/1856, 2/22/1856; Steve Dunkelberger and Walter Neary, "Historic Fort Steilacoom," *Columbia* 13, no. 2, (1999): 22-23.

24. J.W. Forsyth to J.H. Forsyth, late 1856. James W. Forsyth Papers; Coffman, *The Old Army*, 158, 278.

25. *Anacortes American*, 2/27/1913; Suttles, "Economic Life of the Coast Salish," 274; Jeffcott, *Nooksack Tales*, 423.

26. *Anacortes American*, 2/27/1913; Asher, *Beyond the Reservation*, 135.

27. Mrs. Fred March in Jeffcott, *Nooksack Tales*, 425.

28. The Davis family remains at the Menominee reservation. Chad Waukechon to author, 7/21/2010; Alan Caldwell to author, 7/20/2010; Abigail Norderhaug, Wisconsin Veterans Museum files; Gov. Wm. Upham, "Reflections on Jefferson Davis," in Tim Pletkovich, *Civil War Fathers: Sons of the Civil War to World War II* (Vandamere Press, 2006) 266-69; "Last Veteran of Civil War Dead," *Shawano County Journal*, 4/6/1933; "Last Veteran of Civil War Dies Monday," *Shawano Leader-Advocate*, 4/6/1933; Joseph T. Mills, "Jefferson Davis in the '30s," *Milwaukee Sentinel*, 11/10/1895. All newspaper articles courtesy of Chad Waukechon.

29. J.W. Forsyth to Ada Forsyth, 4/30/1859, James W. Forsyth Papers.

30. Amelia Dan interview, 1953. NWEC, CPNWS.

31. *Anacortes American*, 2/27/1913.

32. *Territory v E.C. Fitzhugh* #211 (1858), 3rd District Terr. Court. WSA, NW.

33. Bill Jarman to David Tuck, in Jeffcott, *Nooksack Tales*, 153.

34. Heitman, *Historical Register and Dictionary*, 360.

35. *Pioneer-Democrat*, 8/21/1857, 8/24/1857.

36. Ibid., 8/21/1857.

37. Whatcom County Deeds A, 23, 25. 10/19/1857.

38. Whatcom County Commissioners Proceedings v. 1, 43; *U.S. v William Smith (Sgt.), Michael O'Rourke, and John Fish* #96 (1858). 3rd District Territorial Court.

39. "Petition from Citizens of Whatcom County," 12/30/1857. U.S. Attorney General, "Records Relating to the Appointment." F.A. Chenoweth.

40. Whatcom County Commissioners Proceedings v. 1, 6/18/1858, 2/15/1859.

41. Archdiocese of Seattle, Sacramental Register, v. 3, 107.

42. County Commissioners Proceedings v. 1: 9/8/1858, 2/15/1859, 3/1/1859, 3/2/1859, 8/17/1859, 5/8/1862.

43. Charles Beale interview, Interstate Publishing Co., *Illustrated History of Skagit,* 25; "Oldest Living Skagit Pioneer," *Anacortes American,* 8/11/1921; Carrie White, "Fidalgo Before the Boom"; Charles Beale obituary, *Anacortes American,* 4/19/1923.

44. Interstate Pub. Co., *Illustrated History of Skagit,* 97; *Anacortes American,* 8/11/1921; Olive Munks, quoted in White, "Fidalgo Before the Boom."

45. *Pioneer-Democrat,* 12/9/1859; Charles W. Beale Jr. Affidavit, 1917. Roblin, "Schedule of Unenrolled Indians."

46. *Pioneer-Democrat,* 3/15/1861.

47. *Puget Sound Herald,* 4/11/1861, 5/9/1861, 5/16/1861; *Pioneer-Democrat,* 5/24/1861, 5/31/1861.

48. Leonard Munks, in Jordan, *Yarns of the Skagit,* 391-392.

49. Ibid.

50. *Puget Sound Herald,* 7/11/1861.

51. *Anacortes American, 2/27/1913*; McArthur, *The Enemy Never Came,* 59, 81.

52. Charles Beale, in Interstate Pub., Co., *Illustrated History of Skagit,* 97; *Anacortes American 2/27/1913*; Davis family genealogies, Davis, *Papers*; J.M. Post to C.S. Hubbell, 11/10/1917, Edmond S. Meany Papers.

53. Fred March to Percival Jeffcott, *Nooksack Tales,* 425; Leonard Munks, in Jordan, *Yarns of the Skagit,* 392.

54. Leonard Munks in Jordan, *Yarns of the Skagit,* 392.

55. Robert H. Davis Compiled Service Record, NARA RG94, M269, Roll 314; Dunbar Rowland, *Military History of Mississippi, 1803-1898.* Google books online.

56. 1850 U.S. Census, Warren County, MS; Dave Adams, Auter family research.

57. Davis, Compiled Service Record; Hermann, *Joseph E. Davis,* 114.

58. Hermann, *Joseph E. Davis,* 102-3; Terry Winschel, "Grant's March Through Louisiana," *The Blue and the Gray* 13, no. 5 (1996).

59. Bartholomees, *Buff Facings and Gilt Buttons,* 254.

60. Dave Adams to author, 3/2/2006; Robert Davis Compiled Service Record, Roll of Prisoners of War 6/29/1863.

61. Davis, Compiled Service Record; Memo from A.A. Stevens in 1/29/1865 inspection report, U.S. Dept. of War, *The War of the Rebellion* Series II, vol. 8, Correspondence.

62. Whatcom County Commissioners Proceedings, v. 1, 148.

63. Hannon, "Passing the Time," 83; Edward T. Downer, "Johnson's Island," in W.B. Hesseltine, ed. *Civil War Prisons,* 100, 103; Marcia Garner, *Johnson's Island,* (Toledo: M. Garner, 1992) 5.

64. Hannon, "Passing the Time," 88; Molly Conway autograph album, Johnson's Island U.S. Military Prison Collection. Center for Archival Collections, Bowling Green University, Ohio.

65. Dept. of War, *War of the Rebellion,* Correspondence 9/9/1864, 10/6/1864 and Inspection Report of Lt. Col. E.A. Scovill, 1/22/1865; Hesseltine, *Civil War Prisons,* 226;

66. U.S. Dept. of War, *War of the Rebellion.* Series II, v. 8 Correspondence. 1/13/1865, 1/16/1865, 1/18/1865, 1/20/1865, 1/25/1865.

67. Davis, Compiled Service Record; J.W. Davidson to Commander A.A. Stevens 1/29/1865. U.S. Dept. of War, *War of the Rebellion.* Series II, v. 8 Correspondence; Ruth Williams to author 3/20/2002.

68. U.S. Grant to Sec. of War Edward Stanton, 2/2/1865; Ould to Mulford 2/6/1865; Grant to Col. Wm. Hoffman 2/6/1865. All in *War of the Rebellion.* Series II, v. 8 Correspondence; Camp Hamilton Register entry, courtesy of Ruth Williams.

69. Davis, Compiled Service Record; Cooper, *Jefferson Davis, American,* 562; Ward Calhoun to author, 3/2011.

70. Fisher Funeral Home records, Vicksburg; Dave Adams research.

71. 1870 U.S. Census, Warren County, MS; Dave Adams research; Fisher Funeral Home Records; J.M. Keating, *A History of Yellow Fever: the Yellow Fever Epidemic of 1878* (transcribed by Linda F. Mason, www.rootsweb.com), 244.

72. *Anacortes American,* 2/27/1913.

73. Two books provided most of the general Irish context of James Kavanaugh's family. Richard Killeen, *A Short History of Ireland* (Dublin: Gill and MacMillan, 1994); Robert James Scally, *The End of Hidden Ireland: Rebellion, Famine and Emigration* (New York: Oxford Press, 1995).

74. Tim Kavanaugh, "The Kavanaugh Family History," unpub. ms.

75. Birthdate from James Kavanaugh's birth family's records, documents, and tombstone.

76. Kavanaugh, "Kavanaugh Family History."

77. They landed on June 3, 1846. Kavanaugh, "Kavanaugh Family History." Patricia Scott family research.

78. James kept a correspondence with Morgan. Tim Kavanaugh and Patricia Scott family research; 1850 U.S. census, Warren County, MS.

79. Fred March Sr., oral history.

80. James Kavanaugh letter to *Puget Sound Mail,* 1/20/1883; Fred March, 1969; Jeffcott, *Nooksack Tales,* 414.

81. Fred March, oral history.

82. Jeffcott, *Nooksack Tales,* 413; Fred March, oral history; Margaret Willis, ed., *Cheechacos All* (LaConner: Skagit County Historical Society) 21.

83. Whatcom County Deeds F, 7-8, 5/7/1860; *Territory v Oscar Olney* #247 (1860) 3rd District Territorial Court.

84. Whatcom County Commissioners Proceedings, v. 1, 127; Fred March, 1969.

85. James Kavanaugh to C.H. Hale, 10/16/1862, in Asher, *Beyond the Reservation,* 85. From records of the WA Superintendency of Indian Affairs.

86. James Kavanaugh diary, 5/23/1863. Two incomplete transcriptions and para-phrases of the diary are in public hands which the author synthesized. The original is thought to have been deposited by Sarsfield Kavanaugh with the Swinomish Tribe and is not available to public researchers, and Kavanaugh family members do not know of its location. Each outstanding version omits some events the other includes. Citations name the diary rather than the synthesis manuscript for brevity. See bib-liography under Wellman.

87. James Kavanaugh, Diary, 10/3/1863.

88. Kavanaugh, Diary, 7/23/1863, 7/29/1863, 8/1/1863; William Munks Sr. Diary, 7/23/1863, William Munks Sr. Papers.

89. Kavanaugh, Diary, 8/1/1863, 8/10/1863, 10/12/1863, 10/16/1863, 1/26/1864, 8/11/1865.

90. Kavanaugh, Diary, 8/20/1863; *Territory v William Gibson* #386 (1863). 3rd District Territorial Court.

91. *Puget Sound Herald,* 11/7/1861; Grant Keddie, *Songhees Pictorial: A History of the Songhees as Seen by Outsiders 1790-1912,* (Victoria: Royal BC Museum, 2003) 91; *British Colonist,* 9/26/1863–10/1/1863.

92. Whatcom Deeds F. 48, 50; Kavanaugh, Diary, 10/12/1863.

93. Richard March was born in 1859 and William in 1861. 1870 Whatcom County U.S. Census; John Tennant Journal, 10/25/1863; Kavanaugh, Diary, 10/28/1863, 11/2/1863.

94. Tennant, Journal, 12/9/1863-12/31/1863; Kavanaugh, Diary, 12/13/1863-12/31/1863; *Territory v William Smith* #376 (1863). 3rd District Terr. Court.

95. Tennant, Journal 1/1/1864; Kavanaugh, Diary 1/1/1864.

96. Kavanaugh diary, 8/26/1864, 6/7/1866, 10/22/1869, etc; Whatcom Commissioners Proceedings v. 1, 167-168.

97. Sarsfield and Caroline Kavanaugh 2/15/1917. Roblin, "Schedule of Unenrolled Indians."

98. Kavanaugh, Diary, 6/26/1863, 10/23/1864, 3/3/1865; Fred March, oral history.

99. Kavanaugh, Diary, 8/30/1864; Reg Ashwell, *The Coast Salish: Their Art, Culture and Legend* (Blaine, WA: Hancock House, 1978) 48.

100. Kavanaugh, Diary, 7/12/1865, 8/23/1865.

101. Kavanaugh diary, 10/10 or 10/16/1865; Don and Cathy Munks interview, 9/1/2006; Whatcom Deeds F, 19. 1/14/1861; Jeffcott, *Nooksack Tales,* 414; Tim Wahl, map of land tracts in 1871, in Trebon, *First Views,* 26.

102. Don and Cathy Munks, 9/1/2006; Olive Munks in Loutzenhiser, *Told by the Pioneers,* 2:177.

103. 1870 U.S. Census, Whatcom County.

104. Roberts, *History of the Swinomish,* 79, 156, 168.

105. Kavanaugh, Diary, 6/17/1866, 8/8/1866-8/16/1866, 9/10/66-9/16/66.

106. Ibid., 9/20/1866.

107. Ibid., 10/26/1866, 10/29/1866, 12/31/1866.

108. Ibid., 12/31/1866.

109. Ibid., 11/21/1867, 12/26/1867.

110. The Sacramental Register (v. 3, 63 & 107) noted that Sam was Jefferson Davis' grandnephew and son of Lt. Davis, a rare accurate depiction of the relationships; Kavanaugh, Diary 2/19/1870; Trebon, *First Views*, 12; Map 10/13/1992 by Fred March Jr., Shell Oil Kavanaugh File. WSA, NW.

111. *Anacortes American*, 2/27/1913; William Willis Griffin, "A History of the First Fidalgo Island Schools," unpub. ms. Courtesy of Carleton Howard; Carleton Howard, Griffin family research; Trebon, *First Views*, 29; Kavanaugh, Diary, 9/17/1873; 5/19/1877.

112. Don and Cathy Munks, 9/1/2006; 1870 U.S. Census Agricultural Supplement, Whatcom County.

113. Kavanaugh, Diary, 8/19/1868, 9/1/1868, 6/27/1871 and others; Wm. Munks, Ledgers and Account Books. Munks Papers; Trebon, *First Views*, 27; Conner Store Ledger, 1871-1873 (Skagit County Historical Museum, LaConner, WA).

114. Washington Territory Superintendent of Indian Affairs, reports 1867, 1868, 1869, 1870.

115. Samish Indian Tribe, *Petition for the Federal Acknowledgment*; Sarsfield Kavanaugh 3/6/1927, *Duwamish v U.S.*; Russell Barsh, "Ethnogenesis and Ethnonationalism from Competing Treaty Claims," in Alexandra Harmon and John Borrows, *The Power of Promise: Re-thinking Indian Treaties in the Pacific Northwest (Seattle: UW Press, 2009)*, 224; Susan and Fred Miller, *Samish Island, a History from the Beginning to the 1970s* (Mt. Vernon, WA: Fred and Susan Miller, 2007) 115; James Jr. and Gladys Squires, "Samish Island" in *Samish Gold Memoirs: Samish River Adventures and History* (Lawrence Hanson: 1999) n.p.

116. Samish Indian Tribe, *Petition for the Federal Acknowledgement*, 19; U.S. Dept. of the Interior, BIA "Recommendation and Summary of Evidence"; Suttles, *Post-Contact Culture Change*, 97.

117. Washington Superintendency, Report 10/1/1871, 273; Kavanaugh, Diary, 11/6/1873; Samish Indian Tribe, "Petition for the Federal Acknowledgement"; Roberts, "A History of the Swinomish," 228.

118. Kavanaugh, Diary, 1/29/1873; William Munks diary, 3/14/1872; Don and Cathy Munks, 9/1/2006.

119. Tim Wahl personal research; Kavanaugh, Diary, 6/20/1874; *James Kavanaugh v George Becker #2*, Series 2 (1876) 3rd District; *Territory v George Becker #915* Series 2 (1875), 3rd District.

120. 1880 U.S. Census, Whatcom County; Roberts, "A History of the Swinomish" 289; Sampson, *Indians of Skagit County*, 33; Carrie White, Diary 1882-1884.

121. *Bellingham Bay Mail*, 11/16/1878.

122. Kavanaugh, Diary, winter/spring 1879-1880, 4/16/1880, 9/7/1883, 4/5/1884, 6/11/1876; *Anacortes American*, 1/19/1884; Photo of James Kavanaugh courtesy of Jeff Haner; 1880 U.S. Census Agricultural Supplement.

123. *Puget Sound Mail*, 5/21/1881, 6/7/1881, 7/30/1881.

124. *Puget Sound Mail*, 11/27/1880, 12/4/1880.

125. Kavanaugh, Diary, 4/27/1881, 9/6/1881; Copy of the Kavanaugh patent in *Hiram March v Caroline Kavanaugh, et al.*, #660 (1892), Skagit County Superior Court; *Hiram A. March v Caroline Kavanaugh, Sarsfield John Kavanaugh, Francis James Kavanaugh, and Kate March* #500 (1888), Skagit County Superior Court.

126. Kavanaugh, Diary, 6/11 or 7/11/1876; *U.S. per John O'Keane v Johnny Lachweuse* #159 (1880), Skagit County Territorial Court; 1880 U.S. Census, King County, WA.

127. Wright, ed., *Lewis & Dryden's Marine History*, 261; *Puget Sound Mail*, 12/28/1878; 3/29/1879, 10/11/1879, 10/18/1879, 12/6/1879, 8/17/1881, 4/29/1882, 11/11/1882; Lorna Cherry, *South Whidbey and Its People*, v. 1 (Greenbank, WA: South Whidbey Historical Society, 1983) 132; Fred Beckey, *Range of Glaciers*, 334-36.

128. *Puget Sound Wreck Reports*, 1/17/1874-12/2/1888, 110; Wright, ed., *Lewis & Dryden Marine History*, 313; *Puget Sound Mail*, 1/20/1883; Flora Engle, *Recollections of Early Days on Whidbey Island* (Coupeville WA: Joanne Engle Brown, 2003) 148-49.

129. Kavanaugh, Diary, 1/17/1883.

130. *Puget Sound Mail*, 1/20/1883; *Puget Sound Wreck Reports*, 110; Interstate Publishing Co., *Illustrated History of Skagit*, 131.

131. *Puget Sound Mail*, 1/20/1883, 2/14/1883; Kavanaugh, Diary, 1/11/1885.

132. *Northwest Enterprise* 4/18/1885; Will of James Kavanaugh, 3/22/1885. Skagit County Probate Court #48; Kavanaugh, Diary, 6/9/1885.

133. *Northwest Enterprise* 7/4/1885; *Whatcom Reveille* 7/13/1885; Jackson Funeral Home records; Rosamond Van Miert, *Settlers, Structures and Ships on Bellingham Bay 1852-1889*, 191-92.

134. *Northwest Enterprise*, 7/4/1885, reprinted in the *Whatcom Reveille*.

135. Roberts, "A History of the Swinomish," 240; *Puget Sound Mail*, 8/26/1887, 10/20/1887; Fred March Sr. oral history.

136. No definitive name or history has been found by this author for Caroline's sister Annie/Alice; Tom Wynn Jr. in Jeffcott, *Nooksack Tales* 426; *Anacortes American*, 2/27/1913; Caroline Kavanaugh affidavit 1/15/1917 in Roblin, "Schedule of Unenrolled Indians"; Sophie Walsh, "Trials and Hardships of Anacortes Pioneers: Sarsfield John Kavanaugh," *Anacortes American*, 6/10/1927.

137. Leonard Munks in Ginger Houston, "The Legends of Grandma Kavanaugh," *Fidalgo Magazine*, 8/31/1994, 9/28/1994; Fred March Sr. oral history.

138. *Territory v William Munks* #418 (1887), 3rd District Terr. Court; Skagit County Court Journal B.

139. *U.S. v G.E. Kain and J.P. Olson* #171 (1886), Whatcom Territorial Court.

140. *Territory v William Munks* #472 (1887), 3rd District Territorial Court; *Puget Sound Mail,* 12/15/1887.

141. Skagit County Deeds 5, 680-81; Skagit County Deeds 4, 557-559; *Hiram March v Caroline Kavanaugh, Sarsfield John Kavanaugh, Francis James Kavanaugh, and Kate March* #500 (1888). 3rd District Territorial Court, Skagit County.

142. F.J. Kavanaugh to McEachran and Godfrey, Chattel Mortgage 12/13/1889. Skagit County Chattel Mortgages v. 2, 309-10.

143. *Hiram A. March v Caroline Kavanaugh, Sarsfield John Kavanaugh and Francis James Kavanaugh* #660 (1890). Skagit County Superior Court.

144. *John P. Hayes and George W. Merriam, dba as Hayes and Merriam v S.J. Kavanaugh and F.J. Kavanaugh* no. 1886 (1893); *Charles L. Fowle v F.J. and S.J. Kavnaugh* #1885 (1892). Both in Skagit County Superior Court.

145. Skagit Marriage Certificate #82; 1900 U.S. Census, Skagit County; F.J. Kavanaugh affidavit 8/15/1918. Roblin, "Schedule of Unenrolled Indians."

146. Sampson, *Indians of Skagit County,* photo p. 36; 1880 U.S. Census, Whatcom County; Roberts, "History of the Swinomish," 24, 296.

147. *Martha Kavanaugh v F.J. Kavanaugh* no. 4763 (1905), Skagit County Superior Court; Skagit Count Marriage Certificate no. 2473; F.J. Kavanaugh affidavit 8/15/1918, Roblin "Schedule of Unenrolled Indians"; Jeff Haner to author, 7/19/2010.

148. Life lease #75517, Skagit County Leases and Agreements, v. 5, 329-331. 12/30/1905, filed 1909; Shell Oil Kavanaugh file.

149. Suttles to author 4/19/2004; photos courtesy of Jeff Haner; 1930 U.S. Census, Skagit County.

150. "Sarsfield Kavanaugh" in Loutzenhiser, *Told by the Pioneers,* 24.

151. U.S. Dept. of Interior, BIA, "Recommendation and Summary;" Alexandra Harmon, *Indians in the Making,* 176.

152. Stauss, *Jamestown S'Klallam Story,* 136; Dept. of Interior, BIA, "Recommendation and Summary;" Northwest Federation of Indians Records.

153. Sarsfield Kavanaugh testimony, *Duwamish v U.S.* (1927).

154. Photos of Caroline Kavanaugh courtesy of Jeff Haner.

155. *Anacortes American,* 2/27/1913.

156. Loutzenhizer, *Told By the Pioneers,* 24; J.M. Post to C.S. Hubbell, 11/10/1917. Edmond S. Meany Papers, UW.

157. *Anacortes American* 2/13/1919; *Sunday American-Reveille,* 2/16/1919.

158. Fernhill Cemetery records; *Anacortes American,* 2/13/1919.

159. Harmon, *Indians in the Making,* 179-80.

160. *Anacortes American,* 6/19/1924; Samish Indian Tribe, "Petition for the Federal Acknowledgment," 37-38; Resolution 10/3/1925, Northwest Federation of Indians Records.

161. *Puget Sound Mail,* 5/19/1932.

162. Sarsfield Kavanaugh, 3/6/1927, *Duwamish v U.S.*

163. *Anacortes American* 12/16/1943; Skagit County Death Certificate 12/10/1943; Jackson Funeral Home Records, v. 1, 115.

164. Vaughn Ploeger, 4/27/2011; Samish Indian Tribe, "Petition for Federal Acknowledgment."; Harmon, *Indians in the Making,* 214.

Chapter 3

1. Coll-Peter Thrush and Robert Keller Jr., "'I See What I Have Done': The Life and Murder Trial of Xwelas, a S'Klallam Woman," *Western Historical Quarterly* 26, no.2 (Summer, 1995), 169-83.

2. Manuel Quimper diary, in Jervis Russell, *Jimmy Come Lately: History of Clallam County, a Symposium* (Port Angeles WA: Clallam County Historical Society, 1971), 15; L.L. Langness, "A Case of Post Contact Reform Among the Klallam," in *Shadows of Our Ancestors,* ed. Gorsline, 167; Delbert J. McBride, "Viewpoints and Visions in 1792," *Columbia* (Summer 1990), 21-27.

3. Hilbert, *Siastenu,* 7-9; Hilbert, "To a Different Canoe," in *A Time of Gathering: Native Heritage in Washington State,* ed. Robin K. Wright, 255.

4. Langness, "A Case of Post Contact Reform," 168.

5. Mary's birth year estimated by average age of first marriage, date of her 2nd marriage to E.C. Fitzhugh, Laurie Cepa family research, and errors of fact in censuses which put her birth impossibly late; Boyd, *Coming of the Spirit,* 170; Herbert Taylor Jr., "The Ft. Nisqually Census of 1838-39," *Ethnohistory* 7, no. 4 (1960), 403-4; Langness, "A Case of Post Contact Reform," 168-69; Wayne Suttles, "Central Coast Salish" in *Handbook of the North American Indian,* v. 7, ed. Wayne Suttles, 473; Gunther, "Klallam Ethnography," 181.

6. Lambert, *House of the Seven Brothers,* 7-14.

7. Stauss, *Jamestown S'Klallam Story,* 29, 32, 41; Gunther, "Klallam Ethnography," 216; Suttles, "Central Coast Salish," 458.

8. Stauss, *Jamestown S'Klallam,* 41; Jamie Valadez, interview by author at Port Angeles, WA, 9/9/2016; Candace Wellman, "The Face of Extinction: Ske'xe, The Coast Salish Wool Dog" (Unpub. ms., 2013).

9. Valadez, 9/9/2016; Jacilee Wray, ed., *Native Peoples of the Olympic Peninsula: Who We Are* (Norman: U of Oklahoma and Olympic Peninsula Intertribal Cultural Advisory Committee, 2002), 40.

10. *William Jarman v Alice Jarman,* Skagit County #89 (1879). 3rd District Territorial Court; Camfield, *Port Townsend, An Illustrated History,* 261-62; Patricia Campbell, *A History of the North Olympic Peninsula* (Port Angeles: Daily News, 1977), 9-11.

11. Kah'tai Lagoon no longer exists at the west end of Port Townsend, filled in during the 1960s; James G. McCurdy, *By Juan de Fuca's Strait: Pioneering Along the Northwestern Edge of the Continent* (Portland: Binford & Mort, 1937), 16-17.

12. Boyd, *Coming of the Spirit*, 161, 168.

13. Kennedy, "Quantifying Two Sides," 25, 26.

14. Sampson, *Indians of Skagit County*, 26; Hilbert, *Siastenu*, 34; Ruth Shelton, "Sehome Line," Percival Jeffcott Papers; Kennedy, "Quantifying Two Sides," 22, 119, 127; Lambert, *House of Seven Brothers*, 12.

15. Brumbaugh, interview.

16. Photo of Mary, property of Gordon Lear, photocopy courtesy of Chief William James, 2004.

17. Richard Miller, "Foundation Stones of Stafford County, Virginia" (unpub. ms), 21; *The Free Lance* (Fredericksburg, VA), 9/14/1901; Boscobel chain of title in Fitzhugh Family file, Central Rappahannock Regional Library; George King Papers.

18. William Rasmussen, "First Fitzhughs of Virginia," *American Art Review* 9, no. 2 (1997), 81; Sallie Lee Fitzhugh interview; Central Rappahannock Regional Library, Fitzhugh Family file.

19. University of Pennsylvania, Master Alumni File, Office of Alumni Records; Thomas Fitzhugh of Boscobel will, George King Papers; Dr. Alexander Fitzhugh, Service Record, War of 1812, NARA online; Alexander Fitzhugh obituary, *Alexandria Gazette*, 8/19/1847; 1840 U.S. Census, Stafford County VA; Stafford County Land Tax Books 1834-1850. Microfilm, Library of Virginia.

20. Sallie Lee Fitzhugh interview.

21. Lottie Roth (in *History of Whatcom County 1*) wrote that Fitzhugh attended Georgetown Law School but it did not exist at that time; Elizabeth Clare Fitzhugh obituary, *Alexandria Gazette*, 4/26/1836; *Political Arena (VA)* 9/18/1827, 4/22/1836; "The Fitzhugh Family," *Virginia History Magazine*, 8 (1901), 431; Georgetown University, *Entrance Book 1834-1838*, and 1835 prospectus "Georgetown College, in the District of Columbia." Both at Georgetown University Archives.

22. Lynn Conway to author 9/29/2000 re dismissal, Georgetown University Archives.

23. Evidence suggests that Fitzhugh may have hidden this embarrassment while he lived at Sehome; Leonard, *General Assembly of Virginia*, 390; U.S. Military Academy, Cadet Application Papers, 1805-1866, E.C Fitzhugh File #247. U.S. Military Academy Archives; Sheila Biles, USMA, to author 12/5/2000 re dismissal.

24. William Gwin to Attorney General 3/15/1858, U.S. Attorney General, Records Relating to the Appointment. Edmund C. Fitzhugh; (Fredericksburg) *Democratic Reporter* 9/29/1843; Leonard, *General Assembly*, 423.

25. American Antiquarian Society, online, Misc. Documents 1703-1867, Slavery in the U.S. Collection, 1703-1905; Stafford County (VA) Deed Book OO, 270-272. 6/12/1847.

26. Patricia Fitzhugh research re 1849 departure; *Pioneer-Democrat*, 6/15/1860; Malcolm Rohrbaugh, "No Boy's Play: Migration and Settlement in Early Gold Rush California," in *Rooted in Barbarous Soil*, ed. Starr and Orsi, 25-43; Carl I. Wheat, "California's Bantam Cock," *California Historical Quarterly* 9, 276; Oscar T. Shuck, *History of the Bench and Bar of California* (Los Angeles: Commercial Printing House, 1901), 452.

27. Bancroft, *History of California*, 7:229, 237-242.

28. Joseph Glover Baldwin, *Flush Times of Alabama and Mississippi: A Series of Sketches* (New York: Appleton, 1854), 212.

29. Directory Publishing, *Langley's San Francisco City Directory* (1850, 1854); William Gwin to U.S. Attorney General 3/15/1858; Bancroft, *History of California*, 679; Howard A. DeWitt, "Senator William Gwin and the Politics of Prejudice," www.online. ohlone.edu.

30. *Samuel Brown v Henry Roeder, R.V. Peabody and H.C. Page dba Roeder, Peabody & Company* #185 (1859), 3rd District Washington Territorial Court; William Ellison, "Memoirs of the Honorable William Gwin," *California Historical Quarterly* 19:256; Roeder "Narrative 6/22/1878," (unpub. ms.), Bancroft Library, University of California, Berkeley; Roger W. Lotchin, *San Francisco 1846-1856: From Hamlet to City* (Lincoln: U of Nebraska, 1974), 71.

31. Roth, *History of Whatcom County*, 1:38.

32. *Pioneer-Democrat*, 6/15/1860; Whatcom County Deeds A, 8. 12/16/1853 and 3/2/1854.

33. Ruth Shelton and Harriet Dover to Percival Jeffcott, 2/5/1954. Jeffcott Papers.

34. Shelton and Dover to Jeffcott, 2/5/1954; Dover, *Tulalip from My Heart*, 72; Roth, *History of Whatcom County 1*, 38.

35. Shelton and Dover, 2/5/1954; Dover, *Tulalip from My Heart*, 73.

36. Dover, *Tulalip From My Heart*, 72; Capt. James Tarte in Roth, *History of Whatcom 1*, 932; Shelton and Dover, 2/5/1954.

37. Owens, Reid Family Papers; All records for Mason Fitzhugh are consistent in his birthdate; *Pioneer-Democrat*, 11/6/1857.

38. *Pioneer-Democrat* 11/6/1857; N.V. Sheffer in *Port Townsend Leader*, 12/17/1905.

39. Washington Territorial Volunteer Records, Muster Roll of the Staff of the First Regiment of Washington Territorial Volunteers 10/14/1855-2/11/1856, WSA, Olympia; Roberts, "A History of the Swinomish," 204; Phil Wahl & Earngy Sandstrom interview; August Martin, 1947-1948 interviews by Wayne Suttles, in Suttles research files; Fitzhugh to I.I. Stevens, 2/8/1856, 2/22/1856; Fitzhugh to Michael Simmons, 9/12/1857; Stevens to Fitzhugh 6/4/1856. All in Washington Territory Superintendent of Indian Affairs, Letters Received; U.S. Attorney General, Fitzhugh nomination papers, extract from report of J.Ross Browne re language ability.

40. N. R. Knight, "Early Washington Banking," *WHQ* 26, no. 4 (10/1935): 251-59; Island County, Claim Book, v 2A, 39; *Pioneer-Democrat*, 8/24/1855; Emily Tawes Morhman interview by Howard Buswell, 4/10/1949. HBP, CPNWS.

41. Whatcom County Commissioners Proceedings v. 1; Lang, *Confederacy of Ambition*, 72, 124; U.S. Attorney General, Records relating to the Appointment, Fitzhugh.

42. The criminal case file informs much of the following paragraphs. *Territory of Washington v Edmund C. Fitzhugh* #211 (1858), 3rd District Territorial Court, WSA, NW. Also 2nd District Court, Minute Book, WSA, SW.

43. Fischer, *Albion's Seed*, 403.

44. Lang, *Confederacy of Ambition*, 121-23.

45. Territorial Prosecutor Butler P. Anderson to *Pioneer-Democrat*, 1/7/1859.

46. 3rd District, Court Journal A, 250, 10/10/1858; "One of Mr. Buchanan's Judges," *New York Daily Tribune*, 11/17/1858.

47. *New York Daily Tribune*, 11/17/1858; "Speech of Honorable John A. Tennant," *Pioneer-Democrat*, 2/4/1859.

48. Lucy Washington's son John A. Wilson founded a Lummi Reservation family.

49. 2nd District Terr. Court, Minutes Book, 3/14/1859; *Pioneer-Democrat*, 3/14/1859, 7/22/1859; *Puget Sound Herald*, 4/1/1859.

50. Edson, *Fourth Corner*, 187; Fitzhugh to W.W. Miller, 6/28/1859. Miller Papers.

51. *Territory of Washington v William Strong and E.C. Fitzhugh*, #465 (1860), 2nd Judicial District; *Puget Sound Herald*, 12/17/1858; *Pioneer-Democrat*, 3/23/1860; Lang, *Confederacy of Ambition*, 128.

52. *Pioneer-Democrat*, 3/23/1860.

53. *Pioneer-Democrat*, 5/25/1860; *Daily Alta* (Sacramento), 11/17/1857; Whatcom Deeds A, 65-67, 36-37; August Martin to Wayne Suttles, 1947/48, Suttles research files; Sherry Guzman interview.

54. The author has read all of Fitzhugh's district court cases; Bancroft-Whitney, *Reports of Cases Decided in the Supreme Court of the Territory of Washington*, vol. 1 and vol. 2 by John B. Allen, vol. 3 by Henry Struve, (San Francisco: Bancroft-Whitney, 1889); *Benjamin Madison v Lucy Madison* #169 (1859), 3rd District Territorial Court; John B. Allen, *Reports of Cases Determined in the Supreme Court of the Territory of Washington from 1854-1879*, v. 1, new series. (Olympia: C. B. Bagley, 1879), 60-63.

55. Fitzhugh to W.W. Miller, 6/28/1859, Miller Papers; *Puget Sound Herald*, 7/15/1859.

56. Sherry Guzman interview; Shelton and Dover to Jeffcott, 2/5/1954. PRJ, CPNWS.

57. Shelton and Dover to Jeffcott, 2/5/1954; Dover, *Tulalip*, 73.

58. Shelton and Dover to Jeffcott, 2/5/1954.

59. Miller to O.B. McFadden, 6/16/1860; Fitzhugh to Miller, 7/22/1860. Both in Miller Papers.

60. *Pioneer-Democrat* 4/5/1861; Stephen T. Moore, "Cross-Border Crusades" *PNW Quarterly* (Summer 2007), 132; Ken Mather, *Buckaroos & Mud Pups: The Early Days of Ranching in British Columbia* (Vancouver, B.C.: Heritage House, 2010), 38; David C. Keehn, *Knights of the Golden Circle: Secret Empire, Southern Secession, Civil War* (Baton Rouge: LSU Press, 2013), 134.

61. Marriage notice, *Fredericksburg Star*, 6/7/1861; Cora Fitzhugh obituary, *Alexandria Gazette*, 1/3/1863; Pete McLallen, Bowie family genealogy research.

62. *The North-West*, 7/18/1861.

63. Island County Deeds & Mortgages Record Book 2, 73-75 and 265-267; *The North-West*, 7/18/1861.

64. *Alexandria Gazette*, 1/3/1863.

65. *Orrington Cushman and B. Franklin Shaw v Edmund C. Fitzhugh,* Series 1, #367 (1862) 3rd District Territorial Court; E. C. Fitzhugh to B. Franklin Shaw, Island County Deeds and Mortgages, Record Book 2, 258-59.

66. Much of Barkhousen's family died in an 1832 cholera epidemic in Rushville, Illinois. He spent his childhood within sight of the mass grave that contained his father and siblings.

67. Carol Ericson, Lear family research; photocopy of Mary Phillips photograph, courtesy of Chief William James.

68. Heitman, *Historical Register,* 621; Ericson research; Patricia A. Neal research and Lear timeline.

69. Heitman, *Historical Register,* 621; Carol Ericson, Martha Holcomb, and Patricia Neal research on William King Lear. Their work informs much of the section on Lear's activities.

70. Isabella married her stepfather's brother and her intricately woven baskets are the foundation collection at Maryhill Museum, Goldendale, WA. Ericson, Holcomb, and Neal research; Isabella Underwood obituary, *Mt. Adams Sun,* 11/25/1936; Amos Underwood obituary, *Skamania County Pioneer,* 12/27/1917; *Hood River Glacier,* 7/27/1905.

71. Dr. Caleb Burwell Rowan Kennerly account book #5, 4/1858; Kennerly to Spencer Baird, 6/13/1858. Both in Kennerly Papers, Smithsonian Archives, Washington, D.C.; *Pioneer-Democrat,* 7/9/1858.

72. 1860 U.S. Census, Whatcom County; Carol Ericson, Bill James, and census information about the marriage date, birth date; map of Fort Bellingham in Joseph Mansfield, *Report of the Inspector of Fort Bellingham, 12/28/1858.* NARA, NW. Copy at WSA, NW; Shelton and Dover to Jeffcott, 2/5/1954, Jeffcott Collection.

73. Patricia A. Neal, *Fort Wrangel, Alaska: Gateway to the Stikine River 1834-1899* (Greenwich CT: Coachlamp Productions, 2007), 46-48; 1900 U.S. Census, Alaska; Bill James to author 3/28/2002, 11/10/2005; Neal personal research; Holcomb, personal research and newspaper clipping.

74. Aaron Collins was sometimes known as Isaac in records; John Campbell diaries 1853-1894, UW Library Special Collections; diary entry 6/24/1870 noted that Mary Campbell was writing to Fitzhugh; Robert Reid & Julie Owens in Reid Family Papers.

75. Campbell diaries, numerous entries in the 1860s; Shanna Stevenson, "Rebecca Groundage Howard," www.blackpast.org.

76. Reuben and Julianne Reid moved for his logging jobs, finally to Port Townsend. She re-established her relationship with her mother Julia Barkhousen, had a large family, and was a well-known city matron. Robert Reid & Julie Owens, Reid Family Papers; Julie Owens to author 9/12/2000.

77. Jean Barman, "Taming Aboriginal Sexuality: Gender, Power, and Race in B.C. 1850-1900." *BC Studies* #115-116, (1997-98), 237-66.

78. 1870 U.S. Census, Whatcom County; HBP, CPNWS; Affidavits by her children in Seattle Archdiocese Sacramental Register v. 3, 78; *Sounder* 9/10/1997; Steve Kenady, "Cultural Resources at Port Langdon: Turn of the Century" typescript and map for Cultural Resources Management, Eastsound, WA, 1994; *The Sounder*, 9/10/1997; Lucile McDonald, "Memories of Orcas Island in the 70s," *Seattle Times*, 12/18/1960.

79. Arthur Wotten undated interview re the lime kiln work, San Juan Island Historical Museum files.

80. Seattle Archdiocese Sacramental Register v 3, 103, 78; Whatcom County Marriage Book B, 19.

81. McDonough Account Book AA, 105 and A, 47. Buswell Papers; *Bellingham Daily Mail*, 5/27/1876, 6/3/1876; Roth, *History of Whatcom 1*, 196.

82. Mason Fitzhugh photo, CPNWS; Pearl Fitzhugh Little, 1944 affidavit in *Little, Pearl F., In the matter of the estate of*; Photos of Julianne Reid, granddaughter Cristina. Reid Family Papers; 1900 U.S. Census, San Juan County.

83. Homer D. Musselman, *Stafford County in the Civil War* (Lynchburg, VA: H. E. Howard, 1995), 46-47.

84. Edmund C. Fitzhugh, Service Record. "Compiled Service Records of Confederate General and Staff Officers and Non-Regimental Enlisted Men." Library of Virginia; Bartholomees, *Buff Facings and Gilt Buttons*, 17-34.

85. George and Elizabeth Grayson Carter Bible, Oatlands Plantation archives, Leesburg VA; Loudoun County (VA) Circuit Court Clerk, Index to Marriage Bonds, 204; Fitzhugh genealogy by Patricia Fitzhugh and others; Wyatt-Brown, *Southern Honor*, 217.

86. Eppa Hunton, *Autobiography* (Richmond; William Byrd Press, 1933) 118; Fitzhugh Service Record; William A. and Patricia C. Young, *56th Virginia Infantry* (Lynchburg VA: A. E. Howard, 1990), informs the account of Fitzhugh's service in the regiment.; R.A. Brock, *The Appomattox Register* (New York: Antiquarian Press, 1962 reprint of 1887 edition), 83-84.

87. *Puget Sound Mail*, 1/13/1883.

88. Carter, " Journal," 5/1865-6/1865.

89. Ibid., 8/1865, 5/1866.

90. *Walla Walla Statesman*, 6/15/1866.

91. Historical Illustrative Co., *Illustrated Fort Dodge* (Des Moines, IA: Historical Illustrative, 1896), 345; 1870 U.S. Census, Webster County, Iowa (inaccurate ages recorded).

92. *Bellingham Bay Mail*, 7/19/1873, 9/13/1873; 1880 U.S. Census, Loudon County, VA.

93. *Bellingham Bay Mail*, 12/7/1874; *Puget Sound Mail*, 1/13/1883.

94. Campbell, Diary 6/24/1870.

95. Shelton and Dover to Jeffcott, 2/5/1954.

96. Directory Publishing, *Langley San Francisco*, 1881-1882, 1883; George Mendell on www.alcatrazhistory.com; "1878 Great Register," California Information File, San Francisco Public Library; U.S. 1880 Census, San Francisco.

97. Directory Publishing, *Langley San Francisco*, 1883; What Cheer Hotel photo, Bancroft Library; San Francisco County Health Dept. "Record of Deaths 1882-1889", v. 3; San Francisco Health Dept., "Interments transferred from Masonic Cemetery," MF Reel 2. Both at San Francisco Public Library.

98. Lillian Schlissel, "Family on the Western Frontier," ed. Lillian Schlissel, Vickie Ruiz and Janice Monk, *Western Women: Their Land, Their Lives* (Albuquerque: U of New Mexico, 1988), 85-86.

99. Seattle Archdiocese Sacramental Records v. 4, 38; Roberts, "Indian and Half-Blood Burial Information"; "A Sad Accident," *Bellingham Bay Mail*, 5/26/1877; Gordon Keith, ed. *The James Francis Tulloch Diary*, 32.

100. *Territory v Mary Phillips* #1070 (#45 Series 2) (1879). 3rd District Washington Territorial Court. This case file is the source of the following account of the homicide and trial, unless noted. Individual testimonies are named.

101. McDonough Store Account Book B, 133. HBP, CPNWS.

102. *Territory v Mary Phillips*.

103. *Orcas Islander*, 12/14/1944; Keith, *James Francis Tulloch Diary*, 33.

104. Charlie Kahana interview, 4/11/1956. Oral History Tapes, HBP, CPNWS.

105. Mary Phillips, John Pearson testimony, 12/26/1878 inquest; Kahana to Buswell, 1956; *Bellingham Bay Mail*, 1/11/1879.

106. Pearson testimony, 12/26/1878.

107. Kahana to Buswell, 1956; James Tulloch, Mary Phillips, John Pearson testimonies, 12/26/1878.

108. Tulloch, Phillips, Pearson testimonies, 12/26/1878.

109. Ibid.

110. Mary Phillips, Mason Fitzhugh, Enoch May testimony, 12/26/1878.

111. All witnesses corroborated that Phillips said to Mason that he had no other friends. Mason Fitzhugh to H. M. Stone, in Stone's testimony, 12/26/1878.

112. Mason to H.M. Stone that night, paraphrased by other witnesses;. Mason Fitzhugh to H. M. Stone, in Stone's testimony, 12/26/1878.

113. Mason Fitzhugh, Enoch May testimonies, 12/26/1878. Inquest results.

114. Mason Fitzhugh, James Tulloch testimonies, 12/26/1878.

115. Tulloch testimony, 12/26/1878.

116. 1880 U.S. Census, San Juan County; San Juan County marriage license, 2/1874.

117. Mason Fitzhugh, Enoch May, H.M. Stone, James Tulloch testimonies, 12/26/1878.

118. W.H. Gifford to Clerk of Court. 1/6/1879.

119. Roberts, "Indian and Half-Blood Burial Information."

120. *Puget Sound Argus*, 1/2/1879; George Phillips, Probate of Estate (1879), San Juan County Probate Journal, Bk. 2.

121. *Seattle Post-Intelligencer* reprint in *Bellingham Bay Mail*, 1/11/1879; *Washington Standard* 1/11/1879.

122. *Puget Sound Argus*, 3/6/1879; Naylor, *Frontier Boosters: Port Townsend*, 70; Emma Balch to Wayne Suttles, 9/1950, Suttles research files.

123. *Puget Sound Argus*, 2/27/1879; O.F. Vedder and H.S. Lyman, *History of Seattle, Washington*, ed. Frederick James Grant (New York: American Publishing and Engraving, 1894), 466; www.rootsweb.com; "Judge Greene's Review of Marriage Laws," *Bellingham Bay Mail*, 6/14/1879.

124. Jefferson County Historical Society, *With Pride in Heritage*, 358; Camfield, *Port Townsend: City That Whiskey Built*, 87; 3rd District Court Journal F, 523.

125. After Mary's trial, he moved to Colfax, WA, and became a prominent lawyer and judge. Biographical Note, William Inman Papers, Washington State University.

126. C. H. Hanford, "Members of the Seattle Bar Who Died Young," *Washington Historical Quarterly* 17, no. 1 (1926) 18-19.

127. List of grand jurors in *Puget Sound Argus*, 2/27/1879; Camfield, *Port Townsend: The City That Whiskey Built*, 48-49; 3rd District Court Journal E, 537.

128. 3rd District Court Journal E, 532 and case file.

129. Ibid. 543.

130. Thomas Phillips believed that he was born on the 23rd, but she was still pregnant that day. Delayed birth certificate, Washington State Dept. of Health, 4/18/1942; Subsistence bills in the case file.

131. *Puget Sound Mail*, 9/20/1879.

132. Charlie Kahana to Howard Buswell, 1956. HBP, CPNWS; Emma Balch to Wayne Suttles, 1950. Suttles research files.

133. Butler, *Gendered Justice*, 90. Diane L. Goeres-Gardner, *Murder, Morality and Madness: Women Criminals in Early Oregon* (Caldwell, ID: Caxton Press, 2009) xv-16.

134. Thurston County Historic Commission. www.co.thurston.wa.us.

135. Butler, *Gendered Justice*, 229, 5-6; Corcoran, *Bucoda*, 19.

136. Corcoran, *Bucoda*, 25; U.S. Dept. of the Interior, National Park Service, *National Register of Historic Places Inventory Nomination Form*, "Seatco Prison," 1975; Nix, *History of Lewis County*, 8.

137. WA State Dept. of Corrections. "Inmate Register, Penitentiary, WA Territory." WSA, Olympia; "Seatco Prison at Bucoda, 1877-1888," vol. A, 3. WSA; France, *Struggles for Life*, 279.

138. France, *Struggles for Life*, 246; 1880 U.S. Census supplement, Seatco Penitentiary.

139. National Park Service, National Register nomination form; Corcoran, *Bucoda*, 26-27; France, *Struggles for Life*, 250, 279, 295.

140. France, *Struggles for Life*, 280.

141. Corcoran, *Bucoda*, 26, 29.

142. Corcoran, *Bucoda*, 26; Balch to Suttles, 9/1950. Suttles research files.

143. *Washington Territory v Thomas Clark, Jr. and Susan Clark* #127 (1880), 3rd District Territorial Court.

144. Butler, *Gendered Justice*, 17, 84; France, *Struggles for Life*, 279-80.

145. *Puget Sound Mail*, 9/4/1880.

146. *Puget Sound Mail*, 9/4/1880; 1880 US Census, Seatco Prison.

147. Granddaughter Virginia Brumbaugh to author, 10/16/2004; Balch to Suttles, 9/1950. Suttles research files.

148. George Phillips, Probate. San Juan County Probate Journal, Bk 1 and 2.

149. San Juan County Marriage Records, vi, 49; 1880 U.S. Census, San Juan County; 1900 U.S. Census, Orcas Island.

150. McDonough Account Book E, 3; 1887 Washington Territorial Census and others indicate that Laurinda Fitzhugh was born in July 1881.

151. Balch to Suttles, 9/1950; August Martin to Wayne Suttles, 1947/48, Suttles research files; McDonough Account Book E, 213. HBP, CPNWS.

152. Archdiocese of Seattle, Sacramental Register v 4, 38 and 108.

153. George Phillips Probate, San Juan County Probate Journal Bk. 2.

154. Angie Bowden, *Early Schools of Washington Territory*, 474-75.

155. Archdiocese of Seattle, Sacramental Register v 4, 127.

156. John(ny) Pearson also received an allotment and married one of Chief Henry Kwina's daughters; U.S. Surveyor General, 1884 Lummi Reservation Allotment map, copy at Lummi Nation Library; August Martin to Wayne Suttles, 1947/48, Suttles research files; Aurelia Celestine to Howard Buswell, 11/29/1954. HBP, CPNWS. Sacramental Register v4, 249; Whatcom County Certificate of Marriage Book 1, 142 and Marriage Return 11/23/1891.

157. Henry Kwina to "Mr. Meade," 7/19/1886. McDonough Papers, HBP, CPNWS; Charlie Kahana re Mary hop picking. Buswell Audio Collection, CPNWS; *Whatcom Reveille*, 9/7/1883; Paul Fetzer, field notes, author's copy, courtesy of Wayne Suttles.

158. Raibmon, *Authentic Indians: Episodes of Encounter*, ch. 4, informs this description of hop picking life.

159. *Puget Sound Mail*, 9/20/1879; Crisca Bierwort, *Brushed by Cedar*, 206.

160. Raibmon, *Authentic Indians*, 91.

161. Ronimus Nix's cabin was among those of intermarried men burned during the Treaty War. He sold the government the island for McNeil Federal Prison, and the State Fairground is also on Nix land. By the 1989 state centennial, the Nix farm held the record for the farm longest owned by the same family. WA State Dept. of Agriculture, *Washington Centennial Farms* (Olympia: WSDA, 1980), 43; Nix, *History of Lewis County*, 275; Rosalie Nix record in BIA Records of the Puget Sound Agency,

Family Records 1893-1947, NARA, NW; 1890 Lummi Tribal Census; Photocopy of Gordon Lear photo of Billy and Rosalie Lear, courtesy of Chief Tsi'li'xw James.

162. No recorded death date in public or BIA records; 1920 U.S. Census, Whatcom County; BIA census records; Laurie Cepa, Phillips family research; Descendant Sherry Guzman stated that her family had visited the grave at Lummi, 10/16/2004. A descendant of Billy Lear thought she was buried at Madrona Point, 3/22/2004 to author; Mary Regina Phillips and Leah Preston Phillips affidavits, Roblin, *Schedule of Unenrolled Indians*, 1917.

163. Orcas Island Museum, title list; 1885 San Juan County census; 1889 Statehood census, San Juan Islands.

164. 1889 Statehood census, Port Townsend; Julie Owens to author 9/12/2000 re sibling separation.

165. 1900 U.S. Census, Orcas Island; Lummi Tribal census 1895, 1900, 1906. Typescript at WSA, NW; Laura (Squi'Qui) Edwards obituary, *Skagit Valley Herald*, 1/10/1998.

166. Tom She'kla'malt U.S. Homestead Certificate #1639, 4/15/1884; San Juan Cty Marriage Return 6/7/1911; Daniel L. Boxberger, "San Juan Island Cultural Affiliation Study," (1994) prepared for the National Park Service, 25. NWEC, CPNWS; 1900 U.S. Census, San Juan County.

167. Mason Fitzhugh Death Certificate, 10/12/1927, San Juan County; *Friday Harbor Journal* 10/18/1927; Pearl Little is listed as a 1/1/1942 add-on to the Lummi census; *Squol Quol*, 4/1/1977; Kathy Duncan (Jamestown S'Klallam Tribal office) to author re S'Klallam registration, 2/14/2007; Winona Rouleau in Pearl Little probate; Roberts, "Indian and Half-blood Burial Information."

168. Juanita Rouleau interview by author, 4/20/2004, San Juan Island; William Harlan Little Enrollment and Allotment Application. www.ancestry.com.

169. *Pearl Little, in the Matter of the Estate of,* #2088 (1983); Stanley Rouleau in Pearl Little probate re Maggie's wishes about the cemetery.

170. *Whatcom County v Billy Lear* #2295 (1918). Whatcom County Superior Court.

171. *Bellingham Herald* 11/25/1947.

172. Snohomish County Marriage Certificate #264, 4/23/1898; Interstate, *History of Skagit and Snohomish*, 482; Leah Preston Phillips affidavit 4/11/1917, Roblin "Schedule of Unenrolled Indians"; Virginia Brumbaugh to Laurie Cepa, 10/16/2004; Laurie Cepa family research.

Chapter 4

1. Atwood, *Glimpses in Pioneer Life*, 396-397; Rev. David LeSourd, "Sketches of an Itinerant's Career," (unpub. ms.), PRJ, CPNWS; Judson, "My Aboriginal Neighbors"; Judson, *A Pioneer's Search*, 252-53.

2. Alexander McKenzie, Journal 8/16-25/1825 in HBC Journals, Tim Wahl research files; "Dr. John Scouler's Journal of a Voyage to Northwest America." *Quarterly of the Oregon Historical Society* 6, (3/1905-12/1905), n.p.

3. "Captain Roeder, A Little Unwritten History of Interest to the People," *Bellingham Bay Reveille*, 11/10/1893; Lummi elder to Howard Buswell, HBP, CPNWS; Lummi elder to Tim Wahl, 3/17/2003.

4. Lummi elder to Tim Wahl, 3/17/2003.

5. Lummi elders to Wayne Suttles (Suttles research files) and Howard Buswell (HBP, CPNWS); *White River Valley Museum Newsletter*, 4/2001 (Auburn, WA); www.duwamishtribe.org.

6. 1874 annuities list, Bernard McDonough account books, HBP, CPNWS; Lummi elder to Howard Buswell, 3/11/1954; Buswell notes, 4/12/1955, both in HBP; Coll Thrush to author, 4/12/2007; Ada Pyeatt to Miranda Pyeatt, 2/15/1884 re Clara's basketmaking; Tennant family letters.

7. 1870 U.S. Census, Whatcom County; Howard Buswell compilation of family interviews, HBP, CPNWS.

8. Judson, *A Pioneer's Search*, 226.

9. Ibid., 253-54.

10. Interviews with tribal elders, HBP, CPNWS.

11. Marriage 4/16/1865 per Henry Kwina deposition. *In re the Estate of Mary Kwina.* BIA, 1918; "Lummi Chief Calls," *Bellingham Herald*, 10/13/1925; "Old Chief Was Tillicum of Pickett," *Bellingham Herald*, 1/15/1926.

12. "Religious Transformation and the Second Great Awakening," www.UShistory.org.

13. Dick, *The Dixie Frontier*, 192-93; Robert Bearden, "The Romance of Arkansas Methodism," *Flashback* 7, (3/1957): 1-12.

14. "Appointments of Arkansas Methodist Episcopal Conference." *Arkansas Democrat* 11/23/1849, reprinted in *Arkansas Family Historian* 23, no.4 (12/1985), 193; Methodist Episcopal Church, "Minutes of the Annual Conferences," vol. 1. Arkansas United Methodist Archives; Vernon, *Methodism in Arkansas*, 30, 475; Ingersoll, *To Intermix with Our White Brothers*, 110.

15. Gilbert Din, "Between a Rock and a Hard Place: The Indian Trade in Spanish Arkansas," 114, in Jeannie Whayne, compiler, *Cultural Encounters in the Early South: Indians and Europeans in Arkansas* (Fayetteville: Univ. of Arkansas Press, 1995); Bolton, *Territorial Ambition*, 2; Dougan, *Arkansas Odyssey*, 49.

16. Dorothy Jones Core, ed., trans. by Nicole Wable Hatfield, *Abstract of the Catholic Register of Arkansas, 1764-1858* (DeWitt, AR: Grand Prairie Historical Society, 1976), 15; Charles J. Kappler, comp. and ed., *Treaty of Harrington's, Arkansas Territory with the Quapaw, November 15, 1824*. www.councilfire.com.

17. D. Niler Pyeatt family research; Grand Prairie Historical Society, *Bulletin* (1988), 36; Margaret Smith Ross, "Squatter's Rights" parts 1 (6/1956), 2 (9/1956), 3(12/1956), *Pulaski County Historical Review* 4, (1956).

18. S. Charles Bolton, *Arkansas 1800-1860: Remote and Restless* (Fayetteville: Univ. of Arkansas Press, 1993), 112; "Minutes of the Annual Conferences," Arkansas United Methodist Archives; Steve Tennant and Forrest Tennant, interview by author, 5/22/2001, Farmington, Arkansas; Vernon, *Methodism in Arkansas,* 39, 541.

19. Ross, "Squatter's Rights"; "Thomas H. Tennant" land record. www.ancestry.com; "Petition to Congress by Inhabitants of the Territory" 12/21/1832 in Clarence E. Carter, ed., *The Territorial Papers of the U.S.,* "The Territory of Arkansas, 1819-1825," vol. 21 (U.S. Gov't Printing Office, 1954), 682-83.

20. The Gibson genealogy places John Tennant's birth year at 1830, but numerous records created during his lifetime place it at 1829.

21. Lacy P. McColloch, "Apple Industry at Cane Hill, Arkansas," *Flashback* 16, (11/1966), 1-3.

22. Bolton, *Territorial Ambition,* 99; Ruth H. Payne, "The House of Crozier—in Washington County," *Flashback* 14 (7/1964), 33-35.

23. Emory Stevens Bucke, ed., *History of American Methodism, vol. 1,* (New York: Abingdon Press, 1964), 537-39.

24. *Arkansas Gazette,* 10/6/1835; T.H. Tennant to A. Sevier, *Arkansas Gazette,* 5/19/1835; Dougan, *Arkansas Odyssey,* 154.

25. Ancel Bassett, *A Concise History of the Methodist Protestant Church* (Pittsburgh: Press of Charles A. Scott, James Robison, 1877), 143, courtesy of Nancy Britton personal research re Tennant church and school history; Bethlehem M.E. Church, "Register of Members," 104, Arkansas United Methodist Church Archives.

26. Vernon, 542, information from Addison Tennant; Bethlehem M.E. Church, "Register of Members," 104, Archives of the Arkansas Methodist Conference; Britton, personal research.

27. Mabel B. McClure, *The McClure Clan* (Enid, OK: Baer's Printery, 1954), 40-42; Margaret Dunn to Miranda Pyeatt, n.d., Pyeatt-Tennant family letters.

28. Ingersoll, *To Intermix with our White Brothers,* 218; Theda Perdue and Michael D. Green, *The Cherokee Nation and the Trail of Tears* (New York: Penguin, 2008), 139.

29. J.F. Bates, "Murder of the Wright Family–Recollections," *Publications of the Arkansas Historical Association 4* (1917), 204-6. Reprint *Flashback* 6, (1/1956), 21-22; J.P. Neal, "The Wright Murders," *Flashback* 6, (1/1956), 4-10.

30. Gibson, "Thomas H. Tennant Family Tree"; Walter Tennant Sallee, "Life Story of George S. and Sinah H. Sallee" (unpub. ms, 1938), courtesy of Mary Jane King; D. Niler Pyeatt personal family research; Bethlehem M. E. Church, *Register of Marriages,* Arkansas United Methodist Church Archive.

31. General Assembly of Arkansas, "An Act to Incorporate the Bethesda Academy" courtesy of Nancy Britton, personal research; W.J. Lemke, "Early Colleges and Academies," 10-13.

32. Wanda Karnes, "Cane Hill College," *Flashback* 35, (2/1985), 1- 3; Lemke, "Early Colleges and Academies," 14-25; "Souvenirs of the Tennant Family," *Flashback* 4, no. 1 (1954), n.p.

33. Gibson, family research, plus many other sources; John Tennant, U.S. census statements.

34. For complete information on the Cherokee Trail, *see* Jack E. Fletcher, Patricia K.A. Fletcher, and Lee Whitely, *Cherokee Trail Diaries*, vol. 1 and 3 (Caldwell, ID: Caxton Printers, 2001); J.H. Atkinson, "Cattle Drives from Arkansas to California Prior to the Civil War," *Arkansas Historical Quarterly* 28, no. 3, (1969), 276.

35. C.C. Seay, "The 1853 Cattle Drive," *Cincinnati Argus* (1857), reprinted in *Flashback* 42, # 2 (1992) 27-36.

36. Ibid.

37. Whatcom County Auditor, Road Book 1, 4/23/1855.

38. Whatcom County Auditor, Territorial Land Claims, 1854-1861, 11; Tim Wahl, "The Lummi River and Cha-choo-sen Island." *Journal of the Whatcom County Historical Society*, #1 (4/2000), 57-64.

39. John Tennant to W.W. Miller, 2/15/1858. W.W. Miller Papers; Patent Application #4528, U.S. General Land Office, Olympia, WA, 3/16/1872.

40. *Pioneer-Democrat*, 12/10/1858; Washington Territory House of Representatives, "House Journal," 1/10/1859, 1/12/1859. Copies courtesy of Sam Thompson.

41. *Pioneer-Democrat*, 2/4/1859; *Northern Light*, 7/3/1858, 7/17/1858; 3rd District, Wash. Territorial Court Journal A, 2/24/1861, 509 and Probate Journal D, 1/1861; Whatcom County Commissioners Proceedings vol.1, 127. 7/28/1862.

42. Asst. Indian Agent, 4/1859; Deputy Sheriff, 1859. Dates taken from court appearances and correspondence.

43. The following letters inform the paragraphs about the "battle": John Tennant to Territorial Indian Agent M.T. Simmons, 8/8/1859 and 8/11/1859, Puget Sound District Agency, "Correspondence and Accounting Records"; Naylor, *Frontier Boosters*, 67.

44. Tennant to Simmons, 8/11/1859.

45. *Daily Reveille*, 2/14/1893.

46. John's nephew Henry Pyeatt, left out of his uncle's will, seems to be the source of the obituary story that a local historian printed sixty years later without investigation; Jeffcott, *Nooksack Tales*, 137.

47. E.C. Fitzhugh to District Superintendent of Indian Affairs, 6/8/1857. Copy in NWEC, CPNWS; Judson, *A Pioneer's Search*, 253.

48. Conevery A. Bolton, "A Sister's Consolation: Women, Health and Community in Early Arkansas, 1810-1860." *Arkansas Historical Quarterly* 50, (1991), 276-77.

49. "Captain Roeder, A Little Unwritten History of Interest to the People," *Bellingham Bay Reveille*, 11/10/1893.

50. *Puget Sound Herald*, 8/26/1859; *Pioneer-Democrat*, 12/9/1859; Whatcom County Commissioners Proceedings, vol. 1, back leaf, 1858.

51. Jean Barman, "Taming Aboriginal Sexuality," 248. Manuscript copy courtesy of the author; Jean Barman, "Family Life at Fort Langley," *B.C. Historical News* 32, #4 (1999), 20; Dorothy H. Johnson and Percival R. Jeffcott, *James Alexander Tennant: Early Pioneer and Preacher* (Bellingham: Fourth Corner Registry), 40.

52. John Tennant "Farm Journal," 3/11/1864, etc., William James Collection, Lummi Nation Archives.

53. Lummi elder to Wayne Suttles 4/11/1949, Suttles research files; George Swanaset to Paul Fetzer, 8/17/1950, field notes copy in possession of author; Lummi elder to Howard Buswell, 3/12/1954, HBP, CPNWS; Ada Tennant Buchanan to Miranda Tennant Pyeatt, 1883, Pyeatt-Tennant letters.

54. U.S. Census records, Whatcom County and Lummi Reservation; W.J. to author 6/18/2002; Leland Donald, *Aboriginal Slavery on the Northwest Coast of North America* (Berkeley: Univ. of California, 1997), 19.

55. Tim Wahl personal research re land history.

56. Numerous entries for many years in Tennant, "Journal"; John Bennett obituary, *Weekly World-Herald*, 6/21/1901; Dept. of Agriculture, *1913 Annual Report* (copy, University of Chicago online), 450; Vince Randolph, *Ozark Magic and Folklore* (New York: Dover, 1947), 21-22.

57. Bob Keen, interview by author, Arkansas, 5/21/2001; Mentions in Tennant "Journal."

58. Tennant, "Journal"; *David Wight and William Bishop v H.B. Niles no. 151* (1885), Whatcom County Territorial Court, WSA, NW.

59. McDonough Account Book B, 30. HBP, CPNWS; Ada Pyeatt to Miranda Pyeatt, 2/15/1884 re Clara's quilts, Tennant family letters.

60. Tennant "Journal" 1861-1865; *Puget Sound Herald*, 3/2/1862, 3/5/1864.

61. Bob Keen, 9/8/2000; *Fayetteville Daily Democrat, 7/10/1926;* Southern Claims Commission, "Settled Files," Thomas H. Tennant #4160.

62. Ibid.

63. SCC Tennant claim file; Mark K. Christ, ed., *Rugged and Sublime: The Civil War in Arkansas* (Fayetteville: University of Arkansas Press, 1994), 131.

64. SCC Tennant claim file; Thomas S. Tennant to Miranda, Andrew, and Ada Pyeatt, 7/12/1874, Tennant family letters.

65. Maxine Stremler, interview by author, 1/21/2006 re Julia and Tom T'ing; Tennant, "Journal"; Tim Wahl research; *Ferndale Record,* 2/5/1904.

66. *Bellingham Herald,* 7/10/1909; Lummi Reservation allotment map, Lummi Nation Library.

67. Tennant "Journal," 5/13/1863; 6/30/1862.

68. Ibid., 7/16/1863.

69. Tennant, "Journal," 11/27/1863; Archdiocese, Sacramental Register v2, 95.

70. Tennant, "Journal," 1/22/1866–1/28/1866.

71. Ibid., 3/29/1867.

72. Edmund Coleman, "Mountaineering on the Pacific," *Harpers New Monthly* 39 (11/1869), 793-817, reprinted in Majors, ed., *Mount Baker: A Chronicle,* and Roth, *History of Whatcom 1,* 880-897; Miles, *Koma Kulshan,* 17, 22; Tennant, "Journal," 8/6/1866; Beckey, *Range of Glaciers,*11.

73. Tennant, "Journal," 6/1868-8/1868; Miles, *Koma Kulshan,* 44.

74. Miles, *Koma Kulshan,* 29; Edmund Coleman in Majors, *Mount Baker: A Chronicle,* 152, 154; Edmund Coleman in Roth, *History of Whatcom 1,* 894; Thomas Stratton diary, in Majors, *Mount Baker: A Chronicle,* 183.

75. Majors, *Mount Baker: A Chronicle,* 155.

76. Tennant, "Journal," 8/22/1868, 9/5/1868.

77. Washington Territory, 1870 Agricultural Census— Products of Agriculture. Copy at Bellingham Public Library; U.S. Land Office, Tennant Patent Application #4528.

78. Daniel C. Linsley, "Journal of Exploration of the Cascade Mountains, 5/25/1870-8/6/1870." (unpub. ms.) Northern Pacific Railroad Chief Engineer Papers, Minnesota Historical Society, St. Paul, Minnesota; Beckey, *Range of Glaciers,* 222-30.

79. Whatcom County Deeds F, 52; *Bellingham Bay Mail,* 8/16/1873; Whatcom County plat maps, CPNWS; Jeffcott, *Nooksack Tales,* 137; Tim Wahl research files re resurvey of Lummi Reservation boundary.

80. Jeffcott, *Nooksack Tales,* 159; *Puget Sound Mail,* 9/13/1879, 11/19/1881; *Whatcom Reveille,* 6/22/1883.

81. George Swanaset to Fetzer, 9/2/1950, Fetzer field notes; Daphne Sleigh, ed., *One Foot on the Border,* 348.

82. Tennant Patent Application #4528; John Tennant house, "Historical Preservation Survey," Michael Sullivan Collection; Alvord interview re Tennant house, Frank Teck papers; "Local Pioneer Lives in Old John Tennant House, Recalls Log Jam," undated article, Frank Teck Papers, Michael Sullivan Collection.

83. *Bellingham Bay Mail,* 8/1875, quoted in Jeffcott, *Nooksack Tales,* 174.

84. Whatcom County Auditor's Record, 1873-79; *Bellingham Bay Mail,* 9/21/1878.

85. *Bellingham Bay Mail,* 5/12/1877, 8/3/1877; Whatcom County Superintendent of Schools, Record A, WSA, NW.

86. *Bellingham Bay Mail,* 5/4/1878, 10/19/1878, 11/9/1878, 5/3/1879, 5/8/1879, 11/30/1878; Dunagan, *History of Ferndale,* 23.

87. Gertrude Matz Alvord interview, Frank Teck Papers.

88. Tate, "Diaries 1874-1883."

89. John Tennant and Clara "Cellick," Marriage License, 2/10/1876. Whatcom Auditor's Record Book, 1873-1879, 106. Jeffcott, *Nooksack Tales*, 178.

90. Accounts in Tate, "Diary"; Atwood, "Glimpses in Pioneer Life"; Rev. A.J. McNemee, Harlan Jones, ed. *Brother Mack, the Frontier Preacher* (Fairfield WA: Ye Galleon Press, 1980); Tate, 9/13/1877; Charles A. Johnson, *The Frontier Camp Meeting*, (Southern Methodist University Press, 1955) 149; Lou Nicholson Brown to Millie, 7/7/1880. Lou Nicholson Brown Papers, WSA, NW.

91. Ada Tennant Pyeatt Buchanan to Miranda Tennant Pyeatt, 5/30/1878, Tennant family letters.

92. *Bellingham Bay Mail*, 6/1/1878; Ada Pyeatt to Miranda Pyeatt, 1883, Tennant family letters.

93. Percival Jeffcott notes, "Memorial for John Tennant at 10th Session, Puget Sound Conference, 1893." PRJ, CPNWS; Howell, *Methodism in the Northwest*, 57; *Bellingham Bay Mail*, 8/19/1878, 12/7/1878.

94. Jeffcott notes on Tennant Memorial; Judson, *A Pioneer's Search*, 253.

95. Howell, *Methodism in the Northwest*, 290, 328, 330.

96. Howell, *Methodism in the Northwest*, 57; Susan Armitage and Elizabeth Jameson, *The Women's West* (Norman: Univ. of Oklahoma Press 1987), 168.

97. Jeffcott notes, "Conference Reports," 1884, 1885. PRJ, CPNWS.

98. *Daily Reveille*, 2/14/1893.

99. Bob Keen research re Buchanan clan.

100. Ada to Miranda and Andrew Pyeatt, 8/1/1879, ?/1880, Pyeatt-Tennant family letters.

101. Ada to Miranda, ?/1880; ?/1883, Pyeatt-Tennant family letters.

102. Ibid., 4/2/1883.

103. Whatcom County Deeds 15, 104, 8/4/1891 and 106, 7/3/1890.

104. Ada to Miranda, 2/15/1884, 4/21/1884.

105. *Whatcom Reveille*, 6/29/1883; *Pioneer Press*, 3/6/1889; Whatcom County Probate Court, "Record of Wills," vol. 1; Niler Pyeatt, Pyeatt family research.

106. Bayard's name does not appear in records of the similarly named Territorial Institute (later University of Washington) at which local historians have placed him. Distance from Ferndale, church affiliation, and academic prestige indicate that he was in Olympia; Ada to Miranda, 2/15/1884; Judson, *Pioneer's Search*, 254; Newell, *Rogues, Buffoons and Statesmen*, 100.

107. Llyn De Danaan, *Katie Gale: A Coast Salish Woman's Life on Oyster Bay* (Lincoln: U of Nebraska, 2013), 192; Volney Steele, *Bleed, Blister and Purge*, 279; Ada to Miranda, 2/15/1884; H.H. Bancroft, *History of California* 7:704.

108. Ada to Miranda, 3/12/1885. This letter is the source of his death date and the surrounding events.

109. Ada to Miranda, 3/12/1885; Judson, *Pioneer's Search,* 255.

110. Ada to Miranda, 3/12/1885; Nettie Tennant Pyeatt to Miranda Pyeatt, 4/6/1885; Judson, *Pioneer's Search,* 255.

111. Ada to Miranda, 3/12/1885.

112. Ada to Miranda, 5/8/1885.

113. Rev. D. G. LeSourd in Howell, *Methodism in the Northwest,* 57; *Northwest Enterprise,* 11/14/1883.

114. Ada to Miranda, 5/8/1885.

115. Richardson, *This is Our Story,* 11; Ada to Miranda, 1/7/1886.

116. Ada to Miranda, 1/7/1886; Woodsey Kimple, "Building of the Methodist Church Started in 1884," *Orcas Islander,* 5/3/1945; Keith, *James Francis Tulloch Diary,* 84-85.

117. Ada to Miranda, 1/7/1886.

118. Ibid.

119. Thomas Sanford Tennant to Miranda Pyeatt, 2/1/1885; Nettie Pyeatt to Miranda Pyeatt, 2/12/1886; Ada to Miranda, ?–?1886. All in Tennant family letters.

120. Richardson, *This is Our Story,* 11-12.

121. Jeffcott notes, "Third Puget Sound Conference Reports" PRJ, CPNWS; Richardson, *This is Our Story,* 13-14; Orcas Island Museum, Methodist Church file.

122. Jeffcott notes, "Third Conference reports" in Jeffcott Papers; Fred J. Splitstone, *Orcas, Gem of the San Juans* (Eastsound, WA: Fred Darvill, 1954), 52.

123. John Tennant will, 10/31/1887. Whatcom County Deeds 37, 344-45; *Blaine Journal* 11/10/1887, 12/1/1887, 6/21/1887, 7/26/1887.

124. *Pioneer Press,* 11/27/1888, 1/1/1889.

125. Nooksack Indian Mission Methodist Episcopal Church, "Record."

126. *Sunday Reveille,* 4/10/1892; *Daily Reveille,* 4/13/1892.

127. *Daily Reveille,* 2/11/1893, 2/14/1893; *Bellingham Bay Express,* 2/14/1893.

128. Whatcom County Probate Court, Record of Wills v. 1, 64-65; *John Tennant, Estate of,* Whatcom County Deeds 37, 344-45.

129. Judson, *A Pioneer's Search,* 256; Peter James testimony, *Duwamish et al. v U.S.* (1927).

130. Whatcom Marriage Returns, 9/23/1903; *Bellingham Herald,* 12/19/1908.

131. *Evening Herald,* 9/29/1903.

132. George Swanaset and others in Paul Fetzer field notes, 1950; Nooksack Indian Mission Methodist Episcopal Church, "Record"; Tate, "Diary," 9/3/1876; Methodist Episcopal Church, *Annual Reports of the Woman's Home Missionary Society* (Cincinnati: Methodist Book Concern Press). Copies courtesy of Helen Almojera.

133. Judson, "My Aboriginal Neighbors."

134. August Martin to Percival Jeffcott, *Nooksack Tales*, 32; James Selhameten Indian Homestead #1080, 6/30/1880, Whatcom Deeds; *Bellingham Bay Mail*, 4/11/1874.

135. Johnny Richards managed the largest soap factory in the world in Mexico and retired to Dayton, Ohio, where he was friends with early aviation pioneers; Fetzer notes, 8/9/1950; Judson, "My Aboriginal Neighbors"; Dr. Jack Miller, interviews by author, 1994-2003 re John Richards; Robert Emmett Hawley, *Skqee Mus* (Bellingham: Miller & Sutherlen, 1945. Bellingham Museum of History and Art, 1971).

136. A.J. to Fetzer, 10/24/1950. Fetzer field notes; Whatcom Certificates of Marriage, Bk. 1, 11/5/1890.

137. Andrew Smith to Percival Jeffcott, 1/27/1947, PRJ, CPNWS.

138. *Pacific Pilot* (Lynden, WA), 12/3/1903; Judson, *A Pioneer's Search*, 255; George Swanaset, 1954. Fetzer field notes.

139. *Bellingham Herald*, 2/2/1904.

140. *Clara Tennant Yellokanim*, in the matter of, Whatcom County Probate Case File #1080; Probate Orders and Decrees 10, 325-26.

Chapter 5

1. Lucy Lane Handeyside in Nugent, ed., *Lummi Elders Speak*, 71.

2. Tennant, "Journal," 3/1867.

3. Duff, *Upper Stalo*, 16.

4. Carlson, *You Are Asked to Witness*, 89; Agnes James to Paul Fetzer, 12/14/1950, Fetzer field notes; Joe Louie to Jeff Wilner, 5/1/1973. Northwest Tribal Oral History Collection, CPNWS; J.W. Kelleher to Oliver Wells, interview, Oliver Wells Collection.

5. Boyd, *Coming of the Spirit*, 41, 56, 158, 299; Carlson, *You Are Asked to Witness*, 28, 36, 51.

6. Carlson, *A Sto:lo Coast Salish Historical Atlas*, 24, 36, 51.

7. Handeyside in Nugent, *Lummi Elders Speak*, 71.

8. N.V. Sheffer, "A Story of Pioneering, Part 3." *Lynden Tribune*, 8/1910; Henry Roeder diaries, account books. Henry Roeder Papers.

9. Boyd, *Coming of the Spirit*, 172-73, 184-85.

10. St. Helena was the mother of convert Roman Emperor (and saint) Constantine; Kay Cronin, *Cross in the Wilderness* (Vancouver BC: Mitchell Press, 1959), 85, 95; Archdiocese, Sacramental Records v. 3, 63; Boyd, *Coming of the Spirit*, 184.

11. Carlson, *Sto:lo Coast Salish Historical Atlas*, 97.

12. Whatcom County Auditor, Book of Liens H, 100, and Nellie Lane and Daniel Daley marriage certificate, 1/30/1918; Whatcom County Probate, Journal 13 and 14, Case #1836, Nellie Lane Daley; Archdiocese, Sacramental Record v. 3, 63; Mary

Helen Cagey to author, 7/5/2008, and other family members; August Lane, Death Certificate, Whatcom County Auditor, 1917.

13. Carlson, *You Are Asked to Witness*, 50-51.

14. Duff, *Upper Stalo*, 76.

15. Ibid., 79.

16. 1860 U.S. Census, Whatcom County.

17. Interstate Publishing, *Illustrated History of Skagit*, Enoch Compton interview, 98.

18. Edson, *Fourth Corner*, 33; Van Miert, *Settlers, Structures and Ships*, 7.

19. Roeder, Financial Record Book 1856-57 and diary. Both in Roeder Papers; Whatcom County, Deeds B, 24; *Pioneer-Democrat*, 5/1/1857.

20. Whatcom County, Commissioners Proceedings v. 1, 47.

21. 1860 U.S. Census, Whatcom County; Van Miert, *Settlers, Structures and Ships*, 12b.

22. Tim Wahl, personal research re land claims and ownership at the *Noos'kwiem*.

23. Tennant "Journal," 12/8 and 12/9/1862, 2/10/1865, 11/13/1865, 1/23/1866.

24. Roeder, Diary, 7/1862.

25. Nellie Lane Daley, Whatcom County Death Certificate, 1929; U.S. Census, Whatcom County, various; Perry, *On The Edge of Empire*, 172; Charles Miles, *Michael T. Simmons* (Vivian E. Bower, 1980), 4; Coontz, *Marriage, A History*, 172.

26. Handeyside in Nugent, *Lummi Elders*, 71.

27. Ibid.

28. Orcas Island Museum, homestead map; Archdiocese, Sacramental Records v. 4, 270.

29. Charlotte Lane's careful research informs much of the family history here. Charlotte Lane, "Lane Family History," Charlotte Lane Papers.

30. Daniel Woodbury, "History of Lobster Cove in Annisquam" (unpub. ms.), Peterson file, Gloucester City Archives.

31. Gloucester Historic Commission, 1985 architectural survey of 10 Arlington Street, Gloucester City Archives.

32. Charlotte Lane Papers.

33. F.F. Lane's middle name's origin remains a mystery. Research showed no relatives or friends on either side with that name. It may have been a play on the seafaring word "foam;" Topsfield Historical Society, *Vital Records of Gloucester, Massachusetts to the end of the year 1849 vol. 1 – Births*. (Topsfield, Mass.: Topsfield Historical Society, 1917), 412; Charlotte Lane speech 6/6/1892, Charlotte Lane Papers; Charlotte Lane, 1/15/1925 in *The Pittsburgh Advocate*.

34. The local sea monster was seen as late as 1960. Newspaper excerpts about the storm, www.downtosea.com.

35. Diane Kaplan, Yale U. Archives, to author, 10/27/2000 re possible attendance by F.F. Lane; Charlotte Lane Papers; Sylvanus Smith interview 1901, reprinted on www. downtosea.com.

36. Charlotte Lane, "Lane Family History."

37. Oliver G. Lane Papers; Cutler, *Queens of the Western Ocean,* 373, appendix.

38. *Whatcom Reveille,* 8/4/1906, and *1893 Whatcom County Agricultural Census,* 11/1893; 1850 U.S. Census, Sacramento County, California; *Georgia* passenger list (NARA), courtesy of Carleton Howard.

39. *Boston Daily Atlas,* 2/18/1852; ad for the *Victory,* 6/2/1854; Louis Rasmussen, *San Francisco Ship Passenger Lists v. 4* (Colima, CA: San Francisco Historic Record and General Bulletin, 1970), 15; *Whatcom Reveille,* 8/4/1906.

40. *Alta California,* 4/3/1855; Oliver G. Lane Papers; "The New Ship 'Neptune's Favorite'," *Boston Daily Atlas,* 6/21/1854; Mike Mjelde (Puget Sound Maritime Museum) to author 5/27/2000; Charlotte Lane, Charlotte Lane Papers.

41. Charlotte Lane, "Lane Family History."

42. Handeyside in Nugent, *Lummi Elders Speak,* 71.

43. *Puget Sound Mail,* 2/24/1883; *Whatcom Reveille,* 8/4/1906.

44. Carleton Howard personal research re the Griffins and Lanes.

45. *Puget Sound Mail,* 2/24/1883; Whatcom County Deeds D, 273.

46. *Whatcom Reveille,* 11/1893, "1893 Whatcom County Agricultural Census."

47. Whatcom County, Commissioners Proceedings v. 1, 91.

48. Ibid., 93, 95, 96.

49. F.F. Lane diary 1860-61, typescript, PRJ, CPNWS.

50. Ibid., 6/27/1861-7/1/1861, 7/6/1861-7/9/1861.

51. W.W. Griffin, "Frederick Lane," Griffin Family Papers; Martha Almina Griffin Mankins to Lottie Roeder Roth re Captain Griffin's time on the *Harney*. Carleton Howard personal research.

52. W. W. Griffin, "Frederick Lane," Griffin Family Papers.

53. F.F. Lane, Homestead application #637, General Land Office, Olympia; Tennant, "Journal," 2/9/1866, etc.; John Allen to Howard Buswell, 4/13/1948, HBP; Tim Wahl, personal research re homestead boundaries.

54. James Kavanaugh, "Diary," 6/7/1866.

55. *F.F. Lane v Nellie Lane* #6573 (1902), Whatcom County Superior Court; Homestead application #637.

56. Private Lane family photo viewed by author, 6/25/2003.

57. *Bellingham Herald,* 8/4/1906; Edson, *Fourth Corner,* 175.

58. Charlotte Lane Papers; U.S. Census, Lummi Reservation, various years.

59. Washington Territorial Census, 1870, "Products of Agriculture." Microfilm copy at Bellingham Public Library.

60. F.F. Lane Homestead application #637; Final certificate #291; Whatcom County Deeds M, 276-77.

61. Lane children birthdates are documented in Seattle Archdiocese Sacramental Records; Constance Lane Delayed Birth Certificate, Whatcom County Auditor; *Bellingham Bay Reveille,* 11/10/1893; Handeyside, in Nugent, *Lummi Elders,* 71.

62. Whatcom County Auditor, Book of Liens H, 100.

63. Bertha Lane Smith, Helen Lane Jefferson, and Edith Lane Jones to Howard Buswell, 9/10/1953, HBP, CPNWS.

64. *Bellingham Bay Mail,* 10/14/1874, 5/9/1874, 5/16/1874; Whatcom County Superintendent of Schools, Record A, "School Boundaries and Official Records"; Bowden, *Early Schools of Washington Territory,* 294-295; Edith Carhart, *A History of Bellingham* (Bellingham: Argonaut, 1926), 47; Edson, *Fourth Corner,* 165, 175; Whatcom County, Commissioners Proceedings v. 3, 28.

65. *American Reveille,* 2/21/1909.

66. *Bellingham Bay Mail,* 10/14/1876; Roth, *History of Whatcom County,* I, 191; *Puget Sound Mail,* 8/1880; *Daily Reveille,* 7/29/1894.

67. Washington Territorial Census, 1880, "Agricultural Supplement"; Bernard McDonough Account Books A, AA, B. HBP, CPNWS.

68. *Puget Sound Mail,* 7/9/1881.

69. *Electa Fouts v F.F. Lane and Nellie Lane* #173 (1880), Whatcom (Skagit) County Superior Court.

70. *Whatcom Reveille,* 10/5/1883; Whatcom County Deeds 3, 653-54; Whatcom County Genealogical Society, *Cemetery Records of Whatcom County,* 37.

71. Christian Tuttle to Secretary of the Interior, 5/21/1878, copy at Lummi Island Library; Mullen, *Whatcom County, Washington Post Offices,* 25.

72. *Whatcom Reveille,* 7/25/1884.

73. Laura Tuttle Everheart, "Tuttle Genealogy" (unpub. ms.), Lummi Island Library; Hiram Tuttle to Peggy Aiston, 8/9/1975, Aiston research collection. U.S. Census, Whatcom County, 1880, 1900.

74. Handeyside in Nugent, *Lummi Elders,* 50.

75. Whatcom County Auditor, Marriage and Misc. Records C, 47; *Daily Reveille,* 4/26/1895; Bayview Cemetery Records, WSA, NW.

76. U.S. Coast and Geodetic Survey Map #1871 (1888), *Topography of Washington Sound,* Sheet 3. Copy courtesy of Tim Wahl; Handeyside in Nugent, *Lummi Elders,* 34, 38.

77. Handeyside in Nugent, *Lummi Elders,* 34; *Bellingham Bay Evening Express,* 6/28/1894.

78. Handeyside in Nugent, *Lummi Elders,* 38.

79. Handeyside in Nugent, *Lummi Elders,* 50, 72; *Bellingham Bay Mail,* 8/18/1877.

80. Handeyside in Nugent, *Lummi Elders,* 50.

81. *Bellingham Reveille,* 1/25/1905.

82. *Daily Reveille,* 4/8/1892.

83. Handeyside in Nugent, *Lummi Elders,* 107.

84. *Daily Reveille,* 12/2/1892, 11/8/1893, 2/2/1894.

85. *The Blade,* 6/14/1898.

86. Art Granger to Howard Buswell, 11/20/1956. HBP, CPNWS; Mullen, *Whatcom County, WA Post Offices,* 12; Bobbie Hutchings, Thurid Clark and Beth Hudson, *Shared Heritage: A History of Lummi Island* (Lummi Island: Lummi Island Heritage Trust, 2004), 36.

87. Handeyside in Nugent, *Lummi Elders,* 92.

88. Peggy Aiston Collection; *Bellingham Herald,* 11/10/2003.

89. Peggy Aiston Collection.

90. Granger to Buswell, 10/12/1956, HBP, CPNWS; *Ferndale Record-Journal,* 7/26/1972.

91. Peggy Aiston notes, Aiston Collection; Sharlene and Ted Nelson, "Washington's First Lights," *Columbia* (Fall 1995), 23; Gwen Parker, "Music Teacher Nearly Back Where She Started From," *Bellingham Herald,* 7/25/1971; Photos of the Lane Spit light, Aiston Collection.

92. Whatcom County Deeds 28, multiple entries; *The Blade,* 5/16/1899, 7/1/1899; *Daily Reveille,* 7/13/1899.

93. *U.S. v F.F. Lane* #1576 and #1577 (1899). U.S. District Court, Western District of Washington.

94. U.S. District Court, Criminal Register v. 2, 287.

95. *F.F. Lane v Nellie Lane* #6573 (1902), Whatcom County Superior Court, WSA, NW. The case file informs the following description of events.

96. Whatcom Deeds 67, 260.

97. Handeyside in Nugent, *Lummi Elders,* 92; Delia Keeler to Howard Buswell, HBP, CPNWS.

98. Handeyside in Nugent, *Lummi Elders,* 44; *Samuel Gross Insolvency,* #2-231 (1879). 3rd District Washington Territorial Court.

99. Handeyside and Stella Lane Nicholsen in Nugent, *Lummi Elders,* 44; *Daily Reveille,* 8/30/1903.

100. Ernestine Gensaw to author 7/12/2013, Whatcom County.

101. Handeyside in Nugent, *Lummi Elders,* 34.

102. U.S. Coast Guard, Register of Lighthouse Keepers, RG 26, MF 1373, NARA, NW; June Reynolds to Peggy Aiston, n.d., Aiston collection.

103. Photos of F.F. Lane, courtesy of Frank Allen; Portrait of F.F. Lane by S.J. Ballard, William James owner.

104. Carlisle Indian School, Student Record #2051.

105. Whatcom County Auditor, Deeds 68, 96; Deeds 91, 133; Deeds 91, 133-34.

106. Ibid., Power of Attorney 17, 185.

107. Whatcom County Coroner's Register 1, 208; *Bellingham Herald*, 2/22/1909.

108. *American Reveille*, 2/22/1909.

109. The following are all in Whatcom County Probate Records: Probate Case #1746 (F.F. Lane); Probate Journal v. 13: 249, 262 and 478, 527, 530, 579; *In the Matter of the Guardianship of Charles and Lucy Lane*, #1846. Probate Docket G, 1836, 607 for Probate journals 12-15; *In the Matter of the Guardianship of Daniel Swanaset* #1324, Probate Journal 13.

110. Whatcom County Probate Journal vol. 14, 150, 305, 335, 523; also some in vol. 15; *Bellingham Herald*, 12/22/1909; *Nellie Lane v Oscar and Lucy Lane, William and Mary Showers* #9847 (1910), Whatcom County Superior Court; Whatcom County Auditor, Power of Attorney 17, 185; Deeds 68, 96; Deeds 91, 133; Deeds 102, 330; Deeds 113, 367.

111. *Lane v Lane and Showers* #9847, Whatcom County Superior Court.

112. *Bellingham Herald*, 4/23/1911; Whatcom County Auditor, Deeds 119, 360-61.

113. *Bellingham Herald*, 9/18/1915; Whatcom County Auditor, Marriage Certificate #3650, 1/30/1918.

114. Daniel Daley died in Deroche, B.C., 6/29/1937. Vital Event Death Register, B.C. Archives online; Nellie Lane Daley Will, 8/14/1917, copy in Aiston Collection, none filed in the county; Whatcom County Auditor, Deeds 162, 616-17.

115. Mary Helen Cagey to author, 6/5/2008, Lummi Reservation.

116. Whatcom County Death Certificate #280; "Nellie Lane Daley, Pioneer of County, Passes at Marietta," *Bellingham Herald*, 6/28/1929.

117. Vernon Lane, *Bellingham Herald*, 10/8/1990; Ann Nugent, *The History of Lummi Fishing Rights* (Bellingham: Lummi Communications, 1979), 18-26, 28-32; *Bellingham Herald*, 4/15/1915–6/3/1915; *American Reveille*, 5/2/1916, 5/7/1916, 5/31/1916.

118. Whatcom County Auditor, Marriage Record Book C, 102, 247; Aiston Collection; *Daily Reveille*, 4/26/1895; Bayview Cemetery records; Gwen Parker, "Music Teacher Nearly Back Where She Started From," *Bellingham Herald*, 7/25/1971; *American Reveille*, 10/30/1918; *Bellingham Herald*, 11/6/1918.

119. Jernigan, "C.C. Finkbonner Family Genealogy;" Stella Lane Nicholson, in Nugent, *Lummi Elders Speak*, 96, 73, 68, 45, 39; *Daily Reveille*, 2/28/1895, 7/7/1895; Whatcom County Auditor, Marriage Returns, Oscar Lane and Lucy Finkbonner; Whatcom County Auditor, Patents v. 3, 370; BLM Record #WAORAA083800 (www.glorecords.blm.gov); *American Reveille*, 5/2/1916; *Bellingham Herald*, 9/26/1918, 4/19/1937.

120. Mark Karlansky, *The Last Fish Tale: The Fate of the Atlantic and Survival in Gloucester, America's Oldest Fishing Port and Most Original Town* (NY: Riverhead Books, 2008), 62; *Daily Reveille*, 5/1/1895; Aiston Collection; Splitstone, *Orcas, Gem of the San Juans*, 57; Jones-Lamb, *Native American Wives*, 22-26; San Juan County Clerk, Certificates of Marriage, 4/21/1902.

121. "Aunt Tot of Cape Ann," *The Pittsburgh Advocate*, 1/15/1925; *Gloucester Daily Times*, 1/1925; Charlotte Lane Papers; U.S. Census, Whatcom County 1900-1930; *Bellingham Herald*, 1/20/1906; Aiston Collection; WCGS, *Cemetery Records*, Lummi Island and Greenacres Cemeteries.

122. Carlisle Indian School, Student Record #1137; The general summary of life at Carlisle is taken from many issues of *The Carlisle Arrow*, *Indian Helper*, and Jenkins, *The Real All-Americans*.

123. *Indian Helper*, Christmas 1897; Carlisle, Student Record #1137; *The Blade*, 4/17/1900, 8/9/1900; Whatcom County Auditor, Marriage Return #1036; *Bellingham Herald*, 3/27/1908, 3/13/1924; Aiston Collection.

124. Carlisle, Student Record #1137; *Bellingham Herald*, 5/2/1910; *Indian Craftsman, by Indians* (Carlisle) 1/1910, 44; Aiston Collection; Art Granger to Howard Buswell, 11/20/1956, HBP, CPNWS.

125. *The Indian Helper* 14, #38, 7/14/1899; Carlisle, Student Record #2051; Bureau of Indian Affairs, "Chemawa Indian School, Register of Pupils Admitted 1880-1927," NARA, NW; *Bellingham Herald*, 4/23/1911; WCGS, *Cemetery Records*, 37.

126. Carlisle, Student Record #2148; Seattle Archdiocese, Sacramental Records v. 4, 218; Ann Nugent, *Schooling of the Lummi Indians Between 1855-1956*, (Bellingham: Lummi Indian Business Council, 1981) 27, 30; *Carlisle Arrow* 8, 10/30/1908; Helen Lane Finkbonner in Nugent, *Lummi Elders*, 49.

127. Jenkins, *The Real All Americans*, 214; Carlisle, Student Record #2148; *Carlisle Arrow*, 10/2/1908, 10/30/1908, 3/19/1909, 10/1/1909.

128. *Carlisle Arrow*, 4/9/1909; Lucy Lane Handeyside in Nugent, *Lummi Elders*, 93.

129. *Carlisle Arrow*, 4/2/1909, 4/9/1909, 5/21/1909, 4/23/1909; Nugent, *Schooling of the Lummi*, 30; Helen Lane Finkbonner in Nugent, *Lummi Elders*, 106.

130. *Carlisle Arrow*, 12/15/1911; *Helen DeKoff v Jack DeKoff* #13632 (1918), Whatcom County Superior Court; Jernigan, "C.C. Finkbonner Family Genealogy" and personal research notes.

131. Carlisle, Student Record #3887.

132. *Bellingham Herald*, 5/25/1907; *Carlisle Arrow*, 5/15/1914.

133. *Carlisle Arrow*, 3/7/1913.

134. Moses Friedman to Nellie Lane, 10/14/1913, in Carlisle, Student Record #3887; *Carlisle Arrow*, 11/14/1913; U.S. Patent #834534. www.glorecords.blm.gov.

135. Charles Dagenett to Moses Friedman, 1/16/1914. Friedman to Dagenett, 1/20/1914. Reports by W.C. Shambaugh, E.E. McKay, 1/20/1914. All in Carlisle, Student Record #3887; *Carlisle Arrow*, 5/15/1914; Frederick Hoxie, *Parading Through History: The Making of the Crow Nation in America* (NY: Cambridge U. Press, 1995), 289-91.

136. Whatcom County Auditor, Marriage Certificate #2536, 10/26/1915.

137. Carlisle, Student Record #2598; Lucy Lane Handeyside in Nugent, *Lummi Elders*, 92.

138. Carlisle, Student Record #2598; Handeyside in Nugent, *Lummi Elders,* 92; *Carlisle Arrow,* 12/15/1911, 3/22/1912, 1/17/1913, 1/24/1913, 10/24/1913, 9/18/1914.

139. Nugent, *Schooling of the Lummi,* 30.

140. *Star and Sentinel,* 1/31/1914; *Adams County News,* 1/31/1914; *Gettysburg Times,* 2/13/1914; unknown newspaper clipping, 2/15/1914. All courtesy of Barbara Landis.

141. Nugent, *Schooling of the Lummi,* 17; Whatcom County Auditor, Deeds 162, 616-617; *Bellingham Herald,* 3/3/1925, 8/29/1950, 5/21/1978; Frances Lane James, interview by author 12/3/2008, Lummi Reservation.

142. *Bellingham Herald,* 7/2/1981.

Bibliography

Abbreviations for endnotes and bibliography:

CPNWS = Center for Pacific Northwest Studies, Western Washington University, Bellingham

HBP = Howard Buswell Papers

PRJ = Percival R. Jeffcott Papers

NWEC = Northwest Ethnohistory Collection

NARA = National Archives & Records Administration

NARA, NW = NARA, Pacific Northwest Region, Seattle

PNWQ = *Pacific Northwest Quarterly*

WHQ = *Washington Historical Quarterly*

WSA, NW = Washington State Archives, Northwest Region, Bellingham

Sources used only once, or in passing, in the notes are not included in this bibliography.

Abbott, T.O. *Real Property Statutes of Washington Territory from 1843 to 1889.* Olympia: State Printing and Pub. Co., 1892.

Adams, Dave. Research re Robert Hugh Davis and Katherine Auter. Courtesy of Dave Adams.

Aiston, Peggy. Research Collection. CPNWS.

Alvord, Gertrude Matz. Interview, *Ferndale Record-Journal,* undated clipping in Frank Teck Papers. CPNWS.

Anacortes Museum. Fernhill Cemetery records.

Archdiocese of Seattle. Sacramental records, vol. 1-4. Archdiocesan Archives, Seattle, Washington.

Archuleta, Margaret, Brenda Child, and K. Tsianina Lomawaina, editors. *Away From Home: American Indian Boarding School Experiences.* Phoenix: Heard Museum, 2000.

Arkansas United Methodist Church Archives. Bailey Library, Hendrix College. Conway, Arkansas.

Asher, Brad. *Beyond the Reservation: Indians, Settlers, and the Law in Washington Territory, 1853-1889.* Norman: University of Oklahoma Press, 1999.

Atwood, Rev. A. A. *Glimpses in Pioneer Life on Puget Sound.* Seattle: Denny-Coryell, 1903.

Bancroft, H. H. *History of California, Vol. VII, 1860-1890.* San Francisco: History Company, 1890.

Barman, Jean. *French Canadians, Furs and Indigenous Women in the Making of the Pacific Northwest.* Vancouver: University of British Columbia Press, 2014.

——. "Taming Aboriginal Sexuality: Gender, Power and Race in British Columbia, 1850-1890." *BC Studies* no. 115-116, (Autumn-Winter 1997-1998): 237-66.

Bartholomees Jr., J. Boone. *Buff Facings and Gilt Buttons: Staff and Headquarters Operations in the Army of Northern Virginia, 1861-1865.* University of South Carolina Press, 1998.

Bataille, Gretchen M. and Kathleen Mullen-Sands. *American Indian Women: Telling Their Lives.* Lincoln: University of Nebraska Press, 1984.

Beckey, Fred. *Range of Glaciers: The Exploration and Survey of the Northern Cascade Range.* Portland: Oregon Historical Society Press, 2003.

Bethard, Wayne. *Lotions, Potions, and Deadly Elixirs: Frontier Medicine in America.* Lanham, MD: Taylor Trade, 2004.

Bolton, S. Charles. *Territorial Ambition: Land and Society in Arkansas, 1800-1840.* Fayetteville: University of Arkansas Press, 1993.

Bowden, Angie Burt. *Early Schools of Washington Territory.* Seattle: Lowman and Hanford, 1935.

Boyd, Robert. *The Coming of the Spirit of Pestilence: Introduced Infectious Diseases and Population Decline Among Northwest Coast Indians, 1774-1874.* Seattle: University of Washington Press, 1999.

Britton, Nancy. Research re Tennant church and school history. Courtesy of Nancy Britton.

Brown, (Captain) Fred. R. *History of the Ninth U.S. Infantry, 1799-1909.* Chicago: R.R. Donnelley, 1909.

Brown, Dee. *The Gentle Tamers: Women of the Old Wild West.* New York: Putnam, 1958.

Browne, J. Ross. *Indian Affairs in the Territories of Oregon and Washington.* Fairfield, WA: Ye Galleon Press, 1977.

Brumbaugh, Virginia. Interview by author, Marysville, Washington. 10/16/2004.

Buswell, Howard. Papers. CPNWS.

Butler, Anne M. *Gendered Justice in the American West: Women Prisoners in Men's Penitentiaries.* Urbana: University of Illinois Press, 1997.

California State Library, compiler. California Information File, 1846-1985. Microfiche. San Francisco Public Library.

Camfield, Thomas. *Port Townsend: The City That Whiskey Built.* Port Townsend, WA: Ah Tom Pub., 2002.

Campbell, John. Diaries 1853-1894. University of Washington Libraries, Special Collections. Seattle.

Carlisle Arrow (Carlisle Indian School, Pennsylvania). Copies courtesy of Barbara Landis.

Carlisle Indian School. Student Records 1878-1918. RG75, File 1327. NARA. Copies courtesy of Barbara Landis.

Carlson, Keith Thor, ed. *A Sto:lo Coast Salish Historical Atlas.* Seattle: University of Washington Press and Sto:lo Heritage Trust, 2001.

Carlson, Keith Thor. *You Are Asked to Witness: The Sto:lo in Canada's Pacific Coast History.* Chilliwack, BC: Sto:lo Heritage Trust, 1997.

Carter, Elizabeth Grayson. "Journal no. 1, 7/1/1860-10/31/1872." Typescript. Oatlands Plantation Archives, Leesburg, Virginia.

Central Rappahannock Regional Library, Fredericksburg, Virginia. Fitzhugh family files.

Cepa, Laurie. Fitzhugh-Phillips family research. Courtesy of Laurie Cepa.

City of Bellingham, Washington. Bayview Cemetery Records. WSA, NW.

Clinton, Catherine. *The Plantation Mistress: Woman's World in the Old South.* New York: Pantheon Books, 1982.

Coffman, Edward M. *The Old Army: A Portrait of the American Army in Peacetime, 1784-1898.* New York: Oxford Univ. Press, 1986.

Coontz, Stephanie. *Marriage, A History: From Obedience to Intimacy or How Love Conquered Marriage.* New York: Viking, 2005.

Cooper Jr., William J. *Jefferson Davis, American.* New York: Vintage Books, 2001.

——. *Jefferson Davis, The Essential Writings.* New York: Random House Ballantine Modern Library, 2003.

Corcoran, Neil B. *Bucoda: A Heritage of Sawdust and Leg Irons.* Bucoda, WA: Bucoda Improvement Club, 1976.

Cronin, Kay. *Cross in the Wilderness.* Vancouver, BC: Mitchell Press, 1959.

Cutler, Carl C. *Queens of the Western Ocean: The Story of America's Mail and Passenger Sailing Lines.* Annapolis: U.S. Naval Institute, 1961.

Davis, Jefferson. *The Papers of Jefferson Davis, Vol. 2. June 1841-July 1846.* Lynda Crist, editor. Baton Rouge: Louisiana State University Press, 1975.

Davis, Robert Hugh. Service record. Compiled Service Records of Confederate Soldiers Who Served in Organizations from the State of Mississippi. NARA, R6 94, MF 269, Roll 314.

De Danaan, Llyn. *Katie Gale: A Coast Salish Woman's Life on Oyster Bay.* Lincoln: University of Nebraska, 2013.

Dick, Everett. *Dixie Frontier: A Social History.* Norman: University of Oklahoma Press, 1948. Reprint 1993.

Directory Publishing Company, compiler. *Langley San Francisco Directory 1881-1882* and *1883.* San Francisco: Francis, Valentine & Company, various dates.

Dougan, Michael. *Arkansas Odyssey.* Little Rock: Rose Publishing, 1993.

Dover, Harriet Shelton. *Tulalip from My Heart.* Seattle: University of Washington Press, 2013.

Duff, Wilson. *The Upper Stalo Indians of the Fraser Valley, B.C.* Victoria: B.C. Provincial Museum, 1952, 1972.

Dunagan, Dessie May. *History of Ferndale Consolidated School District no. 502.* Ferndale, WA: FCSD no. 502, 1968.

Duwamish, et al. v U.S. (1927) F-275. Washington D.C.: U.S. Court of Claims. Copy in NWEC, CPNWS.

Edson, Lelah Jackson. *The Fourth Corner.* Bellingham, WA: Whatcom Museum, 1951. Reprinted 1968.

Ericson, Carol. Lear family research. Courtesy of Carol Ericson.

Fetzer, Paul. Field Notes. Author's copy, courtesy of Dr. Wayne Suttles (originals now at University of Washington Libraries, Special Collections).

Fischer, David Hackett. *Albion's Seed: Four British Folkways in America.* New York: Oxford University Press, 1989.

Fitzhugh, E.C. Service record. *Compiled Service Records of Confederate General and Staff Officers and Non-Regimental Enlisted Men.* NARA. Copy at Library of Virginia.

Fitzhugh, Patricia. Fitzhugh family research. Courtesy of Patricia Fitzhugh.

Fitzhugh, Sallie Lee. Interview by author re Fitzhugh history. Stafford County, Virginia. 9/24/2000.

Fletcher, Jack E., Patricia K.A. Fletcher, and Lee Whitely. *Cherokee Trail Diaries.* 3 vols. Caldwell, ID: Caxton Printers, n.d.

Forsyth, James W. Papers. Courtesy of Dr. Elizabeth Upton (now in University of Washington Libraries, Special Collections).

France, George W. *The Struggles for Life and Home in the Northwest.* New York: I. Goldman, 1890.

Gibson, James. "Thomas H. Tennant Family Tree" and other genealogy research. Copy courtesy of James Gibson.

Gloucester (Massachusetts) City Archives. Annisquam history collections.

Gorsline, Jerry, ed. *Shadows of Our Ancestors: Readings in the History of Klallam-White Relations.* Port Townsend: Empty Bowl, 1992.

Graybill, Andrew R. *The Red and the White: A Family Saga of the American West.* New York: Liveright (W.W. Norton), 2013.

Griffin Family Papers. Courtesy of Carleton Howard.

Gunther, Erna. *Ethnobotany of Western Washington: The Knowledge and Use of Indigenous Plants by Native Americans.* Seattle: University of Washington, 1973.

——. "Klallam Ethnography." *UW Publications in Anthropology,* v. 1, no. 5, pp. 171-314. Seattle: University of Washington Press, 1927.

Guzman, Sherry. Interview re Phillips family by author. Marysville, Washington. 1/16/2004.

Haner, Jeff. Interview by author re Kavanaugh family. Aberdeen, Washington. 7/19/2010

Hannon, Kyle. "Passing the Time: Prison Life at Johnson's Island." *NW Ohio Quarterly* 66, no. 2, (Spring 1994): 82-102.

Harmon, Alexandra. *Indians in the Making: Ethnic Relations and Indian Identities Around Puget Sound.* Berkeley: University of California Press, 1998.

Hawley, Robert E. *Skqee Mus, or Pioneer Days on the Nooksack.* Percival Jeffcott, editor. Bellingham: Miller and Sutherlen, 1945.

Heitman, Francis. *Historical Register and Dictionary of the U.S. Army from its Organization 9/29/1789–3/2/1903.* 2 vols. Washington: Gov. Printing Office, 1903.

Hermann, Janet Sharp. *Joseph E. Davis, Pioneer Patriarch.* Jackson: University Press of Mississippi, 1990.

Hesseltine, William B., editor. *Civil War Prisons.* Kent, OH: Kent State University Press 1972, 1997.

Hilbert, Vi. *Siastenu, Gram Ruth Sehome Shelton: The Wisdom of a Tulalip Elder.* Translation by Vi Hilbert and Jay Miller. Seattle: Lushootseed Press, 1995.

Holcomb, Martha. Lear family research. Courtesy of Martha Holcomb.

Howard, Carleton. Griffin-Lane family and March Point research. Courtesy of Carleton Howard.

Howell, Erle. *Methodism in the Northwest.* Nashville: Parthenon Press, 1966.

Hunton, Eppa. *Autobiography.* Richmond: William Byrd Press, 1933.

Hyde, Anne F. *Empires, Nations and Families: A History of the North American West, 1800-1860.* Lincoln: University of Nebraska Press, 2011.

Indian Helper. Carlisle Indian School, Pennsylvania.

Ingersoll, Thomas N. *To Intermix With Our White Brothers: Indian Mixed Bloods from the Earliest Times to the Indian Removals.* Albuquerque: University of New Mexico Press, 2005.

Interstate Publishing Company. *An Illustrated History of Skagit and Snohomish Counties.* Chicago: Interstate Publishing Co., 1906.

Island County (Washington) records: Auditor, County Clerk, Probate. WSA, NW.

Jackson, John C. *Children of the Fur Trade: Forgotten Metis of the Pacific Northwest.* Missoula: Mountain Press, 1995.

James, Chief Tsi'lixw William. Interviews by author re Lane family and Lummi culture. Lummi Reservation, 2000-2016.

James, Frances Lane. Interviews by author re Lane family and culture. Lummi Reservation, 2000-2014.

Jeffcott, Percival. Collections. CPNWS.

———. *Nooksack Tales and Trails.* Sedro-Woolley: *Courier-Times,* 1949. Bellingham: Sincyrly Ours, 1995 reprint.

Jefferson County (WA) Auditor records. WSA, NW.

Jeffrey, Julie Roy. *Frontier Women: "Civilizing" the West? 1840-1880.* New York: Hill and Wang, 1979. Revised ed. 1998.

Jenkins, Sally. *The Real All Americans: The Team That Changed a Game, A People, A Nation.* New York: Doubleday, 2007.

Jernigan, Irene Finkbonner. "C.C. Finkbonner Family Genealogy." Unpublished manuscript. Courtesy of Irene Jernigan.

——. Finkbonner-Lane family research. Courtesy of Irene Jernigan.

Jette, Melinda Marie. *At the Hearth of the Crossed Races: A French-Indian Community In 19th Century Oregon, 1812-1859.* Corvallis: Oregon State University Press, 2015.

Johannsen, Robert W. "National Issues and Local Politics in Washington Territory, 1857-1861." *PNWQ* 42, 1951: 3-31.

Jones-Lamb, Karen. *Native American Wives of San Juan Settlers.* Bryn Tirion Pub., 1994.

Jordan, Ray. *Yarns of the Skagit Country.* Sedro-Woolley, WA, 1974.

Judson, Phoebe Goodell. "My Aboriginal Neighbors." *Lynden Tribune,* 1912 from 1904 speech.

——. *A Pioneer's Search for an Ideal Home.* Lincoln: University of Nebraska Press, 1984. Originally published 1925.

Kahana, Charlie. 4/11/1956 oral history, transcription. Howard Buswell Oral History tapes. CPNWS.

Kavanaugh, James. Journals (see under Wellman, Candace).

Kavanaugh, Tim. "Kavanaugh Family History." Unpublished manuscript, 2006. Courtesy of Tim Kavanaugh and Patricia Scott.

Keen, Robert. Research files, regional tour, and interview by author re Tennant history. Lincoln, Arkansas. 5/21/2001.

Keith, Gordon, ed., *The James Francis Tulloch Diary 1875-1910.* Portland: Binford & Mort, 1978.

Kennedy, Dorothy. "Quantifying Two Sides of a Coin: A Statistical Examination of the Central Coast Salish Social Network." *BC Studies* no. 153, (Spring 2007): 3-29.

Killeen, Richard. *A Short History of Ireland.* Dublin: Gill and MacMillan, 1994.

King, George Harrison Sanford. Papers 1930-1985. Virginia Historical Society.

Lambert, MaryAnn. *The House of the 7 Brothers of Ste-tee-thlum.* (1961) Port Orchard: Publishers Printing, reprint 1991.

Landis, Barbara. Carlisle Indian School research notes, papers, and website (www.carlisleindianschool.com). Courtesy of Barbara Landis.

Lane, Charlotte. Papers. Gloucester (Massachusetts) City Archives.

Lane, Frederick F. "Diary, 1860 & 1861." Typescript copy. PRJ, CPNWS.

Lang, William L. *Confederacy of Ambition: William Winlock Miller and the Making of Washington Territory.* Seattle: University of Washington Press, 1996.

Lemke, W.J. "Early Colleges and Academies of Washington County, Arkansas." *Bulletin* no. 16. Fayetteville: Washington County Historical Society, 1954.

Leonard, Cynthia M. *The General Assembly of Virginia: 7/30/1619–1/11/1978.* Richmond: Virginia State Library, 1978.

LeSourd, Rev. David. "Sketches of an Itinerant's Career." Unpublished manuscript. PRJ.

Limerick, Patricia Nelson. *Legacy of Conquest: The Unbroken Past of the American West.* New York: W.W. Norton, 1987.

Little, Pearl, In the Matter of the Estate of. (1983) San Juan County (WA) Superior Court no. 2088.

Loutzenhiser, F.H. and J.R., editor. *Told By the Pioneers, vol. 2.* WPA Project no. 5841, Secretary of State Ernest Hutchinson, 1938.

Lummi Island Library. Lummi Island history files, collections.

Lummi Tribe. *Nooh-whlummi: A Brief History of the Lummi.* Lummi Tribe (Nation), n.d.

Majors, Harry M., editor. *Mount Baker: A Chronicle of Its Historic Eruptions and First Ascent.* Seattle: Northwest Press, 1978.

Mansfield, Joseph. "Report of the Inspector of Fort Bellingham, 12/28/1858." NARA, PNW.

Marschner, Janice. *California 1850: A Snapshot in Time.* Sacramento: Coleman Ranch Press, 2000.

McArthur, Scott. *The Enemy Never Came: The Civil War in the Pacific Northwest.* Caldwell, ID: Caxton Press, 2012.

McKay, Harvey J. *St. Paul, Oregon 1830-1890.* Portland: Binford & Mort, 1980.

Meany, Edmond. Papers. University of Washington Libraries, Special Collections.

Mihesuah, Devon A. *American Indians: Stereotypes and Realities.* Atlanta: Clarity Press, 1996.

Miles, John C. *Koma Kulshan: The Story of Mt. Baker.* Bellingham: Chuckanut Editions, 2010. Revised edition.

Miller, William Winlock. Papers. Bienecke Library, Yale University.

Milliken, Emma. "Choosing Between Corsets and Freedom: Native, Mixed-blood, and White Wives of Laborers at Fort Nisqually, 1833-1860." *PNWQ* (Spring 2005): 95-101.

Morris, Christopher. *Becoming Southern: The Evolution of a Way of Life, Warren County and Vicksburg, Mississippi 1770-1860.* New York: Oxford University Press, 1995.

Mullen, Neil. *Whatcom County, Washington Post Offices and Postmasters, 1857-1985.* Bellingham: 1986.

Munks, Don and Cathy. Interview by author re March Point history. Skagit County. 9/1/2006.

Munks Sr., William. Papers. University of Washington Library Special Collections.

Naylor, Elaine. *Frontier Boosters: Port Townsend and the Culture of Development in the American West, 1850-1895.* Montreal: McGill-Queen's University Press, 2014.

Neal, Patricia. William King Lear research and manuscripts. Courtesy of Patricia Neal.

Newell, Gordon. *Rogues, Buffoons and Statesmen.* Seattle: Hangman Press, 1975.

Newman, Roger. Territorial marriage laws and Seatco Prison research. Courtesy of Roger Newman.

Nix, Alma and John, ed. *The History of Lewis County, Washington.* Chehalis: Lewis County Historical Society, 1985.

Nooksack Indian Mission Methodist Church records. Transcript by Rev. Charlotte Osborn, 1996. Copy courtesy of Rev. Osborn.

Northwest Ethnohistory Collection. CPNWS.

Northwest Federation of American Indians (NFAI). Records. NARA, NW. RG 75.

Northwest Oral History Collection, CPNWS.

Nugent, Ann. *The History of Lummi Fishing Rights.* Bellingham: Lummi Communications, 1979.

——, ed. *Lummi Elders Speak.* Blaine, WA: Pelican Press, 1982.

——. *The Schooling of the Lummi Indians Between 1885-1956.* Lummi Indian Business Council, 1981.

Orcas Island Museum. Collections. Eastsound, WA.

Owens, Julie Chandler. Interview by author re Julianne Fitzhugh. 10/2000.

Pascoe, Peggy. *What Comes Naturally: Miscegenation Law and the Making of Race in America.* New York: Oxford University Press, 2009.

Perry, Adele. *On the Edge of Empire: Gender, Race, and the Making of British Columbia, 1849-1871.* Toronto: University of Toronto Press, 2001.

Ploeger, Vaughn. Interview by author re Kavanaugh family. Eastsound, Washington, 4/27/2011.

Puget Sound District Agency. Correspondence and Accounting Records of the Puget Sound District Agency, 1854-1861 and the Tulalip Agency 1861-1886. RG 75 microfilm. NARA, PNW.

Puget Sound Wreck Reports. NARA, NW.

Pyeatt, D. Niler. Tennant, Hacker and Pyeatt family research. Courtesy of Niler Pyeatt.

Ragland, Mary Lois S. *Fisher Funeral Home Records, Vicksburg, Mississippi 1854-1867.* Heritage Books, 1992.

Raibmon, Paige. *Authentic Indians: Episodes of Encounter from the Late 19th Century Northwest Coast.* Durham, NC: Duke University Press, 2005.

Reid family papers. Courtesy of Julie Chandler Owens.

Richards, Kent D. *Isaac I. Stevens: Young Man in a Hurry.* Pullman: Washington State University Press, 1993.

Richardson, Allan and Brent Galloway. *Nooksack Place Names: Geography, Culture and Language.* Vancouver: University of British Columbia Press, 2011.

Richardson, Allan. *Nooksack Indian Homesteading: A Study of Settlement Ethnohistory.* Bellingham: CPNWS, revised edition 1978.

Richardson, David. *This Is Our Story: Orcas Island Community Church from 1884 to the New Millennium.* Salt Lake City: Publishers Press, 1999.

Riley, Glenda. *Building and Breaking Families in the American West.* Albuquerque: University of New Mexico Press, 1996.

———. *Women and Indians on the Frontier, 1825-1915.* Albuquerque: University of New Mexico Press, 1984.

Roberts, Lynn, compiler. "Indian and Half-blood Burial Information for Orcas Island 1858-1900." Unpublished manuscript. Courtesy of Irene Jernigan.

Roberts, Natalie. "A History of the Swinomish Tribal Community." Unpublished dissertation, University of Washington, 1975. University of Washington Libraries.

Roblin, Charles E. "Schedule of Unenrolled Indians." U.S. Dept. of the Interior, Office of Indian Affairs, 1919. NARA, NW.

Roeder, Henry. Papers. University of Washington Libraries, Special Collections.

Ross, Margaret Smith. "Squatters Rights." Parts 1 (6/1956), 2 (9/1956), and 3 (12/1956). *Pulaski County Historical Review* 4.

Roth, Lottie Roeder, ed. *History of Whatcom County.* 2 vols. Seattle: Pioneer Historical Pub., 1926.

Samish Indian Tribe. "Petition for the Federal Acknowledgement of the Samish Indian Tribe." 1979. Copy in NWEC, CPNWS.

Sampson, Chief Martin J. *Indians of Skagit County.* Des Moines, WA: Lushootseed Press, 1998.

San Juan County (Washington) records: Auditor, County Clerk, Superior Court Clerk, Probate Court. WSA, NW and Friday Harbor, WA.

Sandstrom, Chief Earngy (Snoqualmoo). Interview by author re Treaty War. 6/16/2003, Bellingham, Washington.

Scally, Robert J. *The End of Hidden Ireland: Rebellion, Famine and Emigration.* New York: Oxford University Press, 1995.

Scott, Patricia. Kavanaugh family research. Courtesy of Patricia Scott.

Seay, Christopher Columbus. "The 1853 Cattle Drive." *Cincinnati Argus,* 1857. *Flashback* 42, no. 2 (1992) reprint.

Shell Oil Company, Kavanaugh farm file. WSA, NW.

Shelton, Ruth, and Dover, Harriet Shelton. Letter to Percival Jeffcott 2/5/1954. PRJ, CPNWS.

Skagit County (WA) records: Auditor, Probate Court, Skagit Territorial Court, Superior Court. WSA, NW.

Skagit County Oral History Preservation Project. Microfilm, WSA, NW.

Sleigh, Daphne, ed. *One Foot on the Border: A History of Sumas Prairie and Area.* Deroche, BC: Sumas Prairie and Area Historical Society, 1999.

Smith, Sherry L. *The View from Officer's Row: Army Perceptions of Western Indians.* Tucson: University of Arizona Press, 1990.

Soldiers Who Served in Organizations from the State of Mississippi. NARA, RG 94, MF269, Roll314.

Southern Claims Commission, Settled Files for Claims Approval 1871-1880. Thomas H. Tennant File no. 4160. Records of the Accounting Office of the Dept. of the Treasury. NARA RG 217, Box 115.

Splitstone, Fred John. *Orcas, Gem of the San Juans.* Eastsound, WA: Fred Darvill, 1954.

Starr, Kevin and Richard J. Orsi, ed. *Rooted in Barbarous Soil: People, Culture and Community in Gold Rush California.* Berkeley: University of California Press, 2000.

Stauss, Joseph H. *The Jamestown S'Klallam Story: Rebuilding a Northwest Coast Indian Tribe.* Sequim WA: Jamestown S'Klallam, 2002.

Steele, M.D., Volney. *Bleed, Blister and Purge: A History of Medicine on the American Frontier.* Missoula MT: Mountain Press, 2005.

Sterne, Netta. *Fraser Gold 1858! The Founding of British Columbia.* Pullman: Washington State University Press, 1998.

Sullivan, Michael. Collections. CPNWS.

Suttles, Wayne. *Coast Salish Essays.* Seattle: University of Washington Press, 1987.

——, editor. *Handbook of the North American Indian: Vol. 7, Northwest Coast.* Smithsonian Institution, 1990.

——. "Post-Contact Culture Change Among the Lummi Indians." *BC Historical Quarterly* 18, no. 1 & 2, (Jan-April, 1954): 29-102.

——. Research files, interviews, correspondence, and conversations with author.

Swindle, Lewis J., *The Fraser River Gold Rush of 1858 as Reported by the California Newspapers of 1858.* Victoria: Trafford Pub., 2001.

Tate, Rev. Charles. Diaries, 1874-1883. Chilliwack (British Columbia) City Archives.

Teck, Frank. Papers. In Michael Sullivan Collection. CPNWS.

Tennant family letters, 1874-1906. Courtesy of Ed Pyeatt. Oakland, California.

Tennant, John. Farm Journals 1862-1872. William James Collection, Lummi Nation Archives. Used with permission of Chief William James.

Thrush, Coll. *Native Seattle: Histories from the Crossing-Over Place.* Seattle: University of Washington Press, 2007.

Trebon, Theresa L. *First Views, An Early History of Skagit County: 1850-1899.* Mt. Vernon, WA: Skagit Valley Herald, 2002.

Tremaine, David. *Indian and Pioneer Settlement of the Nooksack Lowland, Washington to 1890.* CPNWS, 1975.

Turner, Nancy J. *Food Plants of Coastal First Peoples.* Vancouver: University of British Columbia Press, 1995.

———. *Food Plants of Interior First Peoples.* Vancouver: University of British Columbia Press, 1997.

———. *Plant Technology of First Peoples of B.C.* Vancouver: University of British Columbia Press, 1998.

U.S. Attorney General, Records Relating to the Appointment of Federal Judges and U.S. Attorneys and Marshals for the Territory and State of Washington, 1853-1861. NARA RG60, MF 1343.

U.S. Census 1830-1930. Washington: Whatcom, Island, King, Skagit, San Juan, Snohomish counties, Lummi Reservation, Seatco Prison; Washington County, Arkansas; Mississippi: Warren, Wilkinson; Alaska Territory; Webster County, Iowa; Loudoun County, Iowa. Microfilms at NARA, NW and Seattle Public Library. Whatcom County Genealogical Society typescripts.

U.S. Coast Guard. Register of Lighthouse Keepers. Dept. of the Treasury. RG 26. MF 1373. NARA, Seattle.

U.S. Department of Agriculture. *1913 Annual Report.* Online, University of Chicago Library.

U.S. Department of the Interior, Bureau of Indian Affairs. *Recommendation and Summary of Evidence for Proposed Finding Against Federal Acknowledgment of the Samish Indian Tribe.* 1982. NARA, NW.

———. Records of the Puget Sound Agency. NARA, NW.

U.S. Department of the Interior, National Park Service. National Register of Historic Places Inventory Nomination Form. Seatco Prison, Bucoda, Washington. 5/2/1975.

U.S. Department of War. *The War of the Rebellion: A Compilation of the Official Records of the Union and Confederate Armies.* Series II, vol. 8. Correspondence. Washington: Government Printing Office, 1902.

U.S. District Court, Northern Division, Western District of Washington. Seattle District Court Records. RG 21. NARA, NW.

———. Case files. Copies in NWEC, CPNWS.

U.S. General Land Office Records (Olympia, Washington). NARA, NW.

U.S. Surveyor General. Map of 1884 Lummi Reservation Allotments. Copy at Lummi Nation Library, Northwest Indian College. Lummi Reservation (WA).

Utley, Robert M. *Frontiersmen in Blue: The U.S. Army and the Indian, 1848-1865.* Lincoln: University of Nebraska, 1967.

Valadez, Jamie. Interview by author re S'Klallam life. 9/9/2016, Port Angeles, Washington.

Valencius, Conevery Bolton. *The Health of the Country: How American Settlers Understood Themselves and Their Land.* New York: Basic Books, 2002.

Van Kirk, Sylvia. *Many Tender Ties: Women In Fur Trade Society.* Norman: University of Oklahoma Press, 1980.

Van Miert, E. Rosamond Ellis. *Settlers, Structures and Ships on Bellingham Bay, 1852-1889.* Bellingham: Rosamond Van Miert, 2004.

Vernon, Walter N. *Methodism in Arkansas, 1816-1976.* Little Rock: Joint Committee for the History of Arkansas Methodism, 1976.

Vouri, Mike. *The Pig War: Standoff at Griffin Bay.* Seattle: University of Washington Press, 2013.

Wahl, Phillip. Interview by author re Treaty War. 6/16/2003, Bellingham, Washington.

Wahl, Tim. Whatcom County geography research. Courtesy of Tim Wahl.

Washington Territorial Census: 1870, 1880, 1885, 1887, 1889. Copies at WSA, NW.

Washington Territorial Court, Third District. Records. Jefferson County Superior Court Clerk. WSA, NW.

Washington Territorial Court. Second District. Records. WSA, Olympia.

Washington Territory Superintendent of Indian Affairs. Records. NARA, NW. Copies in NWEC.

Washington Territory v E.C. Fitzhugh no. 211 (1858). 3rd District, Territorial Court. WSA, NW.

Washington Territory v Mary Phillips no. 1070 (no. 45, Series 2) (1879). 3rd District, Territorial Court. WSA, NW.

Washington Territory v William Strong and E.C. Fitzhugh no. 465 (1860). 2nd District, Territorial Court. WSA, SW (Olympia).

Waterman, T.T. *Puget Sound Geography.* Vi Hilbert, Jay Miller and Zalmar Zahir, editors. Federal Way, WA: Lushootseed Press, 2001.

Waukechon, Chad (Menominee Reservation). Research and knowledge re Joseph Davis. Courtesy of Chad Waukechon and Alan Caldwell.

Wellman, Candace. "The James Kavanaugh Diary 1863-1885: An Annotated Synthesis of Two Versions." Unpublished manuscript, 2010.

Wells, Oliver. *The Chilliwacks and Their Neighbors.* Ralph Maud, Brent Galloway, and Marie Weeden, editors. Vancouver: Talonbooks, 1987.

Whatcom County (Washington) Records: Auditor, County Commission, Probate Court, Superior Court Clerk, Superintendent of Schools. WSA, NW and microfilm at Whatcom County Courthouse.

Whatcom County Genealogical Society. *Cemetery Records of Whatcom County.* Bellingham: WCGS, 1996.

White, Carrie. "Diary 1882-1884." University of Washington Libraries, Special Collections.

——. "Fidalgo Before the Boom." Paper for Historical Society of Anacortes. 9/13/1898.

Williams, Jacqueline B., *The Way We Ate: Pacific Northwest Cooking 1843-1900.* Pullman: Washington State University Press, 1996.

Wright, E.W., ed., *Lewis and Dryden's Marine History of the Pacific Northwest.* Portland: Lewis and Dryden, 1895.

Wyatt-Brown, Bertram. *Southern Honor: Ethics and Behavior in the Old South.* New York: Oxford University Press, 1982.

Index